The Witness

'. . . a dramatic tale of war and survival.' —*Sydney Morning Herald*

'*The Witness* stands alone as the most comprehensive account to date of the Sandakan survivor Bill Sticpewich . . . Gilling has produced a sharp and compelling account of events through the eyes of key witnesses. In writing this book, Tom Gilling has helped keep the memories of the lost souls of Sandakan alive, and for that, he has done Australia a great service.' —*The Australian*

'A compelling story indeed.' —*Australian Defence Magazine*

Bastard Behind the Lines

'The horror and heroism of the Pacific war are evoked by Tom Gilling in a way that is vivid and compelling as well as multi-faceted.' —*The Age*

'Gilling has produced an engrossing book, vividly bringing to light disturbing facets of Australia's Pacific War . . . a sobering reminder of a horrific era that should never be forgotten. An extraordinary true tale.' —*Newcastle Herald*

'Not for the faint-hearted . . . This cloak and dagger real-life story will have you on the edge of your seat.' —*The Chronicle*

Lost Battalions

'[Gilling] has made superb use of an Australian Army History Research Grant to afford us a greater understanding of what the lost Australian warriors on Java experienced as a consequence of failed imperial wartime policy.' —*The Australian*

'An engaging account . . . Gilling makes good use of diaries, memoirs and interviews with survivors.' —*Good Reading*

THE DIGGERS OF
KAPYONG

THE STORY OF THE AUSSIES WHO CHANGED
THE COURSE OF THE KOREAN WAR

TOM GILLING

ALLEN&UNWIN
SYDNEY·MELBOURNE·AUCKLAND·LONDON

First published in 2024

Allen & Unwin
Cammeraygal Country
83 Alexander Street
Crows Nest NSW 2065
Australia
Phone: (61 2) 8425 0100
Email: info@allenandunwin.com
Web: www.allenandunwin.com

*Allen & Unwin acknowledges the Traditional Owners of the Country
on which we live and work. We pay our respects to all Aboriginal and
Torres Strait Islander Elders, past and present.*

A catalogue record for this
book is available from the
National Library of Australia

ISBN 978 1 76106 869 0

Maps by Mika Tabata
Index by Garry Cousins
Set in 12.75/16.75 pt Adobe Garamond Pro by Midland Typesetters, Australia

Printed and bound in Australia by the Opus Group

10 9 8 7 6 5 4 3 2 1

The paper in this book is FSC® certified.
FSC® promotes environmentally responsible,
socially beneficial and economically viable
management of the world's forests.

For my parents

CONTENTS

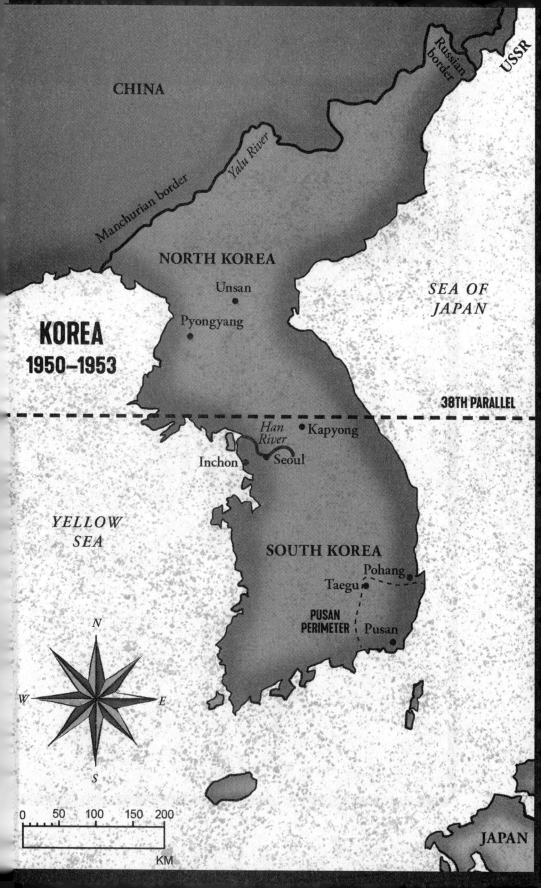

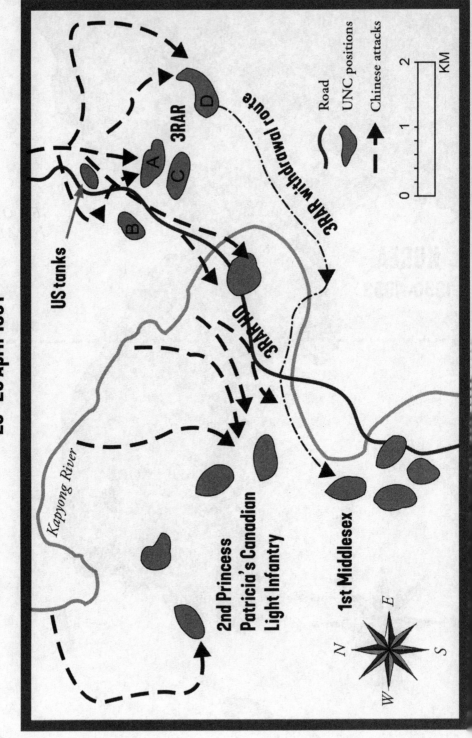

KAPYONG BATTLEFIELD
23–25 April 1951

US tanks

3RAR

D

A

C

B

3RAR withdrawal route

3RAR

Kapyong River

2nd Princess
Patricia's Canadian
Light Infantry

1st Middlesex

Road
UNC positions
Chinese attacks

0 1 2
KM

N
W   E
S

INTRODUCTION

When the veteran US journalist and author David Halberstam was researching his book on the Korean War, he visited a library in Florida where he found 'eighty-eight books on Vietnam and only four on Korea'—a disparity, he wrote later, that 'more or less sums up the war's fate in American memory'.

In Australia, the war began to be forgotten while it was still being fought. After being wounded, evacuated to Japan and then sent back to Korea, Sergeant Jack Gallaway returned to Australia in February 1952, more than a year before the war's end. He recalled 'walking into hotels where I met old friends who said, "Where have you been?" And I said, "Korea." And they said, "What the hell were you doing over there?"'

Some Korean War veterans remembered being rebuffed by RSL clubs because 'that wasn't a proper war'.

While inevitably overshadowed by the two world wars that preceded it, the Korean War was one of the defining events of the 20th century, a product of Cold War machinations whose outcome remains bitterly contested to this day. After three years of savage fighting up and down the Korean Peninsula, the border between the communist North and the democratic, pro-American South had hardly moved. The war ended without a formal peace treaty between the two Koreas. The armistice signed on 27 July 1953 left hostilities unresolved.

As many as two million soldiers became casualties—dead, wounded or missing. Perhaps another two million Korean civilians died. Australian servicemen were more than twice as likely to be killed in Korea as in Vietnam.

The Royal Australian Navy (RAN) and the Royal Australian Air Force (RAAF) both played significant roles in the conflict, but most of the hard fighting was done on the ground by soldiers of the Royal Australian Regiment (RAR). Of its three battalions, it was the 3rd Battalion—3RAR—that served during the most intense period of the conflict, when the war came close to being lost.

This book is the story of a desperate battle fought by a few hundred Australian soldiers for a strategic hilltop in South Korea, and of the events that led up to it. During the long night of 23–24 April 1951, Major Ben O'Dowd's A Company suffered nearly 50 per cent casualties fighting off wave after wave of Chinese infantry. As day broke, the surviving diggers, running out of food, water and ammunition, were reduced to scrounging bullets from their fallen mates.

American accounts of the Korean War rarely mention the Battle of Kapyong, although President Harry S. Truman recognised its importance with a Presidential Unit Citation that credited the 'courageous, indomitable and determined' Australians with stopping an enemy breakthrough and turning 'defeat to victory'.

Before 3RAR landed at Pusan on 28 September 1950, the United Nations' army had been clinging to a foothold at the south-eastern tip of the Korean Peninsula. General Douglas MacArthur's daring amphibious assault at Inchon, more than 160 kilometres behind the enemy lines, turned the war on its head. Within a fortnight of 3RAR's arrival, the battalion was spearheading the UN army's pursuit of the retreating North Koreans.

After a string of small engagements, 3RAR took part in its first major action at Yongju on 21–22 October, in what became known as the Battle of the Apple Orchard. Battles at Pakchon (23–26 October) and Chongju (29 October) took the battalion to within a few kilometres of the Chinese border. Chongju was as far north as the diggers would go.

The dramatic intervention by the People's Republic of China (PRC) sent the UN army into headlong retreat, and 3RAR was withdrawn hundreds of kilometres to a new defensive line south of Seoul. When the UN forces went back on the offensive, 3RAR again took the lead, fighting the Chinese for control of a series of wooded hills before arriving at the Kapyong Valley, north-east of Seoul, a traditional invasion route for attacks on the capital.

It was here that Corporal Raymon Wilson, already carrying wounds from Pakchon and the Battle of the Apple Orchard, was wounded for a third time. Wilson had been pegged by his fellow diggers as unlucky and destined to be killed in Korea; before every firefight they would rib him and ask for their pick of his belongings.

Wilson's platoon was attacking a hill when the assault was held up by an enemy trench. The position of the trench halfway up the tree-covered slope made it impossible for the Australians to bring it under direct fire, so Wilson and his mate Ron Cook crawled forward with two grenades and an Owen submachine gun.

'I was just looking for a way to throw through [the trees] when we got rained with grenades,' Wilson recalled later.

> Ronnie went down, he got a piece of shrapnel . . . I got up, tossed my two grenades . . . just after I threw them we got another shower of grenades . . . I dropped down to the ground again and I felt this thing hit my back and the next thing I know it exploded . . . I thought it had broken my back.

One Chinese grenade had worked its way under Wilson's haversack before detonating. Luckily for him, grenades explode upwards.

If the grenade had been underneath him, it would have killed him. As it was, Wilson's thick pile jacket took much of the blast. Though not fatal, the injury to his back was serious enough for Wilson to need evacuating—first to a mobile surgical unit and then to Japan.

Strapped to a wire basket attached to the side of an army helicopter, the wounded digger was on his way out of Korea, and out of the war. His mates, meanwhile, hunkered down on the rocky slopes of Hill 504 for a battle that would cost more Australian lives than any other single engagement, and change the course of the Korean War.

1

THE FINEST TROOPS
IN THE WORLD

The diggers' journey to Korea had begun on Morotai, a mountainous island in the North Moluccas, in the aftermath of the Pacific War. It was here that Australian soldiers came to join the occupation force that would disarm and demilitarise the defeated Japanese.

The British Commonwealth Occupation Force (BCOF) was the result of an offer made by the Australian prime minister, Ben Chifley, three days after the Japanese surrender, to supply an independent Australian force to take part in the occupation of Japan. The War Cabinet decided that Australia's contribution would be made 'not as a subsidiary, but as a principal Pacific power which has for so long borne the heat and burden of the struggle against Japan'.

General MacArthur, however, wanted a united Commonwealth force, not ragtag contingents from individual nations, and was determined to maintain American control over the administration of post-war Japan. Eventually, Canberra agreed to a British proposal for a Commonwealth force under Australian command. MacArthur ensured that BCOF would take its operational orders from local US commanders.

Needing around 10,000 men to meet the Australian government's promise of three battalions, the army called for volunteers from among serving troops. Veterans from Bougainville and Borneo, New Guinea and the Netherlands East Indies gathered on Morotai to form the 34th Brigade. They included veterans of costly and unnecessary 'mopping up' operations on Japanese-occupied islands, which had claimed the lives of many diggers. Having endured months of bloody jungle fighting in New Guinea and Borneo, many were looking forward to an easier time in Japan, where they thought they would do little more than show off their ceremonial drill.*

The diggers had been ready to sail since early December 1945, but Washington was procrastinating and some of the troops on Morotai were starting to wonder if they would ever move to Japan. On the night of 8 January 1946—beer night, as canteen sergeant Keith Lewtas noted in his diary—their patience finally snapped. After lights-out, they leapt out of bed and marched on brigade headquarters, hurling insults at their officers and screaming, 'When do we go to Japan? We've had it!'

Four days later, the men repeated their protest. Brushing their officers and sergeants aside, other ranks from all BCOF units marched 'in perfect unison' to brigade HQ, where they outlined their grievances. 'The leaderless troops were addressed by a lieut[enant] colonel,' Lewtas wrote, 'who partially satisfied them as regards sailing etc.' Brigade HQ chose to turn a blind eye to the revolt and no disciplinary action was taken.

Alarmed by news of the 'jack-up' on Morotai, the deputy prime minister and minister for the army, Frank Forde, flew up to speak to the diggers. He conceded that the men 'had some cause for grievance' and attributed the delay to the difficulty of finding accommodation

---

*   When word came down that no artillery units would be taken to Japan, gunners who had waived their rights to repatriation in order to join BCOF begged to join the infantry; some even offered to revert to the rank of private to be part of the force.

in war-ravaged Japan and to the Americans' 'unreadiness . . . to accept us'.

While the diggers waited, the press at home was increasingly sceptical about the occupation. American troops had been in Japan since August and it was widely believed that by the time the Australians arrived—if they ever did—the serious business of demilitarising the country would be over. Critics scoffed that the occupation would be nothing more than a holiday for BCOF troops, and that venereal disease (VD) would be rampant among Australian soldiers fraternising with Japanese prostitutes.

As the months dragged on with no embarkation in sight, the diggers' early enthusiasm began to wane. After the second protest, the commander of the 34th Brigade, Brigadier Robert Nimmo, issued a statement to be read out to all ranks. Nimmo promised to deny any press reports that came to light of VD in the occupation force, and to take action to 'dispel the possible public impression that the Force is to be catered for on a large scale by Japanese entertainment women and that the Force is merely on a pleasure tour'.

Nimmo also assured the troops that 'suitable publicity' would be created at home 'with a view to emphasising the fact that this Force will play an important role as a component of BCOF in Japan'. As far as publicity in Japan was concerned, 'arrangements have already been made for press correspondents to accompany the Force and therefore news of your doings will be fully reported in Australia . . . it is well for us to remember when we are there that the blaze of publicity will be upon us!'

Despite the order from brigade HQ that no disciplinary action was to be taken against the protesters, the army quickly weeded out ringleaders and other 'undesirables' and drafted them home to Australia. The 'jack-up' on Morotai had its desired effect, however, and a month later the first Australians were on their way to Japan.

Sailing through channels that had been swept clear of mines, the American troopship *Pachaug Victory* steamed around the

Japanese coastline before crossing the inland sea. Its destination was the former Japanese naval base at Kure, on the south-east coast of Honshu Island. Five kilometres away lay the devastated city of Hiroshima.

As the *Pachaug Victory* entered Kure Bay, it passed the cruiser HMAS *Hobart*, part of the naval force that had supported the allied landings at Tarakan and Balikpapan, in Borneo. There were no port-holes on the American ship, so diggers crowded the decks to wave at the sailors on the *Hobart*—some of whom seemed to think the soldiers had come from Australia rather than from Morotai, as they yelled, 'What's the beer like at [Melbourne hotel] Young and Jackson's?'

'We wouldn't know,' the diggers shouted back. 'We haven't been home for three years!'

Kure had been a major target of American bombing raids. Amid the ruins of the naval dockyards lay wrecked midget submarines of the type that had infiltrated Sydney Harbour in 1942. The city, too, had been flattened. Lewtas joined the other sergeants and warrant officers in a 'long, cold, windowless hut' that was heated by a single woodburning stove. This was to be their mess and sleeping quarters until better accommodation could be built.

Their first impressions of Japan and its cowed and desperate population were not encouraging, and some of the diggers were soon wondering how they would be able to stick it out. Others were deter-mined to make the best of their time in Japan, buying cigarettes and candy cheaply from the army canteen and selling them for ten times the price on the black market.

'The Japanese were short of everything, absolutely everything,' Private Stan Connelly recalled.

We had our own stores where things that were available to us were not available to the Japanese: soap, washing powder, coffee, tea, sugar . . . So you could get your wages at the end of the fortnight . . . go and spend it all on commodities, walk out of the gate of the camp and somebody would be there waiting . . . to buy it from you for double what you paid for it.

While the main BCOF headquarters was in Kure, there was a secondary HQ at Ebisu, in Tokyo. The Ebisu barracks was surrounded by a three-metre-high wall.

'Such was the level of trust between the Japanese buyers and the Australian sellers,' Connelly recalled, 'that you could walk to the wall, shout out and get a response from the other side, throw the bag of merchandise over the wall and the person on the other side would throw the bag back with the currency in it . . . Nobody defaulted. There was absolute trust.'

But Connelly saw no point in trying to make a fortune out of the black market. 'You could fill your pockets with Japanese yen but all you could buy was cigarette cases or lighters or little knick-knacks [as] . . . mementos.'

Many diggers were curious to visit Hiroshima. Years later, Lewtas recalled entering the Asahi Press building, one of few structures to have survived the atomic blast:

We walked into the charred interior and ascended the crumbling stairway, where the corroded banisters had fallen away and the elevators remained as heaps of ashes at the bottom of the wells. From the roof of this many-storied shell we viewed with awe the four square miles of rubble with only a pattern of lanes cleared through them to make communication possible. Below us, we saw twisted and broken metal girders in heaps on the ground; to the north, we noticed the Chamber of Manufacturers Building ruins . . . and the well-known 'T'-shaped bridge which was the target point for the detonation of the dreadful bomb.

Kure was full of prostitutes, who looked to the BCOF troops for their own and their families' survival. Rates of VD rocketed.

All cases had to be reported to BCOF medical units, and 'self-treatment [and] private treatment by BCOF, Japanese or other doctors' was prohibited.

By April 1947 the incidence of VD among the Australian contingent was so high that a special annexe to the hospital had to be built. This became known as 'the house that Jack built', 'Jack' being a colloquial term for gonorrhoea.

BCOF initially reacted by stopping all leave, declaring nearly all Japanese places out of bounds and implementing a strict 'no fraternisation' policy. Private Japanese houses were subject to raids, and if any soldier was spotted walking on the street with a Japanese woman, she would be seized by the provosts and taken for a medical examination, while the soldier was put under arrest.*

But, given the impossibility of keeping lonely and homesick Australian soldiers and Japanese women apart, and the fact that American troops—other than being banned from geisha houses—were relatively free to mix with Japanese locals, the decision was discreetly made not to police the 'no fraternisation' order. After visiting Japan in 1947 and speaking to the new BCOF commander, Lieutenant General Horace 'Red Robbie' Robertson, and other senior officers, Frank Forde even hinted that the order should be 'quietly cancelled before it dies completely'.

As a canteen sergeant, Keith Lewtas saw little of BCOF's military activities, which consisted primarily of dismantling Japan's war-making capacity by finding and destroying armaments and military installations, or converting them to civilian use. Around 100,000 tonnes of explosives and ammunition and 5000 tonnes of poisonous gas were estimated to be stored in the Hiroshima prefecture alone, much of it hidden in tunnels and caves. Explosives

---

*   Keith Lewtas used to meet one of his many girlfriends, 'an ex-Kure dance girl' named Michiko, three nights a week in a secluded hide-out behind her hotel 'to avoid being caught by the MPs'.

and ammunition that could not be dumped at sea were burnt or destroyed on the spot.

From its headquarters at Kure, BCOF was responsible for around 9 million Japanese people across six prefectures, but by the time Lewtas was listing his personal aspirations for 1947 ('an army job, interesting travel, plenty of wealth, and contented social well-being'), the role of the occupation forces was changing. The job of pacifying the Japanese had turned out to be much easier than expected, and the next two years saw a dramatic reduction in the size of BCOF.

From a maximum strength of more than 37,000 (including nearly 12,000 Australians) at the end of 1946, it had dwindled to just 12,000 by April 1948, and was expected to number less than 7000 three months later. The withdrawal of the Indian and New Zealand contingents and the bulk of the British at the end of June 1948 left the Australians carrying out the bulk of BCOF operations.

In the three years since BCOF's arrival in Japan, the occupation had changed from a strict military occupation to what MacArthur characterised as the 'friendly guidance of a protective force'. While BCOF's focus shifted to guard duties and training, the diggers continued to make the most of the social and business opportunities that came their way.

The Australians were prolific black marketeers. To deter soldiers from slipping in and out of camp via gaps in the perimeter fence, the battalion command issued a draconian warning:

1. The perimeter fence WILL NOT be interfered with in any way and will NOT be used by any member as an entrance or exit.
2. The fence will be booby trapped as part of the unit security plan and each trap will contain sufficient explosive to seriously wound a man or woman. All personnel are hereby warned against the danger of close contact with fence.

3. Any person found entering or leaving the area by any other
    means than an authorized entrance will be immediately
    charged and will be severely dealt with.

At home, negative publicity continued to be a problem, and
BCOF soldiers were cautioned against giving reporters off-the-record
interviews while they were on leave in Australia. After visiting the
troops in July 1948, a parliamentary delegation attempted to correct
the public's 'grave misapprehension' about the quality of the BCOF
troops and the role they were playing, with one member informing
the parliament that '[w]e have in Japan what I consider to be the finest
body of troops, in peace-time, that now exists in the world'.

In Korea, peace was looking increasingly fragile. After its annex-
ation in 1910, Koreans had endured 35 years of oppressive Japanese
rule. During the Pacific War as many as 200,000 Koreans were
mobilised to fight in the Imperial Japanese Army, while a similar
number of Korean women were forced to serve as 'comfort women'
to Japanese troops. As the war neared its end, Soviet troops went
into action in northern Korea, with American troops landing in
the south a month later. After the Japanese surrender, both powers
agreed on the 38th parallel as a convenient border for their divided
military occupation.

Unlike China and Western colonies seized by Japan during the
war, there was no indigenous government or colonial administration
waiting to take over in Korea when the war ended. Most claimants
to power had been living in exile overseas.

A period of 'international trusteeship' was intended to pave
the way for an independent, unified Korea. In 1947, over Russian
objections, the United States referred the future of Korea to the
United Nations, which determined there should be UN-supervised
elections, followed by Korean independence and the withdrawal of
all foreign forces. A communist boycott meant that voting only took
place in South Korea, leading to the election of a pro-American

government in Seoul and the consolidation of a pro-Soviet regime in Pyongyang.

In late 1948 tensions between the North and South exploded in a short border war that left thousands dead. Cross-border incidents continued to occur, and it seemed only a matter of time before a larger war broke out on the peninsula.

To soldiers like Keith Lewtas and Sergeant Jack Gallaway, war with Russia felt inevitable, although Lewtas's military contribution to it was likely to be negligible. In August 1948 he failed his rifle training, scoring only 98 hits out of a possible 200.* By his own admission, he was also 'hopeless' with a Bren gun.

At the end of 1948, Australia withdrew two of its three BCOF battalions.** In the view of the parliamentary Defence Committee, the diminished BCOF—consisting of just one army battalion and one RAAF squadron—was now unable to make a useful contribution to 'any military situation which may arise in Japan'.

Long starved of reinforcements in anticipation of its withdrawal, 3RAR now consisted of three understrength rifle companies, a bare-bones headquarters company and no support company. Those reinforcements who did arrive were generally deemed to be of 'poor quality', with the unit diary noting that reinforcement drafts 'thrown up' as a result of the reorganisation of other BCOF units were responsible for an increase in both petty crime and venereal disease. A 'critical' shortage of officers was at least partly alleviated in March 1949 with the arrival of fourteen new Duntroon graduates.

---

*   The pass mark was 105, a score Lewtas claimed he 'would have reached if I had not fired on the target of the man next to me by mistake, thus losing possibly 40 points'. This might have been optimistic. A terse diary entry four months later recorded that Lewtas had 'failed to qualify at musketry at the annual practice'.

**   Originally the 65th, 66th and 67th Australian Infantry Battalions, they were now designated the 1st, 2nd and 3rd Battalions of the Australian Regiment, later renamed the Royal Australian Regiment.

Companies took turns to guard the Imperial Palace in Tokyo, and every year the battalion underwent a month's field training at Haramura. 'The Officers' and Sergeants' Messes enjoyed an atmosphere of luxury,' Lewtas noted, 'as there was almost an unlimited selection of efficient Japanese labour available to cook, serve the tables, deliver the drinks, and the monthly formal dinner in the Sergeants' Mess was one of unparalleled grandeur.' As far as Lewtas and his mates were concerned, the occupation 'could go on for another thirty years'.

Lewtas was not the only Australian soldier to be dismayed when news came through on 26 May 1950 that 3RAR was to be returned to Australia. 'Today the fateful news came over the radio that the Commonwealth Government had decided to withdraw after four years' glorious "holiday" in Japan,' Lewtas wrote in his diary. 'I regret, with many others, leaving here and am going to find it hard to change my way of life and to live on in Australia.' The announcement 'came as a sort of blow to all, both military and civilian, as nobody wants to go home . . . troops are worrying to make provision for maintenance of their half-Japanese children* and 75 per cent are planning to return to the Japanese girls they love'.

'No Australian Digger had ever had it so good,' Jack Gallaway wrote later. 'Most of those who stayed would have been content for the occupation to last forever.'

Rumours of a rear party remaining in Japan after the main body had left prompted many to volunteer, but they were warned that it would be for six months only and that they could not escape the inevitable: they would all have to go home in the end.

At the start of June 1950, a solitary Australian battalion remained of the 15,000 troops from five Commonwealth countries that comprised BCOF three years earlier. The only battles Lewtas

---

* The Japanese called them 'fifty-fifty babies'.

was contemplating as 3RAR prepared to go home were 'battles of domestic and housing strife'.

As the battalion's officers prepared for what was to be the last mess party before their return to Australia, six North Korean divisions were moving into place above the 38th parallel. North Korean engineers were hard at work mending railways and strengthening bridges on the main roads south to enable them to carry heavy Russian tanks.

On 22 June the 3RAR unit diary recorded that lieutenants Butler and Townsend caught a train for Tokyo to attend their friend Lieutenant Allen McCann's wedding. The commander-in-chief of BCOF, Lieutenant General Robertson, inspected a guard of honour and 'complimented the guard commander on the bearing and turnout of the guard'.

Two days later, Lieutenant McCann married Miss Billy Jo Fisher, formerly of Kentucky, USA, at St Luke's Chapel in Tokyo. The following day, 25 June 1950, seven North Korean divisions—around 90,000 men—crossed the 38th parallel into South Korea.

2

LOSING THE COLD WAR

The North Korean dictator, Kim Il Sung, yearned to unite North and South under communist rule, just as the South's president, Syngman Rhee, dreamt of creating a unified non-communist Korea with himself at its head.

Both were unsavoury characters. Kim, a former guerrilla who had fought the Japanese in Manchuria, became a Stalinist while serving as a sniper with the Russian army. Fiercely patriotic and devoted to the communist cause, he knew he needed Soviet backing to become leader and arrived in Pyongyang after the war in the uniform of a Red Army major.

Rhee had spent most of his life in exile in the United States, lobbying for Korean independence while acquiring a glittering education at Harvard and Princeton, before returning after the war. His Christian faith, as well as the backing he received from the Chinese Nationalist leader, Chiang Kai-shek, gave him influence in Washington, and his arrival in General MacArthur's plane left no doubt that he was America's man, although many Americans did not trust him. The commander of US troops in South Korea,

General John Hodge, described him as 'devious, emotionally unstable, brutal, corrupt and wildly unpredictable'.

Rhee pestered the Americans constantly for hardware that Washington refused to provide, fearing he would use it straightaway to invade the North. At the same time, Kim took every opportunity to press his own demands on the one man whose permission he needed for an invasion: the Soviet dictator Joseph Stalin.

Both sides regularly instigated clashes across the border. Propaganda broadcasts from Pyongyang fuelled talk of imminent invasion by the communists. With Cold War tensions rising in Europe, the Middle East and Indochina, both the United States and the Soviet Union decided their military manpower would be more use outside Korea. Moscow withdrew its troops from North Korea in 1948, and the following year President Truman bowed to the wishes of his Joint Chiefs of Staff by pulling the last 7500 American occupation troops out of South Korea, leaving only 500 advisers. As compensation, Congress approved a US$100 million economic and military aid package for South Korea. MacArthur concurred with the US withdrawal, believing that the training and combat readiness of the Republic of Korea (ROK) army meant it was now capable of defending the country by itself.

Since 1945, Truman's priority had been paying off America's US$250 billion wartime debt. In five years he pruned the defence budget from 38 per cent of gross domestic product to less than 5 per cent. In that time, the number of American servicemen and women fell from 12 million to 1.5 million. Hardware was not modernised and munitions were left to run down. The armed forces were left undermanned, undertrained and underequipped. In just a few years they had become a mockery of the fighting machine that had defeated the Japanese in the Pacific and the Nazis in Europe.

In his book *The Coldest Winter*, David Halberstam described an army so short of funds that:

artillery units had not been able to practice adequately because there was no ammo; armoured groups . . . lacked gas for real manoeuvres; and troops . . . were being told to use only two sheets of toilet paper each time they visited the latrine. There were so few spare parts for vehicles that some enlisted men went out and bought war surplus equipment at very low prices, using their own money, in order to break it down for spare parts.

Things were hardly better for the occupation army in Japan. Almost every regiment in MacArthur's four divisions was a battalion or battery short; every company had lost a platoon. US Army studies would reveal that more than 40 per cent of the enlisted men thrown against the invading North Koreans were rated as either Class IV or Class V—the bottom two categories—for ability and intelligence. Their training and readiness for war, for which MacArthur himself was ultimately responsible, were abysmal.

This was the strategic climate in which Kim Il Sung sought Stalin's permission to invade South Korea and eliminate the pro-American regime in Seoul.

Visiting Moscow in March 1949 to ask for more economic support, Kim assured Stalin that South Koreans were waiting with open arms to welcome his troops, and that the poorly equipped and unmotivated ROK army could be defeated in days—the same fallacy that, 70 years later, convinced another Russian leader to invade neighbouring Ukraine. It was the right time to attack, Kim told Stalin, because the Korean People's Army was stronger than the ROK army, communist partisans would support the invasion, and Rhee's regime was despised by the people.

Military tension between the two Koreas suited Stalin, who was happy to stir the pot as long as it did not risk a direct confrontation with the United States. Prodding Kim to 'strike the Southerners in the teeth' was one thing, but giving him permission to invade was another. A record of their conversation shows that Stalin responded coolly to Kim's proposal:

Kim Il Sung: Comrade Stalin, we believe that the situation makes it necessary and possible to liberate the whole country through military means. The reactionary forces of the South will never agree on a peaceful unification and will perpetuate the division of the country until they feel themselves strong enough to attack the North.

Now is the best opportunity for us to take the initiative into our own hands. Our armed forces are stronger, and in addition we have the support of a powerful guerrilla movement in the South. The population of the South, which despises the pro-American regime, will certainly help us as well.

Stalin: You should not advance to the South. First of all, the Korean People's Army does not have an overwhelming superiority over the troops of the South. Numerically, as I understand, you are even behind them. Second, there are still American troops in the South that will interfere in case of hostilities. Third, one should not forget that the agreement on the 38th parallel is in effect between the USSR and the United States. If the agreement is broken by our side, it is more of a reason to believe that Americans will interfere.

Kim Il Sung: Does it mean that there is no chance to reunify Korea in the near future? Our people are very anxious to be together again to cast off the yoke of the reactionary regime and their American masters.

Stalin: If the adversary has aggressive intentions, then sooner or later it will start the aggression. In response to the attack you will have a good opportunity to launch a counterattack.

Then your move will be understood and supported by everyone.*

Fearful of provoking a conflict with the United States that he was not sure he could win, and believing that a premature war might result in the destruction of North Korea, Stalin refused to sanction Kim's invasion plans. Forbidden from crossing the 38th parallel except in response to an attack by the South, Kim would have to bide his time.

A speech by the US secretary of state in January 1950 did nothing to reassure the South Koreans. In his address to the National Press Club, Dean Acheson identified America's 'defensive perimeter' in the Pacific as a line running through Japan, the Ryukyus (a chain of islands between Japan and Taiwan) and the Philippines, thereby excluding Korea—not to mention her steadfast wartime allies Australia and New Zealand. Many Australians refused to believe him, Lieutenant General Gordon Bennett telling reporters, 'I cannot visualise America allowing any aggressive Power to come south to a point where it might outflank the American line to the Philippines.'

By placing the Korean Peninsula outside America's 'defensive perimeter', Acheson seemed to be suggesting that the United States would stay out of any war in Korea. Diplomatic cables show that Acheson's comments unnerved the government in Seoul, although it is unclear whether his speech directly influenced either Stalin's or Kim's actions.

But Acheson's words were out of step with the political mood in Washington, which was increasingly conditioned by Senator Joseph McCarthy's red witch-hunt and by the bitterness many

---

* The text of the conversation, quoted by Kathryn Weathersby in her paper '"Should We Fear This?" Stalin and the danger of war with America', is from Evgeniy Bajanov's and Natalia Bajanova's unpublished manuscript *The Korean Conflict, 1950–1953: The Most Mysterious War of the 20th Century—Based on Secret Soviet Archives*.

Americans felt about the 'loss' of China to Mao Zedong's communists. Russia's successful detonation of an atomic bomb in August 1949 only seemed to confirm financier Bernard Baruch's assertion to President Truman that the United States was 'losing the Cold War'. With foreign policy the top priority in Washington, the State Department ordered a comprehensive review of US strategic and military objectives. The result, National Security Council Paper NSC-68, was delivered to the president in April 1950.

Led by the State Department's hardline head of Policy Planning, Paul Nitze, the authors of NSC-68 argued that the Soviet Union was 'animated by a new fanatic faith' inimical to the United States, the ultimate purpose of which was 'the complete subversion or forcible destruction of the machinery of government and structure of society in the non-Soviet world, and their replacement by an apparatus and structure subservient to and controlled by the Kremlin'.

NSC-68 suggested a range of possible responses to Soviet aggression, including a return to US isolationism, but in the end concluded that the only effective deterrent to communist expansion was the massive build-up of the US military and its nuclear and conventional weaponry, to be paid for by increasing taxes and reducing other spending.

A number of officials, including the defense secretary and several senior diplomats, disagreed with NSC-68's conclusions, but the North Korean invasion two months later forced Truman's hand and the authors' recommendations effectively became US government policy. Between 1950 and 1953, the Truman administration would nearly triple its military spending as a percentage of gross domestic product, from 5 per cent to more than 14 per cent.

NSC-68 was classified top secret and would not be declassified until 1975. Had Stalin been aware of it, it is unlikely he would have so seriously underestimated America's resolve to come to South Korea's aid. It was, in the words of historian Max Hastings, a document 'whose secrecy destroyed its very purpose'.

But in April 1950 there was little sense outside the Truman administration of the hardening attitudes that were beginning to shape America's Cold War thinking.

While still awaiting Stalin's permission to invade, Kim was successful in extracting Soviet guarantees of increased military aid. In return for nine tons (over 8000 kilograms) of North Korean gold and 40 tons (over 36,000 kilograms) of silver, Moscow agreed to supply arms, ammunition and technical equipment.

In April, three months after Acheson's National Press Club speech, Kim made another visit to Moscow, where he met the Soviet leader three times. According to historian James Matray, Stalin confirmed to Kim that the international environment had sufficiently changed to permit a 'more active stance on the unification of Korea'. He pointed to Mao's victory in the Chinese civil war as having 'improved the environment' for action in Korea, because Beijing was no longer distracted and would be able to devote more energy to assisting North Korea. Significantly, the pair also discussed the possible use of Chinese troops.

Mao's triumph, Stalin told Kim, had 'proved the strength of Asian revolutionaries, and shown the weakness of Asian reactionaries and their mentors in the West, in America. Americans . . . did not dare to challenge the new Chinese authorities militarily.'

More significant than Acheson's speech was the signing, a month later, of the 'Sino-Soviet Treaty of Friendship, Alliance and Mutual Assistance'. This received wide coverage in Australia, with many commentators smelling a rat. In an editorial headlined 'Hard bargaining in Moscow', *The Sydney Morning Herald* commented that while the treaty 'remove[d] any lingering doubts that the policies of Moscow and Peking are now firmly linked', it would be 'naive to assume that the published text has any but the most general relationship to the real and secret agreement which must have been reached in Moscow'.

According to Matray, Stalin told Kim that the Sino-Soviet treaty had made the United States 'more hesitant to challenge the Communists in Asia'—a comment he would hardly have made had he known of the existence of NSC-68. The prevailing US mood, Stalin told Kim, was 'not to interfere', because Russia now had the atomic bomb and 'our positions are solidified in Pyongyang'. Mao reportedly told the North Koreans that there was no need to be afraid of the United States, as the 'Americans will not enter a third world war for such a small territory'.

Although still wary of US involvement, Stalin finally gave his permission for Kim to invade on the proviso that Kim also obtain approval from Mao. He wanted the war to be 'quick and speedy' and made it clear that Moscow would not countenance direct military intervention. If Kim needed reinforcements, they would have to be Chinese. The attack was set for late June.

Stalin's generals were not impressed by Kim's invasion plans, considering them too 'defensive'. According to retired US Navy commander Richard Mobley, the Soviets drafted a new plan requiring Kim's army to advance fifteen to twenty kilometres per day, to occupy Seoul within three days, and to complete its 'main' military activity within 27 days. After Kim approved the revised plans, the Russian embassy in Pyongyang commented that the North Korean leader appeared 'very confident of a quick victory'.

Kim duly obtained Mao's approval for the invasion, along with advice to follow the example of Mao's victorious campaign against the Nationalists. The Korean People's Army, Mao said, 'must act swiftly, go around big cities not wasting time on their takeover, concentrating their efforts on destroying the armed force of the adversary'.

Kim's confidence in a quick victory was based in part on his belief that a North Korean attack would inspire an uprising of 200,000 communists in the South, and that guerrilla fighters would flock to the aid of his soldiers. He was not alone in expecting a communist uprising. Syngman Rhee's fear of what he called the 'north wind' led to an orgy of state violence against perceived leftists inside South Korea. According to the historian Bruce Cumings, between 100,000 and 200,000 South Koreans were killed as a result of political violence before the war began, at the hands of either their own government or the American occupation force. The Korean War scholar Hun Joon Kim has calculated that at least 300,000 people were arrested and either executed or 'disappeared' by Rhee's security forces in the months following the communist invasion.

But even without the predicted communist uprising, Kim had good reason to be confident of victory. The return of thousands of Korean soldiers from the Chinese civil war had given him an army of highly motivated and well-trained soldiers equipped with modern Russian weapons, nearly half of whom had combat experience. Crucially, Kim's armoured brigade boasted 150 Russian-built T-34 tanks, which the ROK soldiers' obsolete bazookas were powerless to stop.

Facing Kim's disciplined communist troops was a chaotic, poorly trained and poorly armed ROK army led by an officer corps steeped in corruption. Brave as many of them were, too many South Korean officers were—in the words of historian Clay Blair—'venal opportunists who used their newly acquired power for personal gain. Among this element theft, bribery, blackmail and kickbacks were commonplace.'

A typical South Korean soldier at the outbreak of the war was an illiterate villager carrying a clapped-out rifle left over from World War II. In keeping with the US policy of giving Rhee nothing that might tempt him to invade the North, the ROK army had little artillery and virtually no tanks.

American generals were well aware of South Korea's military weakness. A confidential circular written by the head of the Korean Military Advisory Group, Brigadier General Bill Roberts, revealed an army at breaking point due to logistical problems caused by the fragile South Korean economy and by the doubling of troop numbers from 50,000 to 100,000 men. Roberts reported that 10–15 per cent of the army's weapons and 30–35 per cent of its vehicles were useless. According to the army department in Washington, spare parts due in 1950 would not arrive until 1952, and the Korean economy was incapable of making up the shortfall from its own production or from foreign exchange. Roberts concluded that without further support the ROK army could not hold out against a North Korean attack for more than fifteen days. 'In short,' he wrote, 'Korea is threatened with the same disaster that befell China.'

This did not stop Roberts from publicly expressing his confidence in the South's military forces: he told *The New York Times* that a 'full-scale attack . . . was just what was needed to complete the training of the South Korean Army'.

It was in Rhee's interests to exaggerate the communist military threat, and on 11 May he sent his defense minister to a hurriedly called afternoon press conference. The minister announced that the arrival of two divisions of Chinese communist troops since the previous August had raised the 'fully-armed, effective fighting force' in North Korea to 183,100. He estimated the total North Korean fighting strength at 'well above 300,000', including 'women whom the northern regime recently began to conscript'. In addition to the North's 173 tanks and 195 aircraft, the defense minister catalogued an ominous inventory of artillery, mortars, anti-aircraft guns and light and heavy machine guns.

Warning of communist troops massing across the border, Rhee told reporters: 'I do not think these North Korean troops are concentrating near the 38th parallel to invade Japan or China.'

In a telegram to Secretary Acheson, the American chargé d'affaires in Seoul, Everett Drumright, poured cold water on the South Korean figures, estimating North Korea's fighting strength at 103,000 and tank numbers at just 65:

If Embassy estimates approximately accurate, it follows Korean figures are exaggerated—probably deliberately so. Purpose of exaggeration undoubtedly is to convince friendly powers, especially US, of disparity of strength between North and South Korean forces and thus enlist for additional military aid . . . That Defense Minister's statement was expressly issued for foreign consumption is indicated by fact Korean press excluded from conference with foreign correspondents and was later given much less detailed report of North Korean military strength. Fear specific figures would alarm ROK populace probably dictated exclusion.

At a meeting in Seoul six weeks before the invasion, Rhee complained bitterly to Drumright about a recent speech by Senator Tom Connally, chairman of the Senate Foreign Relations Committee, that appeared to dismiss Korea as being of no strategic importance to the United States.

State Department records show Rhee 'protest[ing] what he termed failure of US to respond [to] his request for air support capable of containing rapidly growing North Korean Air Force'. Together with Washington's failure to supply the fighter planes he had repeatedly requested and its plans to pull out military advisers, Connally's remarks had shaken Rhee's 'faith in the determination of the United States to assist Korea in the event of North Korean aggression', Drumright wrote in a secret memorandum.

The reluctance of senior US government officials to go to Seoul while visiting General MacArthur in Tokyo struck the vain and volatile Rhee as proof of Washington's waning interest. 'The President was much distressed,' the US ambassador, John Muccio, cabled Dean Rusk (the Assistant Secretary of State for Far Eastern Affairs) on 1 June after the defense secretary became the latest official to turn down a personal invitation to visit Rhee in Seoul. 'This afternoon an Embassy officer learned from those close to the President that he had become depressed and angered at what he took to be not only a slight to Korea but more important that the US Department of Defense was showing its indifference to the fate of Korea.'

On 19 June 1950—a mere five days before the invasion—the US Central Intelligence Agency (CIA) issued a secret memorandum captioned 'Current capabilities of the North Korean regime'. (The word 'current' was a misnomer, since it was based on information that was more than a month old.) The intelligence organisations of the departments of State, Army, Navy and the Air Force all concurred with its findings.

While acknowledging that Kim's ultimate goal was control of South Korea, the memorandum's authors argued that the North's program of 'propaganda, infiltration, sabotage, subversion and guerrilla operations' would not be enough to bring down Rhee's regime, provided that US aid was not substantially reduced. They noted, however, that the communists' capacity for both short- and long-term military operations was being 'further developed', and that the North was superior in armour, heavy artillery and aircraft.

While conceding that the communists already had the capacity to achieve 'limited objectives in short-term military operations against South Korea, including the capture of Seoul', the authors stated that without direct Soviet and Chinese military intervention, it was 'not certain that the northern regime . . . would be able to gain effective control over all of southern Korea'. Moscow was expected to increase its logistical support to the North Koreans, but the authors regarded the 'direct participation' of regular Soviet or Chinese communist military units as unlikely 'except as a last resort'.

Despite the warning signs, the Pentagon pushed ahead with plans to reduce the size of its Korean Military Advisory Group by half from the start of 1951.

3

NO REASON FOR ALARM

At 10 a.m. on Sunday, 25 June 1950, Ambassador Muccio cabled the State Department in Washington with news of the invasion. According to Korean army reports that had been 'partly confirmed' by US military advisers, the action began around 4 a.m., when North Korean artillery opened fire on the town of Ongjin. Two hours later North Korean troops, supported by tanks, began pouring across the 38th parallel, while seaborne troops landed on the east coast. Although details of the invasion were still sketchy, Muccio had no doubt what was happening. 'It would appear,' he wrote, 'from nature of attack and manner in which it was launched that it constitutes all-out offensive against ROK.'

Muccio's telegram was received by the State Department at 9.26 p.m. on Saturday, 24 June, Washington time. Dean Rusk and Secretary of the Army Frank Pace were contacted by telephone and hurried to the department. At 10.30 p.m. Muccio's cable was relayed to the Army Department. Secretary of State Acheson was also notified and agreed to the telegram being sent to the White House for transmission to President Truman at his home in

Independence, Missouri. Acheson rang Truman and the two agreed to call a meeting of the UN Security Council. At 11.30 p.m. news of the North Korean invasion was sent to London, Paris, Moscow, Ottawa, Tokyo, Canberra, Manila, Wellington, New Delhi, Jakarta and Taipei.

Muccio's cable was the first official report of the invasion, but Washington was already abuzz with news that North Koreans had crossed the 38th parallel. The scoop belonged to United Press's Korean correspondent, Jack James, who reported the use of heavy tanks in a 'general offensive' across the border. James described the South Korean 1st Army as 'defeated'. Officials in Washington were getting calls from reporters asking for confirmation. After a failed effort to reach the Seoul embassy by phone, Acheson drafted a short cable asking the embassy to 'Advise urgently'. Before it could be sent, Muccio's telegram arrived, confirming the substance of James's reports.

At thirteen minutes to midnight, the State Department received another telegram from Muccio. This time, the ambassador—known within the department as a careful reporter—did not hold back:

> At 4 o'clock this morning North Korean armed forces began unprovoked attacks against the defense positions of the Republic of Korea at several points along the 38th degree parallel . . .
>
> Korean defense forces are taking up prepared positions to resist Northern aggression. Both Korean officials and the security forces are handling the situation calmly and with ability. There is no reason for alarm. As yet it cannot be determined whether the Northern Communists intended to precipitate all-out warfare.

Efforts to obtain a clearer picture of the military situation continued after midnight, but the Americans were determined to get the case before the Security Council with or without more information, and to do it in time for the morning papers. State Department records confirm that by 2 a.m. 'no further information about the course of events in Korea had been obtained', but it was considered 'of the utmost importance that the decision to present the case to the Security Council should appear in the morning papers simultaneously with the news of the North Korean attack. Therefore the Secretary made the final decision to go to the Security Council shortly in advance of the press deadline.'

After sending his second cable, Muccio hurried to the presidential palace, where he found President Rhee 'under considerable emotional tension, but . . . composed'. Seoul appeared 'calm and normal'. Rhee told the ambassador that his cabinet would meet at 2 p.m. and he was considering proclaiming martial law in the capital. The invasion, he insisted, had 'come as no surprise to anybody . . . he had been warning the people about it a long time and calling upon every man, woman and child to come out and fight with sticks and stones if necessary'.

Muccio's account of his meeting with Rhee reached the State Department at 2.54 a.m., Washington time. Six minutes later, the UN secretary-general, Trygve Lie, was informed by telephone of Washington's request that the Security Council be convened immediately to consider the 'aggression' in Korea.

By now the North Koreans had already broadcast their own version of events across the 38th parallel. 'The so-called "defense army" of the South Korea puppet regime started a surprise invasion of the north along the whole front of the 38th parallel line at dawn on the 25th,' the Home Affairs Bureau of the People's Republic of Korea announced on Pyongyang radio. 'At this moment our security army is putting up stiff counter-operations against the enemy . . . the people's Republic of Korea wishes to remind the South Korea puppet regime of the fact that, unless the puppets immediately suspend their adventurous military actions, the People's Republic will be obliged to resort to decisive countermeasures.'

Muccio commented: 'It will be obvious that . . . North Koreans are attempting to clothe their naked aggression against ROK with patently absurd charges that ROK commenced invasion. Developments during course of day of course wholly disprove this unfounded propaganda.'

When the morning cloud over Seoul cleared, two North Korean air force fighters buzzed the airport without bombing or strafing. In the late afternoon four more enemy fighters appeared in the sky, strafing the airport building and destroying a fuel dump and tanker. Other fighters caught a number of T-6 trainer aircraft on the ground at a military airstrip. It was clear that the North Koreans intended to make full use of their air superiority. 'Future course of hostilities may depend largely on whether US will or will not give adequate air assistance,' Muccio told Acheson.

By night-time on the day of the invasion it was clear that the ROK army was fast running out of ammunition. Muccio warned that its 'modest stocks' would be exhausted within ten days. '[I]t would be catastrophic,' he cabled Acheson, 'for US to permit gallant Korean forces to succumb for lack of ammunition. I am confident that if adequately supplied, ROK security forces will fight bravely and with distinction'.

The US ambassador in Moscow, Alan Kirk, was away from the embassy, but after reading Muccio's 10 a.m. telegram from Seoul, the chargé, Walworth Barbour, cabled Washington, describing the attack as a 'clear-cut Soviet challenge' that constituted a 'direct threat [to] our leadership of free world against Communist imperialism'. The destruction of the Republic of Korea, Barbour wrote, would have 'grave unfavourable repercussions' for the United States in Japan, South-East Asia and other areas.

The view at the Moscow embassy was that President Rhee had either asked already or would shortly ask for US help, but that in any case Washington should offer its support at once, without waiting for a formal request, since any delay might be read by the Soviets as giving them a licence to start making trouble in Indochina. Reiterating the embassy's belief that Stalin was not prepared to risk a full-scale war with the West, Barbour suggested the United States could take advantage of the 'Kremlin's Korean adventure' to demonstrate its own strength and to 'unmask . . . Soviet weaknesses' before the eyes of the world, especially in Asia, where the belief in Moscow's military might was 'grossly exaggerated' due to 'recent Soviet political and propaganda successes'.

John Foster Dulles, who would go on to become President Dwight D. Eisenhower's secretary of state, was in Tokyo to discuss ending the American occupation of Japan when the North Koreans launched their attack. A few days earlier Dulles and his aide John Allison had visited the 38th parallel. The next day Dulles made a speech to the Korean National Assembly, in which he promised that Korea would 'never be alone so long as you continue to play worthily your part in the great design of human freedom'. There was no great urgency behind Dulles' windy rhetoric—in fact, MacArthur's intelligence chief, General Charles Willoughby, had not even raised the possibility of a North Korean attack when he briefed the pair.

Their presence at MacArthur's headquarters when news of the invasion came through gave the pair a chance to observe MacArthur in action. The hero of the Pacific War seemed curiously unconcerned. MacArthur stated his belief that (a) the offensive was not a full-scale invasion; (b) the Soviets were not necessarily behind the attack; and (c) the South would win. Allison recalled MacArthur telling them, 'This is probably only a reconnaissance in force. If Washington only will not hobble me, I can handle it with one arm tied behind my back.'

Dulles and Allison did not share MacArthur's insouciance. At 9 p.m., Tokyo time, on the day of the invasion they sent a top-secret priority telegram to Acheson and Rusk. It was 'possible', they wrote, that the South Koreans might be able to 'contain and repulse' the communist attack by themselves—an outcome they considered to be 'the best way'. Failing that, however, the pair asserted their belief that 'US forces should be used even though this risks Russian counter moves'. To sit by while Korea was overrun by an 'unprovoked armed attack', they wrote, 'would start disastrous chain of events leading most probably to world war'.

According to Halberstam, Allison went to dinner that night with an old friend, Brigadier General Crump Garvin, commander of the Port of Yokohama, and was shocked to be told that Eighth Army intelligence had been passing on reports 'for the past two or three weeks' indicating that civilians were being moved back from the northern side of the 38th parallel and that North Korean troops were massing in the border area. 'Anyone who read the reports could see something was going to happen and soon,' Allison recalled Garvin saying. 'I don't know what G-2 [i.e. General Willoughby] in Tokyo has been doing.'

During the night, with North Korean tanks reported to be just 27 kilometres from Seoul, Ambassador Muccio 'reluctantly' ordered the evacuation of American women and children from the port of Inchon. MacArthur, according to Allison, 'questioned the necessity' of the evacuation, again rejecting the idea that it was an all-out attack supported by the Soviet Union.

In Moscow, Ambassador Kirk had been trying without success to advise the Soviets of Washington's request for an emergency Security Council meeting on Korea. No senior official was available, and a junior employee on duty at the foreign office told Kirk that it was 'difficult' to reach the deputy foreign minister, Andrei Gromyko, on Sundays.

Despite MacArthur's insistence that there was 'no reason to panic', evidence of panic in the presidential palace was clear. Rhee phoned Ambassador Muccio at 10 p.m. on Monday and asked him to come to a meeting with the acting prime minister, Shin Song-mo. Clearly under 'great strain', Rhee babbled 'incoherently' to Shin in a mixture of Korean and English, telling him that the cabinet had decided to flee Seoul for the town of Taejon, an important junction south of the Kum River, on the Seoul–Pusan road. The decision, he kept repeating, had not been made out of any consideration for personal safety, but because 'government must continue, and because if he himself were lost to Communists, it would be a serious blow for his country's cause'. Muccio told Acheson that Shin 'repeatedly said "yes, sir", "I will, sir" to President's instructions . . . but it was obvious that he was very disgusted at President's decision and orders. He finally excused himself, announcing that he would telephone for latest news of fighting.'

Muccio did his best to persuade Rhee to remain in Seoul, pointing out that he still had troops to throw into the fight and that they could use bazookas, anti-tank guns and mines against the North Korean tanks. If the government left Seoul then much of the battle would be lost, Muccio said. If the situation became 'disorganised', it would be impossible to pull things together again. Rhee was unmoved. His own personal safety did not matter, he said; the government must not run the risk of being captured.

When it finally sank in that nothing he said could change Rhee's mind, Muccio agreed that the president could go to Taejon, but he and the male staff at the American embassy would stay in Seoul. Outside the residence, Shin took the ambassador aside and let him know that Rhee had not consulted him before deciding to abandon the capital.

In Australia, most newspapers carried front-page reports of the North Korean invasion, which was generally taken to have been ordered and directed by Moscow. North Korea, *The Sydney Morning Herald* told its readers, was a 'full-blown satellite of the Soviet Union. What it does, militarily, politically, or economically, is inspired or commanded by Moscow.' An American military adviser told reporters that the launch of the attack during heavy rain, which prevented air support, showed that an 'inflexible plan had been laid down some time ago for a full-scale sweep down the peninsula'.

The United Nations, *The Age* said, was facing its 'most crucial test' and Australia would watch developments with 'vigilance and anxiety'.

On Sunday afternoon the United Nations Security Council met at the UN's temporary home at Lake Success, New York. Some members objected to the short notice, which had made it impossible for them to obtain instructions from their governments. The meeting was held without the Russians, their delegate having walked out of the Security Council in January in protest against the United Nations' refusal to give China's seat to Mao's victorious communists. With Russia unable to use its veto, the council passed by nine votes to nil a resolution calling for the immediate cessation of hostilities and demanding North Korea withdraw 'forthwith' its armed forces to the 38th parallel.

More significantly, the resolution called upon all UN members to 'render every assistance to the United Nations in the execution of this resolution' and to refrain from giving assistance to the North Koreans. But for how long could the disintegrating ROK army resist while the United States decided on its military response?

Acheson stressed the need to keep US military advisers on the ground unless the situation rendered it impossible or futile. 'Obviously vigorous fighting by Koreans with what they have and heroic initial effort are essential if any action by us is to have chance take effect,' he cabled Muccio.

The ambassador assured Dean Rusk that the South Koreans had 'made [a] gallant comeback . . . and seem to have stabilized situation', but this was wishful thinking. As the North Koreans rolled towards the capital, the ROK army seemed in danger of complete collapse. Muccio himself warned that it was 'impossible [to] estimate situation which will exist tomorrow in Seoul'.

Less than 48 hours into the war, the loss of the capital seemed inevitable. By 11 p.m. on Monday, Muccio was admitting the 'rapid deterioration and disintegration' of the military situation, which was unravelling so fast that 'we may not all be able to get out'.

Meanwhile, President Truman had returned to Washington from Missouri and issued his first official statement on the crisis, condemning the North's 'unprovoked aggression' and vowing that the United States would 'vigorously support the effort of the [Security] Council to terminate this serious breach of the peace'.

There was now a real risk that the US embassy in Seoul would be overrun. Rhee and most of his cabinet had fled south, but Muccio—anxious to avoid accusations of 'abandonment'—was determined to hang on with a few volunteers 'until [the] bitter end'. This arrived sooner than expected. By the following day Muccio was advising Acheson that he and the remaining embassy staff would be departing at three o'clock that afternoon with the last of the military advisers, leaving behind just two members of an apostolic delegation, who were choosing to remain in Seoul.

As Dulles and Allison prepared to fly back to the United States, they were joined at Tokyo airport by General MacArthur, no longer the cocksure figure who had boasted of winning the fight with 'one arm tied behind my back'. According to Allison's later account, MacArthur that day was 'dejected, completely forlorn'—so forlorn that when a message arrived that the secretary of the army wanted a telecom meeting with him at 1 p.m., Tokyo time, MacArthur told his aides that his chief of staff could deal with it. 'All Korea is lost,' he told his departing guests. 'The only thing we can do is get our people safely out of the country.'

Whether or not the invasion signalled Moscow's willingness to risk all-out war with the United States (unlikely, most felt), none of Truman's top advisers was in any doubt that it was a direct challenge to America's resolve and demanded immediate action. American ambassadors around the world echoed that message. 'US firmness is regarded under test,' the American chargé in Saigon telegraphed Washington, adding that the Vietnamese believed 'if US will not come to aid of Korea where it has invested vastly more prestige and money, then it could not be expected to defend [Indochina] in case of invasion'.

Chiang Kai-shek's offer of Nationalist troops to fight in Korea interested Truman but was rejected by Acheson and, eventually, by most of the Joint Chiefs of Staff—partly for fear of bringing communist China into the war and partly because the feebleness of the Nationalist army had been made all too obvious during the civil war. Without bothering to secure the approval of Congress, Truman committed US air and sea power to protect the evacuation of Americans and to provide 'cover and support' for beleaguered ROK troops. But nobody believed that air and sea power would be enough to turn back the invaders.

Seoul fell. Lee Hun Ku, a former member of the National Assembly, slipped out of the city in disguise four days after the attack and escaped by ferry to Suwon, where he brought Everett Drumright up to date on the situation in the capital. According to Lee, who had obtained his information from 'young people on [the] streets' while he was in hiding, resistance by police and ROK soldiers had been crushed by noon on Wednesday and all prisoners were immediately killed. The enemy troops, Lee reported, were 'surprisingly young and small' compared with South Korean soldiers, and were 'heavily armed with tommy guns'.

Kim Il Sung made a radio broadcast thanking the citizens of Seoul for their help in ridding Korea of the 'Rhee gang', while an unknown communist functionary appointed to lead the Seoul People's Committee handed out free rice 'as evidence of the difference of life under the two regimes'. Prison gates were thrown open and armed prisoners invited to 'take revenge as seemed suitable', while government officials, police and other 'enemies of the people' were hunted down and killed. Some information suggested that the communists were using the American embassy as their headquarters.

It was left to MacArthur to inform Washington of the scale of the disaster he had overseen. Ordered by the joint chiefs to fly to

Korea and inspect the situation for himself, MacArthur reported dismissively that the South Koreans 'have not seriously fought' and 'lack leadership'. The retreating ROK army had lost or abandoned its supplies and heavy equipment; most soldiers had fled with nothing but their rifle or carbine, and it was only through the efforts of American officers sent over by MacArthur himself that South Korean units were being gathered up and given 'some semblance of organisation'. The Korean army, he went on, 'is entirely incapable of counteraction and there is grave danger of a further breakthrough. If the enemy advance continues much further it will seriously threaten the fall of the Republic. The only assurance for the holding of the present line, and the ability to regain later the lost ground, is through the introduction of US ground combat forces.'

If authorised by the joint chiefs, MacArthur proposed sending a regimental combat team (roughly equivalent in size to a brigade) to join the fighting immediately, while building a force of up to two divisions from his army in Japan to mount a counteroffensive. Without a total commitment to ground, sea and land forces, he wrote, 'our mission will at best be needlessly costly in life, money and prestige. At worse [*sic*], it might even be doomed to failure.'

A teletype conference held in the early hours of 30 June ended with the generals in Washington giving MacArthur their congratulations and best wishes. 'Everyone here delighted your prompt action in personally securing first-hand view of situation . . . We all have full confidence in you and your command.'

A few hours later, after a White House meeting with the secretaries of state and defense and the joint chiefs, President Truman formally committed US ground forces, in addition to the already authorised regimental combat team, and ordered a naval blockade of the entire Korean coast. By calling it a 'police action', Truman avoided the necessity of asking Congress to declare war on North Korea. The American troops would fight under the United Nations' flag.

With General MacArthur desperate to get his hands on the RAAF's Mustang fighters, Australia's recently elected Liberal prime minister, Robert Menzies, announced on 30 June that he was sending the 40-odd Mustangs of No. 77 Squadron—'one of the finest units in the Far East', in the words of US general George Stratemeyer—to help defend South Korea.

The next day, Australian newspapers reported that South Korean resistance had collapsed, *The Sun* quoting 'reliable sources' who claimed that ROK soldiers 'refused to mine roads in order to block the Red advance, and walked away from the fight after promising the Americans to continue fighting'.

As MacArthur rushed to get American troops into battle, Brigadier General John Church, the US commander in South Korea, promised that 'if the Russians come down, we will fight the Russkies'. The US Army, he told reporters, was 'through with retreating . . . We are not going any farther back . . . We are going back to the North Korean border.'

4

BUGGING OUT

The North Korean forces, spearheaded by their seemingly indestructible Russian T-34 tanks, poured south, scattering or obliterating the demoralised ROK divisions. Well camouflaged, they avoided the roads and moved largely on foot over the difficult Korean terrain. Perhaps a third of the North Koreans, and a majority of their officers and non-commissioned officers (NCOs), had fought with Mao's communist forces in the Chinese civil war. Emulating the tactics that had defeated Chiang Kai-shek's better-equipped Nationalists, they tried to avoid massed frontal assaults, looking instead to encircle and destroy enemy units through superior manpower. 'They preferred to make early contact,' Halberstam wrote, 'then slide along the flank of their adversaries, hitting the badly outnumbered South Koreans or Americans from the side or rear.' They also sent small parties of soldiers ahead, disguised as fleeing peasants, to scout enemy positions, which then came under 'strikingly accurate' North Korean artillery fire.

South of Seoul, Kim's army halted to regroup. In those opening days the North Korean advance had been disciplined and cohesive, the ROK retreat chaotic and humiliating. But the logistics 'tail' of the communist army needed time to catch up and Seoul had to be secured before Kim's troops could resume their drive towards Pusan, in the far south-east. While the North Koreans reorganised, the Americans joined the fight.

The nearest American unit to Korea was the 24th Infantry Division, in Japan, commanded by Major General William Dean. Based on the southernmost main island of Kyushu, the 24th Division was directly across the Korea Strait from Pusan. Years of occupation duty had left the 24th a badly depleted force. A third of its wartime strength had been lost. Its 2.36-inch bazookas and M24 light tanks lacked punch, and the tanks were in poor repair and prone to breaking down.

MacArthur's hastily configured plan to repel the North Koreans rested on the speedy deployment of a regimental combat team (RCT) to halt the enemy, while two American divisions were brought over from Japan to prepare for an 'early counter-offensive'.* The problem was that MacArthur did not have an RCT available, so the force had to be improvised using two infantry companies from the 21st Infantry Regiment. A full-strength RCT with all its heavy weapons might have been able to do the job, but it would have taken weeks to airlift the equipment and MacArthur's timeframe did not allow for transport by ship. Rather than suit the transport to the force, MacArthur suited the force to the transport. The Joint Chiefs of Staff foresaw the risks, asking MacArthur in a teletype conference on 30 June, 'Can you move heavy equipment

---

* Before the invasion in June 1950, several plans already existed for the defence of the Korean Peninsula. One was Operations Plan SL-17. After the North Koreans attacked, MacArthur's headquarters in Japan asked the Pentagon for 50 copies of Plan SL-17. In his illuminating study of Task Force Smith, John Garrett identified this document as the blueprint for the defensive plan that MacArthur later claimed as his own.

and artillery into that area by air?' MacArthur refused to answer the question and the deployment was approved.

Task Force Smith, led by Lieutenant Colonel Charles B. 'Brad' Smith, was the first American unit to be thrown into battle against the North Koreans. Its two rifle companies, reinforced with recoilless guns, mortars and some 105-millimetre howitzers, were expected to perform the role of a full RCT. According to one assessment, Smith was given an RCT mission with not even 10 per cent of its assets.

That mission was to stall the enemy advance while awaiting the arrival from Japan of the rest of the 24th Division. According to Roy Appleman's official army history, Dean told Smith: 'When you get to Pusan, head for Taejon. We want to stop the North Koreans as far from Pusan as we can. Block the main road as far north as possible ... Sorry I can't give you more information. That's all I've got.'

Bad weather and a lack of transport planes meant it took two days to airlift the task force from Japan. The last group reached Pusan on the morning of 2 July; by the evening, the force was boarding a train to Taejon, midway between Pusan and what was thought to be the front line. Only around one man in six of Task Force Smith had combat experience, including about a third of the officers. Most of the men were still in their teens and had only eight weeks' training.

MacArthur had sent an advance team under Brigadier General John Church to assess the situation, but the crumbling ROK defence had already forced Church to withdraw his headquarters nearly 150 kilometres south. 'We have a little action up here,' he told Smith. 'All we need is some men up there who won't run when they see tanks. We're going to move you up to support the ROKs and give them moral support.'

As the roughly 500 men of Task Force Smith headed north by train to confront the North Koreans, Major General Dean arrived in Taejon to take over from Church as commander of US forces in

Korea. By now MacArthur had sent the 34th Infantry Regiment—minus tanks and heavy anti-tank weapons—together with the rest of the 21st Infantry Regiment to bolster the task force. In anticipation of a victory parade in Seoul, the troops had been told to pack their summer dress uniforms.

Instead of concentrating his troops further south, along the natural barrier of the Kum River, Dean broke them into three groups deployed fifteen kilometres apart, near the village of Osan. Dean was convinced the war would be 'short and easy'; he was not the last American commander to fatally underestimate the fighting qualities and tactical skills of the North Koreans.

At around 7.30 a.m. on 5 July, a column of eight North Korean T-34 tanks was spotted rolling towards Task Force Smith. At a distance of two kilometres, the American artillery started firing, but shells from the 105-millimetre howitzers simply ricocheted off the tanks' armour. As they closed towards the American positions, some enemy tanks received direct hits from 75-millimetre recoilless rifles but none was damaged. Bazookas fired from less than fifteen metres away were equally ineffectual. While some T-34s were eventually damaged, and a couple disabled, Task Force Smith was overrun. In danger of being encircled by North Korean troops sliding down both flanks, the Americans abandoned the battlefield, leaving behind vehicles, equipment and their own wounded, some of whom were shot on their stretchers by the North Koreans. It was, in Halberstam's words, an 'American disaster of the first magnitude, a textbook example of what happens when a nation, filled with the arrogance of power, meets a new reality'.

Kim's infantry and armour swarmed south to confront the 34th Infantry Regiment, which fared even worse than Task Force Smith. After briefly engaging the enemy with mortars and machine guns, the Americans panicked, discarding weapons and equipment as they ran from the North Korean tanks. Appalled and embarrassed by the fiasco, General Dean sacked the commanding officer of the 34th Regiment on the spot for withdrawing without orders. 'Resistance had disintegrated,' Dean recalled years later, 'and now our troops were bugging out.'

It was an ominous start to America's participation in the war. Badly led and poorly armed soldiers had cut and run without causing significant damage to the enemy or holding up its advance. In the first week of fighting, Kim's army had virtually wiped out two American regiments; 3000 US soldiers were either dead, wounded or missing; and the North Koreans had picked up vast quantities of discarded weaponry to turn back on the Americans. In Hastings' damning verdict, 'Terrain, logistics, poor communications and refugees did more to delay the North Korean advance in the first weeks of July than the American infantry in their path.'

For the United States, however, there was no going back, even at the risk of being drawn into a war with the PRC. A top-secret memorandum of a teletype conference, dated 6 July and prepared by the Department of the Army, stated that the United States and the United Nations were committed in Korea to the extent that withdrawal was 'completely unacceptable from a political view-point'. There were, the memo went on, 'no known diplomatic steps' capable of deterring the Chinese communist government from entering the war, although a threat by the United States to use its strategic bomber force to destroy enemy communications might act as a 'psychological deterrent to the Chinese people, including those in the military forces'.

It was now clear to MacArthur that he had horribly under-estimated the strength and ambition of the North Korean invasion. The situation was 'critical', he advised the Joint Chiefs of Staff on 9 July:

We are endeavouring by all means now avail[able] here to build up the force nec[essary] to hold the enemy, but to date our efforts against his armor and mechanized forces have been ineffective. His armored equip[ment] is of the best and the service thereof, as reported by qualified veteran observers, as good as any seen at any time in the last war. They further state that the enemy's inf[antry] is of thoroughly first class quality.

American troops, MacArthur told the joint chiefs, were 'fulfilling expectations' and 'fighting with valor against overwhelming odds', but would need immediate reinforcement—'an army of at least four divisions'—if they were to hold the southern tip of Korea.

As there were only five army divisions available in the entire continental United States, help would be needed from other countries. Truman had stated his desire for the forces aiding South Korea to be 'truly representative' of the United Nations, but the joint chiefs were wary of being swamped by military units too small to be effective, offered by countries keen to show support for the mission but at little real cost to themselves.

While welcoming the offer of ground forces from Australia and the United Kingdom, the joint chiefs advised against seeking contributions from Italy and Saudi Arabia. MacArthur himself proposed accepting only units of the strength of a reinforced battalion (approximately 1000 men), with their own artillery. Preferably, too, their weapons should be able to fire American ammunition. Since they would be attached to US regiments or divisions, they would certainly need enough English-speaking personnel to 'maintain liaison and . . . avoid confusion in combat'. Foreign troops, MacArthur told the joint chiefs, should arrive with enough supplies to last 60 days, after which they would be supplied by the US government (with costs to be reimbursed).

In the end, President Truman decided to provisionally accept all offers of military aid, even if they later turned out to be unusable. But none of the promised ground units was close to being combat-ready. However useful they might eventually prove, it would be months before they could be deployed on the battlefield.

The only American reinforcements capable of immediate deployment were the 25th and 1st Cavalry Divisions, in Japan. Both had been so short of manpower when the war started that soldiers due to be sent home in handcuffs, often for serious offences, were offered the chance to clean their records by volunteering for Korea. It was said that American officers in Tokyo in the days before the Korean War broke out spent much of their time organising courts martial. The American troops coming from Japan were neither elite nor combat-ready, but they were available. The question was, would they arrive before the retreating 24th Division was kicked right off the peninsula?

On 13 July General Walton Walker arrived in Korea. As commander of the US Eighth Army in Japan, he also had operational responsibility for UN ground forces in Korea, but Walker was not MacArthur's man. A veteran of the war in Europe, not MacArthur's Pacific War, and a friend of generals Marshall and Eisenhower, whom MacArthur could not stand, Walker had been constantly undermined in Tokyo and would continue to be undermined in Korea. But Walker was no fool. For all the humiliating defeats the Americans suffered in the first weeks of the war, Walker understood that he was playing for time, not territory. The further south the North Koreans pushed, the harder they would find it to destroy the UN forces before superior American firepower began to turn the tide.

General Dean now had two regiments deployed along the Kum River, but neither they nor the river were any hindrance to the North Koreans. Narrowly avoiding encirclement, Dean withdrew his battered force to Taejon, where several T-34s were knocked out by anti-tank teams armed with new 3.5-inch bazookas. It was not enough, however, to stop the communists from breaking through. With the remnants of his 24th Division retreating south, Dean himself escaped into the hills, where he hid out for a month before being captured.

5

ONCE LEARNT, NEVER FORGOTTEN

On 2 July, seven days after the invasion, Australian Mustang fighters from No. 77 Squadron had taken off from their base at Iwakuni, in Japan, to attack North Korean ground forces. As a precaution against retaliatory attacks on the RAAF base by North Korean fighter bombers, men from A Company 3RAR were hurriedly trained as anti-aircraft gunners, using guns stripped from water transport launches. Guards from 3RAR were also sent to secure the Japanese Oil Storage Company facility at Yoshiura, an installation now deemed vital to the war effort.

Lieutenant McCann and his bride returned from their honeymoon at Kawana, and a live pig raffle was organised to raise money for the New South Wales flood relief fund. With B Company in Tokyo on guard duties and C Company away training, the decision was made to discontinue parades. While packed troop trains carried American soldiers off to join the war, Sergeant Keith Lewtas found time to go picnicking with his Japanese girlfriend, Michiko.

As late as 11 July, the battalion was still making plans for its relocation to Enogerra Barracks, outside Brisbane. The desperate fighting going on in Korea seemed far away. A more immediate threat to the Australians was from Typhoon Grace, which was expected to strike the Japanese coast with 35-knot winds and heavy rain, but in the end brought only 'showers and gusty winds'.

News reached the battalion on 25 July that General MacArthur had asked Lieutenant General Robertson for the use of BCOF ground troops in Korea. The transfer required approval from Canberra, but senior officers were told to prepare for the move. After finally being given the chance to test-fire their guns, A Company's newly trained anti-aircraft gunners were withdrawn from Iwakuni.

'To go to war you had to volunteer,' Stan Connelly recalled.

You couldn't be sent without volunteering . . . So this parade was called . . . to get the troops to volunteer. So here we are . . . standing to attention and the CO [Lieutenant Colonel Stan Walsh] comes out and address[es] the parade and he says . . . 'This battalion has been ordered to join a battle in Korea. Australia will have a battalion in action and it will be the honour of this battalion to accept that assignment,' and he more or less [says], 'And it's voluntary and any lousy, low-down, lily-livered skunk who doesn't want to come [can] march out now and stand over there' . . . of course he didn't use those words but the inference was that if you didn't want to go you weren't a true member of this battalion and you didn't have the right spirit . . . So by not falling out you auto-matically volunteered. Not a man fell out.

Nobody took the war very seriously, Sergeant Joe Veitch told Jack Gallaway:

We were pretty certain that the Yanks would deal with the situation pretty quickly, and when it was over there would be a further period when Australian troops would be stationed in Japan. That suited me. I was in no hurry to go home. I was nicely set up there and it looked as if I would have to leave it all behind and go home . . . I reckoned that the bit of trouble in Korea might see us stay on in Japan for a year or two, so I signed up quick.

On 4 August the battalion marched all day to Haramura, a distance of more than 30 kilometres, before deploying for the night. C Company withdrew before dawn, using a bridge that was later 'demolished' by the assault pioneer platoon. According to the battalion diary, '[M]uch valuable experience was gained, particularly in the laying out of battalion headquarters, the issue of orders, water discipline, road movement and . . . transport.' Keith Lewtas's diary told a different story:

> With equipment and on foot all the way we marched through Nigata and Urajira and up the steep pass, arriving at Haramura at 2000 hrs. Men in the intense heat were falling over like flies and only about half reached their destination without falling out. Sympathetic Japanese provided cold well water on the route, but this was forbidden by the CO as we were supposed to march the full day on our water bottle full. It was intended to march us back the next day but they decided it might be harmful, so we came back in trucks. It was noticeable and remarked by the rest of the [battalion] that the elderly and old chaps stuck the whole march out whilst the younger men couldn't make it. I marched right through without any assistance with all equipment. I was not . . . knocked up like I was during the New Guinea treks.

At 41, Lewtas was one of the 'elderly and old chaps' who put the young to shame on the march to Haramura. But since the official cut-off age for 3RAR personnel wanting to volunteer for Korea was 40, Lewtas worried that he might not be allowed to go. (Corporal George Lang reckoned 'quite a number' of men who enlisted in 'K Force' were born in the 1800s. 'It must be the first war ever where people have put their age down to go to war instead of putting their age up,' Lang quipped.)

With no reinforcements arriving in July, the battalion numbered just 539 officers and men. It was critically short of officers and of specialists such as signalmen and engineers. It had no maps of Korea and lacked sufficient clothing, rations, ammunition and equipment. (One thing the battalion did have, courtesy of its enterprising commander-in-chief, was 50 brand-new American 3.5-inch bazookas, a weapon greatly superior to the obsolete 2.36-inch bazookas with which MacArthur was sending his own troops into battle.)

To bring the battalion up to combat strength, weapons, vehicles and equipment had to be brought from Australia. But what 3RAR needed most of all was soldiers. Even after cannibalising the brigade's other two battalions, 3RAR was still hundreds of men short. There was no time to enlist and train new recruits from scratch, so the army had to look elsewhere. Fortunately, a large pool of experienced Australian soldiers was waiting for the call: diggers from World War II who were still eligible for re-enlistment. Over the next six weeks, battle-hardened gunners, infantrymen and signallers from the Middle East and New Guinea signed up in their hundreds for the newly designated K Force. Applicants had to be at least twenty years old and no older than 40, and they were to serve for three years. A thousand volunteers were needed; by November 1950 the rolls were full.

Watching the K Force men arriving at the Puckapunyal camp in Victoria, signaller Jack Gallaway noted how 'unrefined' many of them were compared with the regular army soldiers. The K Force recruits flooding into Pucka from Australia's four southern states 'retained the attitudes acquired in a rougher environment and there was no time to do very much about it', Gallaway recalled.

The training was very brief but we had to at least find out what they could do, what they were capable of. They had to go on the [rifle] range . . . they had to throw grenades. They had to . . . prove they had the qualities they claimed to have. It was a very rushed affair. Some of them joined up, arrived at Puckapunyal on a Monday and left for Japan to go to Korea just ten days later.

Men and equipment were both recycled from World War II. 'Even the tan boots provided to the recruits were leftovers from the previous conflict,' Richard Trembath wrote in his 50-year retrospective of the Korean war, 'but now they had to be darkened with raven oil.'

Most K Force volunteers adapted easily to being back in uniform. Skills picked up during the previous war were 'much like riding a bike', Max Eberle recalled. 'Once learnt, never forgotten.'

Not much training was done, a couple of days on the rifle range to zero our rifles and numerous lessons on concealment: 'Go down into the bush and conceal yourself until lunchtime etc.' . . . My training completed, I was placed on draft to Japan approximately three weeks after enlisting.

In Japan the battalion command set about undoing the physical effects of the 'glorious holiday' the diggers had enjoyed for the previous four years. On 10 August the transport section acted as the 'enemy' in night-time defensive exercises. Five days later, 3RAR received a visit from the prime minister. Keith Lewtas remembered Menzies telling the troops that 'he would like personally to thank every man who had volunteered for this vital action in Korea, and if it were physically possible and the time were available, he would have liked to shake hands with every man on the parade'.

That same day, the war diary recorded the battalion receiving '20 Jeeps, 12 three-ton trucks and another ambulance' to bring it up to war strength. Instructors from the Eighth Army also arrived to teach the battalion's signallers how to use their new US Army FM wireless sets. Another eight Jeeps arrived a week later, bringing the total to 75, nearly twice the normal allocation, but half of these were in lieu of troop carriers that the battalion would have to do without.

The time set for 3RAR to move was first light on Friday, 25 August, the same day that the British 27th Infantry Brigade was due to leave Hong Kong for Korea. All equipment and ammunition for 'immediate use' in Korea was to be loaded into jeeps and trailers, with heavier and supposedly 'less important' equipment to follow.

The proposed timing of the battalion's departure, which would have seen the Australians arrive in Korea before their British allies, was set by politicians in Canberra. As well as disrupting essential rearmament and training, it would have meant 3RAR leaving Japan before the first K Force reinforcements had even arrived.

On 25 August Lieutenant Colonel Stan Walsh inspected the barracks. An embarkation notice lay on each soldier's bed and every piece of kit was gone. But military sense prevailed over political one-upmanship and the move did not go ahead. The next day Walsh was told that 3RAR would not be deployed in Korea until it had been brought up to strength and supplied with the necessary weapons, stores and equipment.

MacArthur promised that they would all be home by Christmas, but if the war went on for longer, then the Australian troops would receive US Army winter clothing. In Japan, however, it was still summer. Few of the diggers could imagine the freezing conditions they would have to endure in just a few months' time.

The first 48 reinforcements arrived on a chartered Qantas aircraft on 30 August 1950. On arrival, each soldier was given blankets and refreshments before being interviewed and assigned to a company and sent to the Q store for the issue of equipment and clothing. Lieutenant John Wathen and 29 other ranks—all 'specially enlisted' personnel who had volunteered in Australia to fight in Korea—landed the following day. While he judged the standard of reinforcements to be 'good', Walsh noted in his monthly report that all those just arrived from Australia would 'need much hill climbing' to acclimatise.

A regular army officer who started World War II as a lieutenant and ended it as a captain, Walsh had gone through the Australian Staff College before being given command of 3RAR in Japan. Late in the war, Walsh had led a company of the 2/1st Battalion of the AIF during the Aitape–Wewak campaign in New Guinea, but his pedigree as a fighting soldier was not impressive. In Gallaway's words, 'his experience of infantry command in the field was both brief and unhappy'. Walsh was not alone among Australian officers of his rank in having missed the opportunity to prove himself as an infantry commander in battle, but if the experience of the Americans was any guide, then 3RAR would be fighting within days of arriving in Korea. In that event, combat leadership skills would be essential.

At army headquarters in Melbourne, it was felt that Walsh was the wrong man for the job. The man chosen to replace him was Lieutenant Colonel Tom Daly, who had the necessary combat experience from his time as commander of the 2/10th Battalion AIF in New Guinea. But in 1950 Daly was serving as chief instructor at the Royal Military College, and the college would not let him go. The job of commanding 3RAR fell instead to Lieutenant Colonel Charles Hercules Green DSO.

6

FIGHT TO THE LAST

By 22 July the US 25th Infantry Division and the 1st Cavalry Division had both been deployed, giving some respite to the 24th Division, which in less than three weeks' fighting had lost around a third of its strength. 'Bug-out fever' quickly took hold among the reinforcement troops, just as it had with the men of Task Force Smith and the 34th Regiment. A journalist for the *New York Herald Tribune* reported having seen 'young Americans turn and bolt in battle or throw down their arms cursing their government'. Fearful of being encircled by a fanatical enemy that did not hesitate to shoot prisoners, American soldiers deserted en masse as soon as darkness fell. 'It became necessary,' Hastings wrote, 'to set up roadblocks behind the [American] positions, to halt deserters and stragglers leaving the line.'

In a bid to encircle the retreating 25th Division and the 1st Cavalry, a North Korean division bypassed Taejon and got to within 50 kilometres of the key port of Pusan. Only a last-minute dash by units of the 25th Division stymied the communist advance.

Boxed into the far south-eastern corner of the peninsula, the Eighth Army's commander, General Walker, began organising his exhausted forces along a new defensive perimeter behind a loop in the Naktong River. Here the Americans had no choice but to stand and fight. After the battering they had taken in July, conditions now began to swing in their favour. The relentless drive south had left the North Korean lines of communication and supply perilously overextended and vulnerable to attack by air. The compact battle-field allowed Walker to stabilise his own lines while awaiting the arrival of better American troops and other UN forces, including Australia's 3RAR.

If the Pusan perimeter was going to hold, every American unit had to be able to count on its neighbour not to run when the fighting started; there could be no more 'bug-outs'.

'There will be no more retreating, withdrawal, readjustment of lines or whatever you call it,' Walker told them.

There are no lines behind which we can retreat. This is not going to be a Dunkirk or Bataan. A retreat to [the port of] Pusan would result in one of the greatest butcheries in history. We must fight to the end. We must fight as a team. If some of us die, we will die fighting together.

While Walker's troops dug in for the defence of Pusan, the joint chiefs in Washington set about finding MacArthur the extra divisions he needed.

The army hoovered up every man it could find—'from behind desks, out of hospitals, from depots,' in the words of one company commander. Former marines, even those who had not signed up for the Marine Reserves, found that the terms of their contracts made them liable to serve in Korea.

Instead of six weeks' combat training in the United States, they would have to make do with three days' worth of 'special training' once they arrived at Pusan. In the end, there was no time even for that, and GIs found themselves being trucked straight from the port to the battlefield, often without the chance even to adjust their rifle sights.

The British, who had been the first to offer the United States military support, were far from confident that MacArthur would be able to hold on at Pusan, broaching the possibility that the Americans might have to reinvade after being forced off the peninsula. Maintaining that there should be 'no question of using the atomic bomb in Korea', the British Chiefs of Staff in late July expressed their concern that any such reinvasion 'cannot fail to be long, arduous and expensive in human life and material'.

To the British, the war in Korea was and should remain 'a United Nations police action', the purpose of which was not to 'kill thousands of civilians and create a radio-active shambles', but rather 'with the minimum loss of life and expense on either side, to restore the *status quo* and the integrity of Korea'.

MacArthur did not share their view. Convinced that the Cold War would be won and lost in Asia, he urged the joint chiefs to prioritise Korea above all other areas in which America had a strategic interest. MacArthur wanted eight divisions. His intention was not just to repel the communist invaders but to destroy them. But for that to happen, General Walker had to hold Pusan.

The so-called Pusan Perimeter was not an arc but an upside-down 'L', with the long arm following the Naktong River southwards and the short arm heading east to the coast. The remainder of the ROK army, driven inexorably south, protected the right flank of the three American divisions behind the Naktong. The steep hill ranges along both banks of the river formed a strong natural barrier that helped compensate for the fact that Walker did not have the troops he needed to defend his 200-kilometre front. Of the UN force of roughly 95,000 men, half were poorly trained

Americans from the Japan occupation army, and the rest brittle South Koreans.

While fanatical massed attacks by the North Koreans suggested an army of boundless strength and unlimited reserves, the UN forces by August 1950 had a significant advantage over the communists in both troop numbers and weaponry. Nevertheless, Kim's soldiers repeatedly broke through, only to be thrown back by one of the crack units Walker relied on to plug the gaps in his line. According to the *History of the Joint Chiefs of Staff*, the UN defensive line at Pusan was 'stretched almost to the breaking point, which was nearly reached on several occasions. Through the tense days of August, and on into the middle of September, it was never certain whether the beachhead in south-eastern Korea could be held.'

Prime Minister Menzies was eager to fly to Korea, telling Australian reporters in mid-August that he would go 'like a shot' if he could get approval. That could only come from MacArthur, who was prepared to allow visits by military leaders but 'flatly refused' Menzies' request.

Kim's generals were now well aware that they were in a race against time: if the troops inside the perimeter could hang on long enough, the arrival of UN reinforcements would make a communist victory impossible. With the Naktong at its lowest summer level, the weary and battle-sore North Koreans mounted a series of assaults across the river, but each time the combined power of US air and artillery attacks prevented the communists from bringing up reinforcements, which eventually forced the leading elements to withdraw. The mounting losses suffered by the North Koreans, in men, guns and tanks, were unsustainable. By the end of the month their thrust to the sea was losing impetus. On the UN side there was talk of the war being over by November.

In the final days of August, Kim's army summoned up the effort for one final attack. This time the communist tactics were different.

Rather than hitting the UN defences at a number of points in turn, allowing Walker to plug holes as soon as they opened, several North Korean divisions would strike simultaneously against American and ROK units. A key objective was the port of Pohang, in the north-eastern corner of the perimeter. A breakthrough there would give the communists a 'fairly easy ride' to Pusan.

On 29 August Australian newspapers reported that a 'powerful North Korean drive' by 40,000 troops had managed to 'bend' the right wing of the UN line. Walker was said to have 'rushed through a "fight to the last" appeal to the mauled South Koreans battling to hold Pohang against the Northerners, who have orders to get through to Pusan at any cost'.

For nights before the attack, North Korean engineers supervised the construction of log-and-sandbag crossings just beneath the water level. Guns and tanks were brought forward. Intelligence told Walker that an all-out assault was imminent.

It came just before midnight on 31 August. By attacking at night, Kim and his generals hoped to counter the Americans' overwhelming air superiority and make it harder for the UN troops to exploit their greater firepower. Over the next few days, North Korean divisions broke through in several places, driving a wedge through the US 2nd and 25th Divisions and overrunning positions held by the 1st Cavalry.

On 6 September the Australian Associated Press delivered ominous news from Tokyo:

General MacArthur's defence box sagged and broke yesterday in the Korean east coast sector under the hammer blows of 30,000 Communist troops. In driving rain which grounded the Allied air forces the Communists swept past the beleaguered port of Pohang where American and South Korean troops were still fighting and cut south to within three miles [five kilometres] of the vital road and rail junction of Kyongju, only 55 miles [88 kilometres] by air from Pusan. Behind them were another 20,000 Communist reinforcements.

With Pohang lost and the key city of Taegu in danger of falling, Walker was forced to order part of his headquarters back to Pusan. In the face of the communist onslaught, it seemed possible that the entire Eighth Army would have to fall back to its last defensive perimeter, dubbed the Davidson Line. But Walker held his nerve and the danger passed. The North Korean attack, which came so close to succeeding, had burnt itself out.

By the third week of September, the UN forces had broken free, smashing through enemy positions along nearly 120 kilometres of the 200-kilometre front. It was now MacArthur's turn to go on the offensive.

7

CHUCKLES

Ben O'Dowd, then second-in-command of D Company, was sitting in the officers' mess, where it was the custom to tune in after dinner to Radio Australia, when he heard the news of Charlie Green's appointment as the 3rd Battalion's commanding officer. O'Dowd recalled:

> One evening, the group was shocked to hear the newsreader announce that Lt Col Charles Green DSO would take the battalion to Korea. Stan Walsh was embarrassed and justifiably angry at this casual, unethical treatment. The GOC, Gen. Sir Horace C. H. Robertson, was no doubt equally angry at not being informed that a senior officer under his command was to be sacked.

The manner of Walsh's removal was clumsy, but O'Dowd, for one, was delighted to hear that Green—his commanding officer in the 2/11th Battalion during the Aitape–Wewak campaign—was taking over.

Born in 1919 at Grafton, New South Wales, Charlie Green was not a conventional choice to lead the Australians in Korea. Although Green had been with the AIF in North Africa, he had played no part in the intense fighting in December 1940 and January 1941. According to army records, Green spent Christmas 1940 and his 21st birthday (on Boxing Day) in hospital, having been accidentally burnt by a primus stove. The injury caused him to miss the 6th Division's assault on the Italian-held fortress at Bardia, which resulted in the capture of around 35,000 Italian prisoners.

Green first saw combat at Tempe Gorge, on the eastern coast of Greece, in a doomed rearguard action fought by Australian and New Zealand troops on 18 April 1941. Avoiding capture, a small party including Green embarked on a hazardous journey through the Aegean Islands and Turkey, eventually rejoining their unit in Palestine five weeks later. Green was not the senior officer in the group, but his stamina and natural authority made him its leader.

Another member of the party, Captain Bruce Brock, recalled many years later that '[w]hen so many seemed to be flagging, he seemed to be thriving on the sheer physical effort'. In a 50-page account of their escape which he later gave to Green's widow, Brock wrote that Green 'had an infallible sense of what it was safe to do'.

> At times he would advise something. We would disagree. Invariably he was right. He had another exceptional quality. He could always anticipate difficulty or a problem before it arose and had a solution ready, waiting. Or, he was able to avoid the problem before it arose. It was uncanny. That infallibility was one of the major factors that made him the brilliant leader he was.

After garrison duty in Syria and Ceylon, Green's battalion returned to Australia in August 1942. Typhoid and an injured foot initially kept him out of the New Guinea campaign, but in

December 1944, by now promoted to major, Green sailed to Aitape as acting CO of 2/2nd Battalion. Four months later, with a temporary promotion to lieutenant colonel, Green was given command of the 2/11th Battalion—'a unit comprising mostly parochial Western Australians', according to Gallaway, 'to whom their new commander [a New South Welshman] was a total and not altogether welcome stranger'.

At the age of 25, Green was reputed to be the youngest commanding officer of an infantry battalion in the AIF; he was also the first 2/11th Battalion CO to be posted from outside. David Butler, who later served as one of Green's rifle platoon commanders in Korea, commented that '[i]n the circumstances, it was not a comfortable transition'.

Green was further isolated by the lack of a second-in-command. Perhaps inevitably, the battalion found him 'stern and austere' as he struggled to get to know his men while commanding them in battle. The nickname they gave him—'Chuckles'—said something about them as well as him.* Nevertheless, the outstanding leadership and personal gallantry he demonstrated during the Wewak campaign led to him being awarded a Distinguished Service Order (DSO).

Civilian life did not suit Green, and in 1949 he accepted the offer of a commission as lieutenant colonel in the regular army, soon winning a place in the prestigious twelve-month course at the Army Staff College at Queenscliff in Victoria, which was a prerequisite for becoming a general. His studies were cut short when the call came to lead 3RAR into action in Korea.

---

* At the age of eleven Green had suffered a serious accident on the family dairy farm. He almost died after a horse he was harnessing kicked him in the face, smashing his teeth and fracturing a bone in his skull. He missed a year of school while recovering from his injuries, and returned with a complete set of dentures and a scar across his mouth. Butler suggested that Green was self-conscious of his false teeth, and Green's sister said that when he laughed the injury was 'very noticeable'. Some have mentioned this as a reason for his alleged lack of humour.

While the scarcity of men and equipment had been remedied, the battalion Green inherited was seriously out of condition. In Japan the rifle companies had only trained for three months a year, and it was several years since the battalion had last exercised as a unit.

Green took command of 3RAR at midnight on 12 September 1950, having arrived in Japan two days earlier. During those hectic 48 hours, Green interviewed his officers and removed those he didn't trust. Two officers who would be critical to the battalion's fortunes in the months ahead were already known to him: O'Dowd, whom Green had commissioned in the field at Wewak, and Major Bruce Ferguson, a New Zealander who had taken over from Green as a company commander in 2/2nd Battalion and would now be his second-in-command.

At daybreak on 13 September Green led 3RAR to Haramura for a three-day exercise codenamed Bolero. The battalion had now reached its full fighting strength of 960 all ranks. Other BCOF units, controlled by Lieutenant Colonel Walsh in his role as 'exercise umpire', comprised the enemy.

Bolero was an inauspicious start to Green's command. Torrential rain brought by Typhoon Kezia washed away roads and bridges, forcing vehicles to take a different route to the marching troops. On reaching Haramura, the battalion took up defensive positions. During the night Walsh made sure the 'enemy' was very active.

Among other things, Bolero was intended as a trial of the new concept of a support company, whose role was to keep the battalion supplied with men and weapons. But food for the troops arrived cold, late or sometimes not at all. The support company's quartermaster sergeant paid the price for his unit's poor performance, being demoted within an hour of the battalion's return to barracks.

Other aspects of Bolero were more successful: the walkie-talkies and wireless sets performed well, despite the rain, although Gallaway, a signaller himself, noted that with the exception of the American walkie-talkies, none of the wireless sets issued to the Australians was capable of providing communications with US Army units. But serious deficiencies, including the poor performance of transport drivers and a lack of training among the signallers, were impossible to ignore.

In other exercises later in the month, rifle companies rehearsed attacking, defensive and withdrawal manoeuvres, often watched by their commander-in-chief, Lieutenant General Robertson. The battalion looked far from battle-ready. Lieutenant Alf Argent, who as intelligence officer became close to Green, felt that his commanding officer 'could not have been much impressed' by what he saw during those few weeks in Japan:

The basic material was there . . . but there was a distinct lack of cohesion and the standard of sub-unit and unit training was poor . . . in those difficult, tiring days we wondered if we had absorbed the reinforcements and equipment or whether the reinforcements and equipment had swallowed us.

Despite the difficulties, 'the CO remained surprisingly calm and seemingly above all the turmoil'.

One exercise finished with Green ordering the entire battalion to walk the 30 kilometres from Haramura back to Hiro. 'When the signal came through that we had to get back to Hiro, I climbed into my jeep,' Jack Gallaway recalled.

I was just about ready to go with my driver and along came Captain Watson. He said, 'Out.' I said, 'Why?' He said, 'You are walking back.' I said, 'Why am I walking back?' He said, 'Because I'm walking back. The drivers are the only ones going back with the vehicles.' . . . And we got back to Hiro and there were blokes there who would have cheerfully shot Charlie Green, but my god, they respected him.

Whatever reservations Charlie Green might have had about the battalion's competence, he kept them to himself. 'Confidence was high,' Butler wrote later, 'and the minimal state of training did not seem to concern the more senior people in the unit or in the higher HQ.'

The decision to fill out 3RAR with K Force veterans unbalanced its officer ranks: captains and above had all held AIF commissions, while every lieutenant bar one was fresh out of the Royal Military College. The latter had a lot to learn about leading men in the field, as O'Dowd explained:

One of the companies had had a hard day and a long march back to barracks, arriving tired and sweaty. Their three young platoon commanders were seated in the Mess shortly after, freshly showered, neatly dressed and beer in hand. The beer was only half consumed when their World War II vintage company commander appeared, unwashed and in the battle-dress he had been wearing all day.

'Were hot showers available for your men? Have their feet been inspected for blisters? Were disinfectant foot baths available? Have they had a satisfactory meal?'

Blank faces.

'Well, go and find out!'

8

INCHON

3RAR's war diary recorded that on 15 September 1950 Lieutenant General Robertson spent the afternoon inspecting defensive positions constructed for exercise Bolero. That evening, diggers listening to their radios learnt that US Marines had landed behind the North Korean lines at Inchon—an operation that would not only relieve the defenders at Pusan but that seemed likely to bring the war itself to a speedy end.

MacArthur had been planning his amphibious assault on Inchon since early July. During that time, his confidence in its success had never wavered, despite the reservations of the Joint Chiefs of Staff. The issue was not the attack itself but the choice of Inchon, a port 30 kilometres west of Seoul, as the site of the landing. While a successful assault would put the invaders within easy reach of the South Korean capital, with its vital road, rail and air links, the geographical disadvantages were so severe that journalist Rutherford Poats described Inchon as 'probably the worst place ever selected for an amphibious invasion'.

Mudflats extended five kilometres from the shore. Landing craft capable of carrying tanks could only cross the flats when the tides were at least ten metres deep; since this happened on only a handful of days each month, MacArthur's planners had little flexibility in choosing when to launch the attack. The narrow passage that enabled ships to cross the mudflats was treacherous, even in daylight, and was dominated by a garrisoned island—Wolmi-do—whose early destruction would inevitably alert the defenders on the mainland. The city had no beaches, and US Marines would have to clamber over a four-metre sea wall. Lastly, the distance from Inchon to the Pusan Perimeter—160 kilometres at its closest point—would make it difficult for Walker's Eighth Army to link up with the marines in what MacArthur envisaged as a 'nutcracker' that would crush the North Korean forces.

Despite the joint chiefs' misgivings, MacArthur pressed on with his plans for the amphibious landing, demanding a full marines division and an airborne regimental combat team by mid-September. The invasion force was designated X Corps.

The commander chosen to lead X Corps was a MacArthur loyalist, even disciple, Major General Edward 'Ned' Almond. As well as being commander of X Corps, Almond was MacArthur's chief of staff—an extraordinary dual role that guaranteed MacArthur's enduring favouritism. If Inchon was MacArthur's brainchild, it was Almond who supervised the planning and kept the doubters at bay.

MacArthur is said to have spoken of Inchon as a great gamble, a 5000-to-one shot, but he was supremely confident of winning. An 'early and strong effort' behind the enemy's front lines would 'sever his main lines of communications and enable us to deliver a decisive and crushing blow', MacArthur argued, warning that any 'material delay in such an operation may lose this opportunity'. Delaying the operation also risked giving the North Koreans time to mine the harbour, which would make landings all but impossible.

Worried that even if the initial assault was a success, the invasion force might be thrown back into the sea before Walker's troops could break out of the Pusan Perimeter and join the attack, two of the joint chiefs advocated a different site, 160 kilometres south of Inchon. MacArthur wouldn't hear of it.

On 23 August MacArthur called a full-scale briefing at his Tokyo headquarters. General Joe Collins, the army chief of staff; Admiral Forrest Sherman, chief of naval operations; and Lieutenant General Idwal Edwards, the air force operations deputy, flew out from Washington. At the meeting MacArthur brushed aside their concerns, acknowledging the geographical disadvantages but declaring that the marines and the navy would overcome them. It was these disadvantages, he said, that would guarantee surprise.* A safer landing further south would achieve little; only by landing at Inchon could he achieve his goal of cutting the North Koreans off from their base of operations and destroying them. As for the danger of X Corps being driven back into the sea, there were not enough enemy troops to do it: intelligence reports suggested there were just 2000 North Korean soldiers at Inchon. According to the

---

* How the North Koreans allowed themselves to be surprised is something of a mystery. MacArthur did not trust Washington to keep his plans secret, advising the joint chiefs on 21 July that it would be 'unwise' for him to divulge in a message how he planned to use the marines division he was asking for. A few days later he warned the spokesman for the Army Department against 'reveal[ing] our grand strategy in the slightest degree'. Yet in Tokyo the Inchon operation was an open secret. 'Everyone in Tokyo appeared to know what was coming and where and when it was going to take place,' Halberstam commented in *The Coldest Winter*. 'In the Tokyo Press Club . . . it was already labelled Operation Common Knowledge.' Somehow the rumours failed to alert the North Koreans. Unlike Mao, Kim had never taken seriously the possibility of an amphibious landing behind his lines. Chinese agents had noted the American build-up in Japan in the weeks before Inchon. Much of the equipment pointed at an amphibious operation. The Chinese were well aware of MacArthur's use of amphibious landings in the Pacific War, and even identified Inchon as the most likely target. Kim was warned but apparently took no notice.

History of the Joint Chiefs of Staff, MacArthur finished the meeting with what Collins later described as a 'stirring peroration':

> If my estimate is inaccurate and should I run into a defense with which I cannot cope, I will be there personally and will immediately withdraw our forces before they are committed to a bloody setback. The only loss then will be to my professional reputation. But Inchon will not fail. Inchon will succeed. And it will save 100,000 lives.

The joint chiefs consented to a 'mid-September amphibious operation' but took care not to specify Inchon as the location; they asked MacArthur to consider alternatives. But as far as MacArthur was concerned, there were no alternatives. Without telling the joint chiefs, he issued his operations order for the Inchon landing.

The all-out North Korean offensive against the Pusan Perimeter launched on the night of 31 August briefly threatened to derail MacArthur's plans when Walker tried to hold onto troops needed for Inchon. The joint chiefs were worried enough to deliver a final warning to MacArthur of the dire consequences of failing to secure a quick and decisive victory with his amphibious assault.

MacArthur wrote back saying there was 'no question in my mind as to the feasibility of the operation', which he believed to be 'the only hope of wresting the initiative from the enemy'. Walker's situation inside the perimeter was 'not critical', he assured them, and there was 'no slightest possibility . . . of our force being ejected from the Pusan beachhead'. The capture of Seoul, he wrote, would:

> completely dislocate the logistical supply of [enemy] forces now operating in South Korea and therefore will ultimately result in their disintegration . . . Caught between our northern and our southern forces, both of which are completely

self-sustaining because of our absolute air and naval suprem-
acy, the enemy cannot fail to be ultimately shattered.

Seduced by MacArthur's unshakable confidence, the joint chiefs
approved his plan.

On 15 September, 200-kilometre-per-hour winds stirred up
by Typhoon Kezia—the same typhoon that was causing havoc
for the diggers' training in Japan—lashed the armada of battered
World War II–vintage US Navy landing craft taking the marines
to Inchon. The 1st Marine Division took less than two hours to
secure the island of Wolmi-do, and Inchon was taken at a cost of
just twenty marines killed and fewer than 200 casualties. When
the expected counterattack didn't come, the invaders pushed inland
towards Seoul. By the night of 17 September, the US Marines
controlled Kimpo, the country's main airfield. The next day the US
7th Infantry Division came ashore and moved south-east to form
the right pincer of X Corps. North Korean resistance, although
fierce in places, quickly collapsed.

MacArthur had been careful to insist that the 'prompt' link-up
between Walker's Eighth Army and X Corps, although symboli-
cally important, was 'not a vital part' of the Inchon operation. In
fact, the breakout from Pusan proved harder than expected, as the
North Koreans, oblivious to the enemy at their rear, continued to
bear down on the UN lines. It was only when Kim began pulling
units away from Pusan to defend Seoul that communist pressure
faltered. Walker demanded a final push, ordering his forces forward
'without regard for lateral security'.

As communist troops broke and fled, discarding their weapons
and equipment, elements of the Eighth Army raced to encircle
them. Thousands surrendered, while others slipped away to fight on
as guerrillas.

Capturing Inchon had been easy but Seoul would be far tougher.
Kim had moved quickly to reinforce the city. Instead of the 6000

to 7000 North Korean troops MacArthur had expected to find in the Inchon–Seoul area, there were as many as four times that number. American heavy weapons reduced much of the southern capital to rubble as Kim's troops defended the city street by street. Mounting US casualties exacerbated tensions between MacArthur and the joint chiefs, who would have preferred to see him bypass and cut off the capital before joining up with Walker's Eighth Army, in the process trapping most of the retreating North Korean army. MacArthur wanted Seoul taken by 25 September, exactly three months after Kim's troops had invaded—a publicity gimmick, in the view of marines commander General Oliver P. Smith, that was needlessly costing his men's lives.

MacArthur, as usual, got his way. Seoul was declared liberated on 26 September, although sporadic fighting persisted for another two days. Of the 90,000 communist soldiers who crossed the 38th parallel in the last week of June 1950, less than a third straggled back to North Korea.

The recapture of Seoul was a pivotal moment in the war, energising Washington's belief that North Korea could be defeated and both Koreas united under a pro-American government. Within days, the National Security Council recommended to President Truman that UN troops advance into North Korea, provided this did not draw the Americans and the United Nations into a war with the Soviets or the Chinese. On 29 September Truman gave his approval for MacArthur to cross the 38th parallel.

In a cable that became known as the 'blank check', the US secretary of defense, George Marshall, instructed MacArthur to feel 'unhampered tactically and strategically to proceed north of 38th parallel'.

MacArthur immediately prepared a statement to be distributed to the press and to forces under his command, but he was blocked by Washington from sending it. As the joint chiefs explained in a cable dated 1 October 1950, 'Our government desires to avoid having to make an issue of the 38th parallel until we have defeated the North Korean forces.'

Three days later, the UN General Assembly voted by 47 to five to approve a resolution authorising UN forces to cross the 38th parallel. The resolution also called for free elections and the establishment of a 'unified, independent and Democratic Government in the Sovereign State of Korea'.

MacArthur acted quickly on his new mandate. On the afternoon of 7 October, the 1st Cavalry Division sent patrols across the border, with others following on the next night. At 9 a.m. on 9 October, the commanding officer, General Hobart Gay, gave his orders and the division began fighting its way north.

9

YOU'VE GOT A RIDE, BROTHER

Ben O'Dowd was not alone in believing that MacArthur's audacious strategic move signalled the imminent end of the war, and therefore of 3RAR's hopes of seeing action. O'Dowd recalled news of the Inchon landing bringing 'an air of dejection' into the Australian camp as the diggers digested the possibility that their training had been for nothing.

But preparations continued for 3RAR to move to Korea. New automatic weapons and ammunition were issued. Troops received their clothing, gear and inoculations. Vehicles were loaded with equipment. Not knowing whether he was going or not, Keith Lewtas packed up his belongings, sending his bicycle and camera to Michiko.

On 25 September Green left battalion HQ for the RAAF base at Iwakuni, where he and Lieutenant General Robertson caught a flight to Korea. Two days later, amid pouring rain, 3RAR boarded the *Aiken Victory*, a 10,000-ton US Navy troopship that had been in mothballs before being hastily reconfigured to transport the diggers. As the ship had been designed to carry troops only, decking had to be ripped out in order to load the battalion's vehicles. The work was finished in seven days.

Lewtas had to wait until the last minute before being told that his name was in the draft. 'I asked Michiko . . . if she could possibly wash a green jacket and trousers for me before I left. She brought them back after lunch ironed, but still moist, and she apologised and cried because they were still wet and she had not performed the impossible.'

At 7.45 p.m. the battalion—a total of 1037 all ranks—departed Kure Harbour on the *Aiken Victory*—'farewelled', as the unit diary put it, 'by a large number of BCOF and dependants'. The bandsmen who played as the ship prepared to sail would become stretcher-bearers when the diggers went into battle.

Not all 'dependants' were welcome at the wharf. 'The "unofficial dependants", the Japanese wives and sweethearts of some of the troops, were barred from entry to see off the ship,' Lewtas wrote later, 'so they assembled on a wharf some hundreds of yards away and called out and waved enthusiastically in the rain to their Australian friends long after the official parties had gone home.'

As the *Aiken Victory* passed through the Straits of Shimonoseki, she picked up a Royal Navy escort, the destroyer HMS *Comus*, and the pair sailed together at fifteen knots, arriving at Pusan Harbour in South Korea on the afternoon of 28 September. While US and Korean army bands played the battalion's unofficial anthem, Korean girls in national costume performed a ballet on the wharf. Colonel Green, Major Ferguson and the adjutant stood awkwardly as a group of Korean women presented them with flowers on behalf of the republic.

Within a few hours of their arrival, the battalion—minus Green, who flew ahead—were heading by train to Taegu. Lewtas and his mates were unimpressed by the 'primitive train of ancient vintage', with its bare wooden seats and unlit compartments 'reeking with the odour of vegetables and other commodities'.

Four hours out of Pusan, the train shuddered to a halt. Soldiers sat half-asleep in the darkness, wondering whether they had reached their destination. Eventually word was passed back: this was the place. Webbing and rifles were retrieved from the racks and the diggers lined up on the station platform before being ordered into open three-ton trucks belonging to the US Army. They were transported to a dry riverbed, eight kilometres north-east of Taegu, where they bivouacked for the night. 'It was not unduly cold,' Lewtas wrote, 'but a sharp frost thoroughly drenched their ground sheets above them as they slept.' Winter was still some weeks off, but that frosty riverbed was a foretaste of miseries to come.

Having finally arrived in Korea, 3RAR joined the British 27th Infantry Brigade in a combined force designated the 27th British Commonwealth Brigade. Its commanding officer was Brigadier Basil Coad, swiftly nicknamed 'Plonky' or 'Penfolds' by the diggers on account of his prominent red nose. (According to the battalion war diary, the 'high esteem' in which Coad was held by the Australians was reflected in another nickname: 'the greyheaded old bastard'.)

The 27th Infantry Brigade had been performing garrison duties in Hong Kong when it was ordered to Korea. Rushed into the defence of the Pusan Perimeter, it became one of the 'fire brigades' used by General Walker to repel enemy incursions.

Before the arrival of 3RAR, the brigade had consisted of just two understrength battalions, the 1st Battalion of the Middlesex Regiment and the 1st Battalion of the Argyll and Sutherland Highlanders, both lacking their own supporting arms. During its three weeks in Korea, this two-battalion brigade had (in the words of the brigade diary) 'not been a sound tactical force and . . . had to make the best of what it had'. Despite its excellent fighting spirit and morale, the brigade's weakness in strength, organisation and equipment had 'caused many problems and worries in certain situations'. The addition of a full-strength and well-equipped Australian battalion transformed the 27th British Commonwealth Brigade into a formidable fighting unit; it was no wonder the diggers received a warm welcome.

While Walker's Eighth Army charged after the fleeing North Korean troops, the newly formed 27th Brigade found itself with the less heroic task of 'mopping up' communist guerrillas said to be hiding out in the Plum Pudding Hills, west of Taegu. In the words of 3RAR's war diary, its 'immediate role' was to 'clear certain areas that the US Army troops have by-passed in their advance'. Keith Lewtas put it differently: the battalion, he wrote, appeared to have 'missed the bus'.

Determined to beat the Americans across the 38th parallel, two diggers, privates Rex Wilson of Adelaide and Ernest Stone of Melbourne, absconded. The exploits of the 'grimy, bearded' pair were eagerly recounted by the troupe of correspondents sent from Australia to cover the war. 'We joined up to fight,' Wilson told a reporter, 'but when we arrived we found our unit was too far from the front line, so we just took off and headed for the noise of firing.' According to Sydney's *Daily Telegraph*:

Wilson and Stone trudged for several miles along the dusty road northwards until a US convoy overtook them. Both then took off their digger hats and waved them frantically. The leading tank of the convoy stopped. The Australians shouted that they wanted to go to the front.

The tank driver replied: 'You've got a ride, brother, hop aboard.'

At the front the Australians unofficially enlisted in an assault rifle squad. Stone said . . . 'We wanted to be the first Australians over the parallel.'

Discovered in a weapon pit by Australian military police sent from Tokyo to find them, Wilson and Stone—and five of their mates—were shown remarkable leniency by 3RAR's supposedly humourless and disciplinarian commander. 'He simply ordered them back to their platoons without further ado,' Robert O'Neill noted in his official history. The escapade was not mentioned in the war diary.

Meanwhile, the area to be cleared of enemy soldiers had been expanded to roughly 1300 square kilometres, forcing the 27th Brigade to change its approach. Previously, the method had been to make a clean sweep over all hills and valleys, working from the centre outwards until the entire area had been covered. Since this would have taken several months, the brigade devised a new method, clearing roads and passable tracks and then, if there was time, searching more inaccessible areas later. Any reliable sightings of enemy soldiers were to be followed up immediately, wherever they occurred.

According to signals sergeant Jack Gallaway, 3RAR found a few enemy guerrillas as well as some weapon dumps containing mines and small arms, which were duly blown up by the assault pioneers. The Plum Pudding Hills operation saw the first Australian casualties of the war when a Bren gun carrier driven by Private Kenneth Sketchley ran into an unmarked minefield. The carrier flipped over after setting off several Russian wooden-box-type anti-tank mines, killing Sketchley and Captain Kenneth Hummerston.

While the operation was underway, villagers reported numerous sightings of concentrations of between 1000 and 1500 North Korean troops, but despite rigorous ground patrolling and air reconnaissance, no trace of them could be found. There was little doubt, however, that smaller groups of enemy soldiers were heading north, hoping to make it back over the border.

On 4 October all patrolling activity was abruptly halted and the 27th Brigade was ordered to Seoul. Stores would be moved by road, while all personnel were to be airlifted by the US Air Force to Seoul's Kimpo airfield.

While happy enough with the orthodox-looking C-47, a transport aircraft also flown by the RAAF, the Australians were less sure about the C-119 'Box Cars', with their dumpy bodies and twin tail booms. The Box Car could carry a heavy tank, but that was scant reassurance for the diggers waiting on the airstrip, who watched the twin tails of one aircraft snap off as it touched down before careering along the runway in a shower of sparks. As a result of the incident, all C-119s were grounded until they could be inspected. There was a further hold-up when one of the propeller-driven C-47s was mistakenly refuelled with jet fuel. Meals and a stage show laid on by the US Air Force helped pass the time. Brigadier Coad and his three battalion commanders went on ahead by road.

Until now the diggers had been living on Australian rations—'old dog biscuits and bully beef', in the words of Sergeant Tom Muggleton—but at Kimpo they came under the US Army rations system and began receiving so-called C (for 'combat') rations. 'The one we got had three meals in it,' Muggleton recalled, 'and you had various types of meals like . . . chicken and vegetables, ham and lima beans, hamburgers, pork and ham . . . they were very good rations. Plus you got a packet of cigarettes, toilet rolls, two small tins of fruit and they were excellent . . . I liked chicken and vegetables [and] my boss liked ham and lima beans so . . . if you got sick of eating one you'd swap with someone else.'

The canned meal was designed to be eaten cold but tasted better heated, usually by being suspended in a barrel of boiling water. During the freezing Korean winter, soldiers often had to carve the food out of its can with their bayonets.

As well as eating American food, the Australians were taking American orders. The 27th Brigade was put under the command of the 1st Cavalry Division, which had been badly mauled at Pusan and was fighting for control of Kaesong, around 60 kilometres north-west of Seoul and just a few kilometres south of the 38th parallel.

As soon as the area was secured, the Americans would be joined by the 27th Brigade.

Lewtas did not fly to Kimpo with the rest of the battalion, having been sent back by road to Pusan to organise supplies. The return journey, 300 tortuously slow kilometres in trucks packed with stores and equipment, took several days along narrow dirt roads meant for oxen but now clogged with refugees.

On the northern outskirts of Taejon, Lewtas saw the charred wreckage of two Russian T-34 tanks, with a placard stating that they had been knocked out under the supervision of Major General William F. Dean, commander of the 24th Infantry Division.

A combination of inadequate signposting and inaccurate maps meant that the convoy drivers repeatedly got lost. Arriving late at night at Kimpo airfield, Lewtas slept in a marquee that shook every half-hour as American transport aircraft bringing equipment from Japan taxied past. The next morning he was told that his battalion had already left for Kaesong, so the convoy set out on another arduous drive north.

By now the first ROK units had already crossed the border into North Korea, with the leading elements of the Eighth Army not far behind.

The Australians reached Kaesong at dusk on 9 October. The city had fallen earlier that day to the 1st Cavalry Division, and the diggers arrived to see US fighter jets pounding pockets of enemy soldiers in the hills to the north.

The 27th Brigade's new objective was the North Korean town of Kumchon. While the Americans advanced rapidly against generally light opposition, the Commonwealth troops were soon bogged down. Progress on the narrow country roads was painfully slow; in some cases roads marked on the map did not exist. One of the brigade's Sherman tanks lost a track after running over a mine.

Advancing in parallel, 3RAR and the 1st Middlesex battalion flushed out large numbers of enemy soldiers left behind by the retreating North Korean army. On 14 October 1950, for instance, 3RAR and the 1st Middlesex took 32 prisoners, while the Argylls captured another 49.

'[The enemy soldiers] had reversible quilted jackets, white on one side and khaki on the other,' Corporal Len Opie recalled. 'If you saw somebody in white you assumed he was a civilian but if he was moving faster than a slow walk you assumed he was a [North Korean] soldier, and you shot him.'

Inevitably, there were mistakes. 'We used to rush through villages firing into bunkers,' Opie said, 'but half the time we didn't know until later that they were probably civilians. You never knew, so you either tossed a grenade in [or you called] and if you called, nobody came out anyway, so it was hard to tell . . . In those days nobody worried too much.'

In one village the battalion discovered the bodies of eight Koreans who had been shot with their hands tied behind their backs. The corpses appeared to have been lying there for several days.

Heavy traffic and torrential rain churned up the roads. The diggers' morale was not improved by haphazard meals of cold American rations, including canned turnips and sauerkraut.

The mountainous terrain favoured defence and the North Koreans fought tenaciously. By the time 3RAR reached Kumchon, the town was already in the hands of the 7th Cavalry Regiment, part of the 1st Cavalry Division. Kumchon, according to the brigade diary, was left a 'blazing ruin'.

Lewtas recalled the 'piteous plight' of an old Korean man trying to save his thatched mudbrick home from a fire maliciously lit by an Australian soldier. 'If I knew who did it . . . he'd be right up in the forward company [i.e. sent to fight at the front] tomorrow,' a sergeant major told Lewtas. That Korean villager would not be the last to regret the actions of the foreign troops who had come to save him from communist aggression.

While patrolling a few hundred metres north of the 38th parallel, C Company captured three North Korean prisoners, described in the battalion diary as 'stragglers'. Just before midnight another enemy soldier was challenged by the mortar platoon. Pretending to surrender, he threw a grenade that exploded, wounding two men— the battalion's first combat casualties. The North Korean was shot.

Stopping outside an enemy-occupied village, the diggers watched three American Sabre jet fighters circle overhead before attacking the village with napalm. Lewtas recalled seeing 'a vast and deadly flame burst into the air and spread itself over a wide area, instantly burning anybody or anything . . . After this spectacular demonstration of unopposed might, the three jets formed up in a line, wing tip to wing tip, and raced only feet above the tops of the long columns of vehicles halted on the road.'

At dusk the battalion moved off the road into a defensive position—the sort of drill Charlie Green had made them practise in Japan, with headquarters and supply echelons inside a perimeter formed by the fighting companies. The battalion had orders to make contact the following day with an enemy force that was dug in, with light artillery support, on the far bank of a wide river. Few of the Australians slept that night; for many of the younger men, it was going to be their first experience of combat. Lewtas remembered it as a short, sharp encounter as fierce as any he had experienced in Greece, Syria or even New Guinea.

After crossing the river, 3RAR pushed further north, halting at nightfall beside a small farm. Two North Koreans lay dead by the roadside; according to Lewtas, they had 'taken a shot' at a jeep carrying Green's second-in-command and were quickly dealt with. Another lay dead in the garden, killed by communist soldiers, the diggers were told, after he refused to join up and fight with them. On two steep hills overlooking the farm the Australians dug weapon pits. In the distance Lewtas could hear the keening of the dead man's family as they buried him.

On 15 October the temperature suddenly dropped; for 3RAR it was perhaps the worst night so far, with rain falling all night. The following day the 27th Brigade was ordered to take over the advance on Pyongyang from the 7th Cavalry Regiment. The Argylls would lead off, followed by 3RAR.

Impatient to catch up with the retreating North Koreans, the leading diggers were soon on the heels of the Argylls and had to be told to back off. The idea of pursuit operations, O'Dowd explained, was to 'keep right up with the retreating enemy so he is not encouraged to turn and go in defence . . . When enemy delaying troops were encountered, the leading company dismounted, mounted a quick attack, and the pursuit continued.' But the diggers and the Argylls were pursuing faster than the North Koreans could retreat.

Late in the afternoon, the Argylls entered Sariwon, where they came under fire from enemy snipers. The diggers soon learnt to keep low and not 'skyline' themselves. Confused fighting went on as three UN forces converged on the town: the US 24th Infantry Division from the south, the 7th Cavalry Regiment from the north and the 27th Brigade from the east. Corporal Raymon Wilson would always remember Sariwon because the town was in flames—'everything was on fire'—when the diggers went through.

On 17 October at around 6 p.m. the Argylls, unaware that the remnants of a North Korean division were still at large, reported the town to be secure. Before long, they began reporting enemy activity in and around Sariwon, which was the only line of retreat for North Korean units being driven back by the 24th Division. As the Argylls and North Koreans met in the failing evening light, the communist troops mistook the Scots for Russian reinforcements, sometimes parking their vehicles directly alongside. In some cases the Argylls, heavily outnumbered, pretended to be Russians, keeping up the ruse until the odds were more favourable. Gallaway described the scene: 'With cries of "Russki, Russki", the North Korean soldiers fraternised freely for a time before realising their error. Soon, fighting broke out and in the ensuing struggle, the Jocks killed more than two hundred of the enemy without loss.'

In the battalion diary's more sober version of the incident, most of the enemy troops surrendered, including 25 North Koreans captured when their truck was stopped by Lieutenant Eric Larson's 6 Platoon. Another 1600 surrendered before daybreak, although the Argylls' commanding officer and his second-in-command had to hide all night in a ditch after stumbling into a battalion of North Koreans just south of Sariwon.

That night, as Colonel Green made plans for a dawn attack against enemy positions north of Sariwon, the 7th Cavalry Regiment swung south, trapping the North Koreans and taking nearly 1700 prisoners. The next day, 3RAR, travelling north in trucks and on the back of American Sherman tanks, reached Hwangju, about 40 kilometres south of Pyongyang. With the 5th and 7th Cavalry regiments and the 27th British Commonwealth Brigade all fighting for road space, 3RAR had become detached from its sister battalions and was advancing alone. Although Green's plans had been thwarted, the road north lay enticingly open for 3RAR to become the first UN force to enter the North Korean capital. The Americans, however, had other ideas.

Rather than make directly for Pyongyang, Green was ordered to divert to the small coastal village of Samgapo to protect the left flank of the 1st Cavalry Division. After coming under fire from enemy snipers in Samgapo and the neighbouring hills, the battalion hit back with infantry and Sherman tanks, killing five and taking three prisoners while suffering no casualties of its own. The decision to hold back the Australians ensured that it would be the 1st Cavalry Division and not 3RAR that captured the enemy's capital.

Heavy rain and poor roads hampered the Australian advance and many vehicles became bogged, but the difficult route surprised the North Koreans. Two T-34 tanks and a self-propelled gun, sitting in a paddy field and well camouflaged with straw, were destroyed. Their petrol tanks were empty.

After taking part in the capture of one North Korean tank crew, Len Opie returned to find the enemy soldiers had been forced to strip off and sit on the bonnet of a jeep. 'They were blue with cold and I said, "Who did that?" and [another soldier] said, "I did," and he said, "Gooks" . . . and I said, "They're not Gooks, they're enemy and they're captured, and give them their clothes back."'

Shortly after midday on 19 October, the 5th Cavalry Regiment entered Pyongyang, followed by the rest of the 1st Cavalry Division and the ROK 1st Division. It was clear that the hectic retreat from Pusan had left the North Koreans unable to organise a proper defence of the city. Defensive positions were not manned and resistance consisted mainly of intermittent sniper fire.

Many of the inhabitants had fled or were in hiding, but in the hours and days that followed Pyongyang's fall, some civilians came onto the streets to cheer and applaud the conquerors. While the welcome appeared genuine, Commonwealth commanders speculated that it might be the result of 'good training' ingrained during years of dealing with the North Korean military.

The men of 3RAR did not reach the capital until Saturday, 21 October, long after General MacArthur, his staff and a legion of press correspondents had entered the city. Trundling through streets jammed with vehicles, the Australians were galled to read banners that said, 'You are now entering Pyongyang, courtesy of 1 Cav Div.'

No digger ever forgot that slight.

10

OVER BY CHRISTMAS

The day after American troops entered Pyongyang, MacArthur's intelligence chief, General Charles Willoughby, distributed an intelligence summary across Far East Command:

> Organised resistance on any large scale has ceased to be an enemy capability. Indications are that the North Korean military and political headquarters may have fled into Manchuria. Communications with, and consequent control of, the enemy's field units have dissipated to a point of ineffectiveness.

While there were, as yet, no signs that the enemy intended to surrender, Willoughby was confident that the North Koreans' fighting ability would be limited to 'small-scale delaying actions against UN pressure'.

The Prussian-born Willoughby's bearing was aristocratic (he was known to wear a monocle when it suited him), his politics far right and his intelligence lousy. The head of the CIA's directorate of plans,

Frank Wisner, once described him as 'all ideology and almost never any facts'—dangerous characteristics in an intelligence chief. An admirer of the fascist Spanish dictator General Francisco Franco, Willoughby had been a member of MacArthur's staff since the late 1930s, during which time he had managed to author a hagiographical 1000-page biography of his boss.

As MacArthur's intelligence chief in the Philippines, Japan and Korea, Willoughby had learnt to anticipate what MacArthur wanted. It was 'always important to [MacArthur] that his intelligence reports blend seamlessly with what he had intended to do in the first place', Halberstam wrote in a damning appraisal of their double act. 'What that meant was that the intelligence Willoughby was turning over to MacArthur was deliberately prefabricated.'

MacArthur had never liked civilian agencies collecting intelligence on his patch. As Supreme Commander for the Allied Powers, he had sidelined the Office of Strategic Services, and he objected to the CIA setting up operations in Korea, despite the fact that the agency had been running spies in China and North Korea since 1947. Willoughby was equally opposed to having a rival intelligence source supplying information to Washington. When the agency eventually forced its way into Korea, he made sure to keep tabs on it.

According to X Corps' chief of operations, Lieutenant Colonel John Chiles, 'Anything MacArthur wanted, Willoughby produced intelligence for.' What MacArthur wanted was a unified Korea under pro-American rule, and to achieve that, he needed not just to cross the 38th parallel but to drive the North Koreans all the way to the Chinese border. Intelligence suggesting that this risked war with the PRC would not be helpful to him.

As early as mid-July, MacArthur had told the Joint Chiefs of Staff that he intended not only to repel Kim's invasion but to crush his armed forces, which might require the occupation of North Korea. While MacArthur had the support of at least some of the joint chiefs, Truman equivocated.

On 1 September the National Security Council delivered to the president a report, NSC 81, canvassing the risks and benefits of taking the war across the North Korean border. While noting that Moscow was 'unlikely' to 'passively accept' the loss of its control over 'all or most of Korea', the report suggested that the Soviets would be constrained by the need to avoid 'general war'. A decision to order UN forces across the parallel 'would create a situation to which the Soviet Union would be almost certain to react in some manner', but the risk of a wider war could be reduced by allowing only ROK forces to operate in or occupy North Korea. UN operations, it said, 'should not be permitted to extend into areas close to the Manchurian and USSR borders of Korea'.

As to the legality of crossing the border, NSC 81 left no doubt that military actions north of the 38th parallel that went beyond the primary mission of repelling the North Korean invaders were not authorised by existing UN Security Council resolutions. This included attempting to unify Korea under democratic rule. 'Accordingly,' the report found, 'United Nations approval for such further military actions is a prerequisite to their initiation. Should such approval not be forthcoming, accomplishment of this political objective would not be feasible.'

The joint chiefs dismissed the conclusions of NSC 81 as 'unrealistic', since they assumed the stabilisation of a front on the 38th parallel and concurred with MacArthur that the objective had to be the 'destruction of North Korean forces'. A revised version, NSC 81/1, agreed between Secretary of State Acheson and the joint chiefs, removed the prohibition on UN operations in areas 'close to the Manchurian and USSR borders' and instead stipulated that UN forces should not *cross* those borders.

The joint chiefs waited nearly three weeks before giving MacArthur his orders. During that time, UN forces had broken out of the Pusan Perimeter and the marines had achieved total success at Inchon. Kim's army was in chaotic retreat and the only question for America and its allies was how much they could squeeze from their victory. The joint chiefs told MacArthur:

> Your military objective is the destruction of the North Korean armed forces. In attaining this objective you are authorized to conduct military operations, including amphibious and airborne landings or ground operations north of the 38° parallel in Korea, provided that at the time of such operation there has been no entry into North Korea by major Soviet or Chinese Communist forces, no announcement of intended entry, nor a threat to counter our operations militarily in North Korea. Under no circumstances, however, will your forces cross the Manchurian or USSR borders of Korea and, as a matter of policy, no non-Korean ground forces will be used in the north-east provinces bordering the Soviet Union or in the area along the Manchurian border. Furthermore, support of your operations north or south of the 38° parallel will not include air or naval action against Manchuria or against USSR territory.

Confident that the Soviets would not intervene, and that Stalin and Mao were acting in concert, Washington utterly failed to anticipate that the PRC would intervene by itself.

On 9 October the Eighth Army rolled across the 38th parallel. Within a week, North Korean resistance had collapsed. As the 24th Infantry and 1st Cavalry Divisions chased after the retreating communist army, President Truman arrived on Wake Island, roughly halfway between Tokyo and Honolulu, for a conference with General MacArthur. Suspecting that there were political motives behind the meeting—victory in Korea seemed assured and Truman undoubtedly wanted his share of it—MacArthur delivered a calculated snub by shaking the president's hand rather than saluting.

The meeting lasted less than 90 minutes. According to an unofficial transcript taken by a secretary who overheard the conversation through an open door, MacArthur told Truman that victory had been 'won in Korea'. Asked about the risk of Mao sending Chinese troops to intervene on the North Korean side, MacArthur blithely replied:

> Very little. Had they interfered in the first or second months it would have been decisive. We are no longer fearful of their intervention . . . The Chinese have 300,000 men in Manchuria. Of these probably not more than 100–125,000 are distributed along the Yalu River [the border between Korea and China]. Only 50–60,000 could be gotten across the Yalu River. They have no Air Force. Now that we have bases for our Air Force in Korea, if the Chinese tried to get down to Pyongyang there would be the greatest slaughter.

Assistant secretary of state Dean Rusk, who was at the meeting, recalled MacArthur being equally unperturbed by threats the Chinese had been making in private about entering the war if UN forces crossed the 38th parallel. He did not fully understand, he told Rusk, 'why [the Chinese] had gone out on such a limb and . . . they must be greatly embarrassed by the predicament in which they now find themselves'. Predicting that 'formal resistance will end throughout North and South Korea by Thanksgiving', MacArthur said he hoped to be able to withdraw the Eighth Army from Korea 'by Christmas'.

That the Chinese would not enter the war was exactly what MacArthur's intelligence chief had been telling him, despite mounting evidence to the contrary. Some of this came indirectly from Beijing. The intermediary was India's ambassador to the PRC, K. M. Panikkar, who in late September was told by a Chinese official that Beijing would not sit on its hands if MacArthur's troops came all the way to the Chinese border. The message was reinforced on 22 September in a public statement issued by the Chinese foreign ministry that confirmed the PRC's determination to 'always stand on the side of the Korean people . . . and resolutely oppose the criminal acts of American imperialist aggression against Korea and their intrigues for expanding the war'.

On 2 October Panikkar was summoned after midnight for a meeting with the Chinese foreign minister (and future premier) Zhou Enlai, who informed him matter-of-factly that the PRC would intervene in the war if American troops crossed the 38th parallel. Panikkar's report of the meeting was immediately transmitted back to New Delhi, and from there to embassies around the world. If the messenger had been anyone but Panikkar, or anything but Indian, Zhou's warnings might have been taken more seriously, but the perception of Indians as sympathetic to communism, and of Panikkar as a Chinese stooge, meant that Zhou's comments went unheeded.

Six days later, on hearing that MacArthur had been given a green light by the United Nations to cross the border, Panikkar commented ruefully in his diary that America had 'knowingly elected for war, with Britain following'.*

While Mao's intentions remained cryptic, the PRC's potential for military intervention was apparent, even to Willoughby, whose agents had for some time been reporting the movement of troops from central China to Manchuria. At a teletype conference on 30 August, Willoughby told intelligence heads in Washington that there were a quarter of a million communist regulars in Manchuria. Some of these were likely to be Koreans who could be combed out and released to the North Korean government, like the 40,000 to 80,000 ethnic Koreans who had had already been sent back to fight in Kim's army. Willoughby was convinced, however, that while 'infiltration' might take place, there would be 'no organized partici-pation with [division] or corps units'.

---

*   In an account written after the Chinese intervention, President Truman claimed that Zhou's threats to enter the war had prompted him to call the meeting with MacArthur at Wake Island. 'I wanted to get the benefit of his firsthand information and judgement,' Truman wrote. MacArthur, of course, dismissed Zhou's warnings.

The CIA, too, discounted the likelihood of large-scale organised military intervention. On 8 September, a week before the Inchon landings, the CIA issued Intelligence Memorandum 324, 'Probability of Direct Chinese Communist Intervention in Korea', which estimated that 400,000 Chinese communist troops were either near or moving towards the Korean border. The report assumed that Mao was already secretly providing military aid to North Korea, including some infantry replacements, but that any more overt intervention would need approval from Moscow and a willingness to risk global war. While noting that recent communist propaganda 'may be stage-setting for an imminent overt move', the agency concluded that the repercussions would be so grave as to make it more likely that any Chinese intervention in Korea would be 'indirect, although significant' and confined to returning so-called 'Manchurian volunteers' to Korea to fight with Kim's army.

Twelve days later, the CIA was still hedging its bets, warning that the concentration of Chinese troops near the Manchurian border 'constitutes a powerful secondary reserve' for the North Korean forces that, with Moscow's consent, could 'enter the battle and materially change its course at any time', but at the same time suggesting it was 'doubtful that either Soviet or Chinese communist forces will be committed south of the 38th parallel'.

The failure of the Chinese to enter the war after the successful Inchon landing and the subsequent UN thrust into North Korea suggested to some that Beijing had missed its chance to intervene.* Factors that had previously been read as indicators of a possible intervention—such as large-scale troop deployments to the Manchurian

---

* The US ambassador in Moscow, Alan Kirk, believed that the Chinese threat to intervene if UN forces crossed the 38th parallel was a 'bluff', and that if they had wanted to enter the war they would have done so already. On 29 September he cabled Acheson: 'Moment for armed intervention was logically when UN forces were desperately defending small area Taegu-Pusan, when influx overwhelming numbers Chinese ground forces would have proved decisive factor.'

border area, the movement of medical supplies and congestion on the rail network—were now given a less sinister interpretation. Other warning signs—bulk orders of maps of Korea, and the reservation of ferries on the Yalu River for military use—were ignored. As for Zhou's threats to come to Kim's aid, these could be read as theatrical gestures aimed at deterring the United Nations from crossing the parallel rather than portents of future military action.

On 12 October, three days before Truman's Wake Island meeting with MacArthur, and five days after American troops crossed the 38th parallel, the CIA advised the president that while Chinese ground forces, even without air and naval support, were 'capable of intervening effectively, but not necessarily decisively' in the war, it had found 'no convincing indications of an actual Chinese communist intention to resort to full-scale intervention in Korea'. While full-scale Chinese intervention had to be regarded as an ongoing possibility, the agency determined that 'barring a Soviet decision for global war, such action is not probable in 1950. During this period, intervention will probably be confined to continued covert assistance to the North Koreans.'

US intelligence analysts were right about the Soviets' fear of provoking global war. Their mistake, however, was to assume that Mao was taking his orders from Moscow. Nearly a week *before* American troops crossed the parallel, Mao sent a telegram to Stalin that began: 'We have decided to send a part of the armed forces into Korea, under the title of Volunteer Army, to do combat with the forces of America and its running dog Syngman Rhee, and to assist our Korean comrades.'*

---

*   This and other telegrams from Mao are quoted in Thomas Christensen's 'Threats, Assurances, and the Last Chance for Peace: The Lessons of Mao's Korean War Telegrams'. The original source is *Jianguo Yilai Mao Zedong Wengao* (*The Manuscripts of Mao Zedong Since the Founding of the Nation*), vols I–III, September 1949–December 1952 (Beijing: Central Documents Publishing House, 1987 and 1990).

In committing to the war, Mao acknowledged to Stalin the possibility that the United States would declare war on the PRC and might, 'at a minimum, use its air force to bomb many major cities and industrial centres in China'. Destruction on such a scale would be devastating to a nation exhausted and bankrupted by years of civil war, and the Chinese Politburo was divided over the risks of goading America into all-out war. But Mao's domination over his fellow members ensured that the Politburo approved the decision to intervene, provided that Moscow guarantee air support and war materials. On 8 October Mao informed Kim Il Sung by telegram that the PRC intended to enter the war.

Mao was still hoping the Soviets would provide military equipment and air cover over Manchuria, but when Stalin demurred on both requests the Chinese Politburo made the decision to enter the war with or without Moscow's support. Faced with Mao's *fait accompli*, Stalin decided to hand over Soviet aircraft already in China and to move Soviet fighter squadrons into position to defend Chinese territory. According to Chinese historians Hao Yufan and Zhai Zhihai, Soviet pilots were dressed in the uniform of the Chinese People's Volunteers, and if caught by the enemy were under orders to identify themselves as Chinese Russian minority subjects.

As MacArthur drove his forces towards the Yalu River, the Chinese were laying what has been described as the biggest ambush in the history of modern warfare. The further the Americans advanced, the more stretched their supply lines became. Mao, like MacArthur himself, never doubted that he would be victorious. Told by one of his military strategists, Lei Yingfu, that MacArthur was 'famous for his arrogance and stubbornness', Mao is reported to have replied, 'The more arrogant and more stubborn he is the better . . . an arrogant enemy is easy to defeat.'

On the day before the Wake Island conference, the Far East Command daily intelligence summary—authorised, if not authored, by MacArthur's intelligence chief, General Willoughby—estimated that nine armies comprising 38 divisions were dispersed across Manchuria, but that threats to use them if American forces were to cross the 38th parallel were 'probably . . . diplomatic blackmail'.

At Wake Island, MacArthur assured President Truman that the Chinese, if they chose to enter the war, would be incapable of getting more than 60,000 men across the Yalu River. Mao, in a telegram to Zhou Enlai, expressed confidence in moving his entire invasion force of 260,000 men across the Yalu in just ten days.

11

UNCONFIRMED AND UNACCEPTED

On the night of 19 October 1950, four armies of the Chinese 13th Army Group began crossing the Yalu bridges. MacArthur's forces were still heading north but were too far from the Yalu to interfere with the crossing.

Mao understood that surprise would be a key factor in the battle ahead. In his memoirs, the Chinese commander General Peng Dehuai recalled being told by Mao: 'The crossing of the Yalu starts from the evening of 19 October . . . To keep it secret, all crossing should be done in the darkness from dusk till 4 in the morning.' Peng's troops were warned to avoid major highways.

Mao's instructions, outlined in his telegram to Zhou, were notably cautious and called for General Peng to 'build two or three defensive fronts'. If the enemy were to attack, Peng was to 'cut them off and destroy them in front of the positions':

if the Pyongyang American Army and the Wonsan Puppet Army [i.e. ROK troops] come from two fronts to attack, [he is to] attack the route which is relatively weak and isolated . . .

When our forces are fully equipped and trained, and after in the air and on the land we enjoy a state of overwhelming superiority in comparison to enemy forces, then we will attack Pyongyang, Wonsan, etc.

Moving at night to avoid detection from the air, General Peng's ghost divisions advanced silent and unseen towards their chosen positions on the southern slopes of the high mountain range 80 kilometres south of the Yalu. There, hiding in caves they had dug out by hand, Chinese soldiers lay in wait overlooking the corridors through which the Eighth Army would have to enter the mountains.

In the meantime, MacArthur had made the decision to split his forces, carving off General Almond's X Corps, which landed at Wonsan, on the eastern side of the peninsula, and quickly began moving inland. Between General Walker's Eighth Army on the west and Almond's X Corps on the east lay the virtually impassable Taebaek Mountains.

By late October, reports had begun to reach the embassy in Seoul of the capture of Chinese prisoners. On 29 October Everett Drumright, the US chargé, cabled Secretary Acheson with news that five prisoners of Chinese origin had been captured by the Eighth Army in areas north and north-east of Pyongyang (another two had been taken prisoner by X Corps). Two or three of the five wore complete North Korean uniforms, while others wore part North Korean uniform and part civilian dress. Two of the prisoners told interrogators that they had crossed from Manchuria on or about 19 October as part of the Chinese 40th Group Army. Another claimed to have crossed into North Korea with a unit of 2000 Chinese troops.

Sceptical of these prisoner reports, Eighth Army HQ assured Drumright that its field units had not made contact with any 'sizeable' numbers of Chinese troops, and consequently the Eighth Army was 'not inclined to accept reports of substantial Chinese participation in North Korean fighting'.

The reaction at MacArthur's headquarters in Tokyo was even more dismissive. The Far East Command daily intelligence summary for 27 October reported the recent capture of Chinese prisoners but rejected their comments about Chinese units entering Korea, describing these as 'unconfirmed and thereby unaccepted'.

Three days later Drumright reported the capture of five more prisoners of 'Chinese origin' by the Eighth Army and of another sixteen prisoners by X Corps. Details were lacking but some of the sixteen said they were from the 42nd Group Army.

On 30 October General Willoughby flew from Tokyo to X Corps headquarters to personally interrogate the sixteen Chinese POWs. The interview convinced him they were 'stragglers', not members of an organised People's Liberation Army unit.

Willoughby continued to play down the growing evidence of a vast Chinese force moving into Korea, insisting that Chinese fighters were there only in small volunteer units, and that the presence of Chinese soldiers did not signify a whole army but only elements of it. Speaking to General Clark Ruffner, X Corps' chief of staff, Willoughby scoffed at evidence of multiple Chinese divisions in Korea, suggesting they were only elements of different divisions, not full divisions. From a tactical viewpoint, he believed, the auspicious time for large-scale Chinese intervention had long since passed. '[I]t is difficult to believe that such a move, if planned, would have been postponed to a time when remnant North Korean forces have been reduced to a low point of effectiveness,' the Far East Command daily intelligence summary stated on 28 October.

Despite the fact that prisoners had now admitted to belonging to two separate Chinese armies, the 40th and 42nd, Eighth Army intelligence conceded only that 'there may be two *regiments* of Chinese Communists engaged in 8th Army sector [on] north and northwest side of peninsula'. It was unable to say whether the Chinese were fighting as independent units or 'sandwiched among North Koreans'.

Drumright's telegram ended with the disturbing news that South Korean forces fighting further east, near Onjong, had run into 'strong opposition' and speculated that Chinese communist forces 'may be . . . instrumental' in checking the UN advance towards the Yalu.

On 31 October Drumright reported that of approximately 400 prisoners captured in the Eighth Army sector the previous day, 'none were of Chinese origin'. From this, Eighth Army intelligence concluded that there were 'possibly about 2,000 Chinese engaged in Eighth Army sector'. In fact, by the start of November, the number of Chinese aligned against the Eighth Army and X Corps was close to 200,000, and rising.

Bill Train, a 1st Cavalry Division staff officer, said that Willoughby 'got everything wrong . . . what he was doing in those days was fighting against the truth, trying to keep it from going from lower levels to higher ones where it would have to be acted on'.

China specialists in Washington could only parrot the information and flawed analysis they were getting from Willoughby in Tokyo:

The Third ROK Army captured 18 [Chinese] prisoners and preliminary interrogation indicated that they are part of the 370th Regiment of the 124th Division. The strength of the unit is unknown but [intelligence staff in Tokyo] . . . estimate that its strength might be 2,500 men . . . The prisoners taken reported that they had had no food for three days.

Yet another Chinese soldier was captured on 31 October by ROK troops near Unsan, about 100 kilometres north of Pyongyang, but intelligence's assessment of Chinese strength in the Eighth Army sector hardly changed: it now estimated there were two or possibly three Chinese regiments, less than 5000 men in total. By arguing that these 'regiments' consisted of smaller units combed out of the PRC's 39th and 40th Group Armies, the report again excluded the possibility of those armies being present in their entirety.

At dusk on 1 November 1950 the Chinese finally emerged from their hiding places, pouring out of the hills near Unsan, blowing bugles, hurling grenades and firing their 'burp guns'* at the startled American soldiers of the 8th Cavalry Regiment of the 1st Cavalry Division. The 38th Group Army—between 10,000 and 20,000 men, according to Roy Appleman's official war history—seemed to materialise out of nowhere, attacking from three directions as it swarmed around the flanks and over the defensive positions of American and ROK units. The South Koreans protecting the 8th Cavalry's right flank quickly buckled, while two 8th Cavalry battalions retreated in disarray into the city of Unsan.

The next morning, at risk of being wiped out, the Americans tried to fall back, only to run into a Chinese roadblock. Leaving their artillery behind, the survivors fled into the hills, while the last remaining battalion of the 8th Cavalry fought desperately against 'human wave' attacks by an enemy that until now had existed as little more than rumour.

Efforts by the 5th and 7th Cavalry Regiments to reach the 8th Cavalry men failed when they were unable to break the Chinese encirclement. As night fell, small groups of survivors tried to slip through the Chinese lines and escape in the darkness. The 8th Cavalry suffered more than 800 casualities during the initial assaults—nearly a third of the regiment's strength.

Over the following week, further Chinese attacks forced the Eighth Army to withdraw to defensive positions along the Chongchon

---

* The ubiquitous and very reliable Type 50 submachine gun, a locally manufactured version of a Soviet weapon, was dubbed the 'burp gun' by UN troops because of the sound it made when fired.

River, but by 6 November the fighting was over: Peng's army had mysteriously melted away.*

Just two weeks after the PRC's 38th Group Army had driven MacArthur's forces from the Unsan area, the headquarters of the 'Peoples' Volunteer Army' analysed the fighting performance of the Americans in a pamphlet called 'Primary Conclusions of Battle Experiences at Unsan', a copy of which was captured by ROK troops. The Chinese were impressed by the 8th Cavalry's coordinated use of mortars and tanks, and by its 'very active' artillery. They noted that the strafing and bombing of Chinese vehicles by US aircraft had become a 'great hazard to us . . . their transportation system is great . . . Their infantry rate of fire is great and the long range of fire is still greater.'

The pamphlet's authors were scathing, however, about the way American soldiers who found themselves cut off from the rear would 'abandon all their heavy weapons, leaving them all over the place, and play opossum'.

Their infantrymen are weak, afraid to die, and haven't the courage to attack or defend. They depend on their planes, tanks and artillery. At the same time, they are afraid of our fire power. They will cringe when . . . on the advance they hear firing. They are afraid to advance farther . . . They specialize in day fighting. They are not familiar with night fighting or hand to hand combat . . . If defeated, they have no orderly formation. Without the use of their mortars, they become completely lost . . . they become dazed and completely demoralized . . . At Unsan they were surrounded for several days yet they did nothing. They are afraid when the rear is cut off. When transportation comes to a standstill, the infantry loses the will to fight.

---

*   Peng later explained his strategy: 'We employed the tactics of purposely showing ourselves to be weak, increasing the arrogance of the enemy, letting him run amuck, and luring him deep into our areas.'

The Battle of Unsan taught Peng and his generals tactical lessons that would be put to excellent use against the Americans in the weeks and months ahead. The pamphlet summarised these lessons:

> As a main objective, one of the units must fight its way rapidly around the enemy and cut off their rear . . . Route of attack must avoid highways and flat terrain in order to keep tanks and artillery from hindering the attack operations . . . Night warfare in mountainous terrain must have a definite plan and liaison between platoon commands. Small leading patrol groups attack and then sound the bugle. A large number will at that time follow in column.

Above all, Unsan taught the Chinese the need for speed. Speaking to Max Hastings in 1985, a deputy political commissar in the Chinese 4th Field Army said, 'In the Liberation war one might take days to surround a Kuomintang division, then slowly close the circle around it. With the Americans, if we took more than a few hours, they would bring up reinforcements, aircraft, artillery.'

Despite the rout at Unsan, Willoughby dismissed the battle as insignificant and continued to assert that Mao would not intervene in force. On 3 November, with the 8th Cavalry Regiment still fighting for its life against waves of communist infantry, Drumright passed on the latest assessment from Eighth Army intelligence, which highlighted the aptitude of the Chinese for 'infiltration and guerrilla tactics'. Three days later, MacArthur's headquarters estimated the number of Mao's troops in Korea at 34,500, when in reality more than 30 Chinese divisions—300,000 men—had already crossed the Manchurian border.

While Peng's decision to vacate the battlefield rather than follow up a decisive victory seemed to imply a reluctance to be drawn into a full-scale war with the Americans, the opposite was true.

By retreating into the mountains, the Chinese hoped to lure the UN forces into a deadly trap.

The surprise attack at Unsan caused General Almond of X Corps and his Eighth Army counterpart, General Walker, to think twice about the wisdom of continuing their race to the Yalu,* but Eighth Army intelligence saw nothing to be alarmed about, reporting that the Chinese communist forces in its sector 'continue to assume defensive attitude, digging in and refraining almost entirely from offensive operations'. With Willoughby's intelligence assessments still characterising the PRC forces as units rather than entire armies, Walker and Almond prepared to renew the offensive.

---

* After the rout of the 8th Cavalry Regiment at Unsan, Willoughby flew over from Tokyo for a meeting at Pyongyang, where Walker reportedly told him, 'Charles, we know the Chinese are here; you tell us what they are here for.' Willoughby was unable to offer a satisfactory answer.

12

THE CO'S COPPED IT

On 20 October 1950, as American and ROK troops celebrated the capture of Pyongyang, the US 187th Airborne Regimental Combat Team parachuted into Sukchon and Sunchon, roughly 45 kilometres north of the city, in an attempt to block the enemy's retreat. While most of Kim's soldiers had already escaped, the North Korean 239th Regiment was still in position around the town of Yongju.

Finding themselves trapped by a battalion of the 187th Airborne, the North Koreans attacked fiercely in search of a weak point, forcing the Americans to retreat and call for help from the nearest UN unit, the 27th British Commonwealth Brigade. An initial assault by the Argylls succeeded only in driving the North Koreans back onto the Airborne battalion, prompting another request for help. This time it was 3RAR's turn to bail out the Americans. But first they had to find them.

Setting off at 7 a.m. on 22 October, the diggers came under heavy sniper fire in Yongju. As they moved beyond the town, the fighting intensified. North Korean troops hidden in an apple orchard on a hill allowed C Company, commanded by Captain Arch Denness, to pass through them without firing before suddenly opening up from behind.

As enemy bullets zipped around their heads, the Australians scrambled to get out of their transport trucks. Bolts were pulled and the sides fell open to let the diggers jump. From that height it was all too easy to break a leg. 'You've got to move quick and then straight into action,' Private Keith Brunes recalled. 'Kneel or fall to the ground and just keep firing.'

Sandwiched between 3RAR and the 187th Airborne, the North Koreans fought tenaciously. Green's objective was to link up with the Americans, but since nobody could tell him exactly where they were, he was unable to use artillery for fear of hitting them. Rather than wait for confirmation of the Americans' position, Green decided to attack at once through the North Korean position to reach the 187th. He told C Company to fight with what they had: machine guns, grenades and rifles with fixed bayonets.

Green ordered 7 and 8 Platoons to the attack up the hill, with Lieutenant David Butler's 9 Platoon remaining on the road to protect the company's flank. The apple trees were in full leaf and Butler struggled at first even to see the North Korean soldiers firing at him. The man beside him, an AIF veteran, said, 'They're all there. Can't you see them?' but Butler, who had never been in a firefight before, 'couldn't see a bloody one . . . that's how new I was'.

Terrified by the diggers charging towards the apple orchard, many North Korean soldiers leapt out of their weapon pits and ran. The hill was quickly secured. Butler's platoon was then ordered forward along the road, which was blocked by a badly injured horse and its cart. After clearing the road, the diggers found themselves confronted by a North Korean brigade forming up for a final attack against the 187th Airborne. Butler recalled,

> We came off the slight rise where our battle began, and . . . into
> the vast open space, which was a series of paddy fields . . .

Our road, like all roads going through paddy fields, was . . . slightly higher than the paddy fields. This sea of paddy was just full of North Koreans, hundreds of them. They were clearly about to finish off the Airborne and we'd come from the south into the back of them. We'd come so quickly that they couldn't connect it all up and they didn't have the levels of junior leadership that we had. Their people didn't have a grasp of the battle and they hadn't been well enough trained, and they couldn't shoot well enough.

Chest-high stormwater drains, built to carry away the frequent floodwaters, ran along both sides of the road. Using these for cover, Butler's platoon advanced. By the time the North Koreans realised they were there and started firing, the diggers were deep into them.

During lulls in the firing, North Korean troops poured forward to surrender, but a hard core fought on for nearly two hours. In the end, the arrival of four American tanks proved decisive. 'There were just too many [North Koreans] and we had just about run out of puff,' Butler recalled. '[The tanks] made the difference. They gave us the impetus to get through.'

Caught between the Americans to the north and the diggers to the south, many North Korean soldiers attempted to escape by fleeing across the open paddy fields, only to be shot down as they ran.

Private George Lang was startled by a North Korean soldier jumping out from behind an embankment with his hands in the air:

I put my Owen gun on him. I thought, 'Oh, you beauty, I've got my first prisoner.' And next thing, 'Bang!' Someone shot him right between the eyes . . . It was a British soldier. He said, 'We're not taking prisoners, Digger' . . . I thought he was a mongrel for doing what he did because I had been there first and I had taken him prisoner. And he said, 'Wait till you see what they've done to our blokes up there in the hill.'

By midday, C Company was within sight of the 187th Airborne troops and the Battle of the Apple Orchard was effectively over. Denness and Butler found the Americans in a very bad way. 'They'd really been belted,' Butler recalled, 'and their RSM equivalent . . . who was obviously a man they revered greatly, had been shot in the jaw and was lying on a stretcher . . . One of their senior officers had broken down and they had to ship him out quickly. The poor devils, they thought we were about to do them over.'

According to Butler, when the traumatised American soldiers saw the diggers walking towards them in their heavy greatcoats, they thought they were Russians and surrendered to them.

Not everything ran like clockwork during the Battle of the Apple Orchard. Private Joe Vezgoff was part of a mortar crew with his mate Shuftie Frazer, an AIF veteran. 'Inside his mortar he would carry cigarettes and handkerchiefs, biscuits, pens, socks and so forth, so it took about five minutes to empty this mortar out,' Vezgoff recalled.

We saw these North Koreans running across a rice field and between us and the enemy . . . was this American tank . . . I said to Shuftie, 'Okay, Shuftie, there's some enemy there . . . beyond where the tank is, let's fire some rounds' . . . we'd been carrying these mortars around for quite a few weeks under all sorts of weather conditions and the cartridges had become somewhat damp, and we let one go . . . It went sort of 'pop' and we watched in amazement as this mortar [bomb] slowly climbed out of the 2-inch mortar and . . . landed near the tank and the tank commander yelled out . . . 'Goddamn, the gooks are mortaring us!' So the tank went west . . . and we went north. We left the rest of the mortar bombs there, they were fairly well useless.

The battalion diary recorded approximately 150 North Koreans killed and 239 taken prisoner in the Battle of the Apple Orchard, at a cost of just seven Australians wounded. The brigade diary noted 3RAR's casualties were 'amazingly light', given that a full-scale infantry battle had been fought and high casualties inflicted on the enemy.

Several Australians, including Butler, were decorated for their role in C Company's successful attack. Considering the size of the enemy force, Butler felt that Green would have been justified in waiting for another company to come forward and mounting a battalion attack:

> We'd never done one before, so it would have taken a bit of time. The chances are we would have been at it all day . . . and yet [Green] said, 'Come on. Let's get going' . . . we succeeded because we were on them before they realised it, before they were able to organise themselves, and it saved a lot of casualties.

On 24 October the 27th Brigade began crossing the Chongchon River, only 100 kilometres from the Yalu. The 1st Middlesex was to cross first in assault boats, with 3RAR ready to go to their aid if the enemy tried to hold the far bank. As it turned out, the river itself was a more dangerous adversary than the North Korean army, which had disintegrated in the course of its retreat from Pusan and was incapable of mounting any organised resistance. Small groups of enemy soldiers were now all that remained, Kim's generals having sacrificed all the territory between Pyongyang and the Chongchon River along the line of the UN advance.

With a rise and fall of seven metres and muddy banks in which a soldier could sink up to his waist, the fast-flowing Chongchon was a formidable obstacle. Crowds of villagers turned up early in the morning to cheer and laugh as the troops struggled to keep their assault craft from being dragged off course by the current. In the absence of army engineers to act as boatmasters, some locals took pity and helped the soldiers across in their fishing boats.

Pakchon, fifteen kilometres further on, was 3RAR's next desti- nation. Green's orders were to cross the Taeryong River via a partly demolished bridge a couple of kilometres south of the town. A platoon with makeshift ladders managed to scramble across the damaged bridge before noticing a group of about 40 unarmed North Korean soldiers dressed in white and waving white flags, apparently keen to surrender. As the group came towards them, other North Koreans lying in high ground beyond the bank started firing at both the Australians and their own comrades. Warned by a spotter plane that two more companies of enemy soldiers were hiding on top of the bank, the Australians beat a quick retreat across the river, taking ten prisoners with them.

Green was now faced with a dilemma: either keep his forces on the near bank and allow the North Koreans to dig in strongly before a daytime assault, or risk a night attack to dislodge them. He chose the latter.

With daylight fading, Green called for an air strike on the North Koreans sheltering among the ridges. After following up with an artillery and mortar barrage, he sent two companies across the broken bridge. They reached the west bank without opposition (the battalion diary described it as a 'quiet occupation by moonlight'), only to be counterattacked by an enemy company supported by a T-34 tank. The battalion's new 3.5-inch bazookas jammed in the freezing winter temperature, allowing the tank to breach Green's defensive perimeter and fire off a few erratic rounds before it was driven off.*

---

*   According to Sergeant Tom Muggleton, the diggers arrived in Korea in such a
      hurry that hardly anyone knew how to fire the new bazookas. 'They were a very
      good weapon but you've got to have time and be taught how to use 'em,' Muggleton
      recalled. 'People thought they had had enough time to learn but they didn't
      because some of them still had grease in them and they wouldn't fire and some
      of them [were] hooked up incorrectly.' One team had been carrying a bazooka
      for several days but 'didn't know how to [fire it] . . . Someone said, ". . . we're not
      within enemy contact and [someone should fire] the rocket launcher." And the
      bloke said, "I don't know how to fire it," and the bloke carrying the rocket said,
      "I don't know how to fire it either." So there was an American . . . a sergeant who
      knew something about rocket launchers and he just taught 'em.'

At 4 a.m. an enemy force of about 60 soldiers, supported by two tanks and seemingly unaware that Australians had crossed the bridge, began moving towards A Company. The Australians held their fire until the last moment before opening up on the North Koreans, who turned and fled, abandoning two Russian jeeps, one of which was souvenired by the diggers for future use.

Among the dead was a North Korean colonel who had been directing the tanks from one of the jeeps. Documents found on his body revealed that the tank brigade defending the road to Pakchon had twenty tanks, and that the colonel was the unit's senior culture and propaganda officer. His rueful remarks about the brigade's morale and performance confirmed what was already clear to the UN commanders: North Korean supply lines were breaking down and air support was a decisive factor in the success of UN ground forces.

The colonel's comments were corroborated by a notebook found on another body, which stated that frontline troops were short of ammunition, and that in order to rectify this 'members of the Culture Sect. were sent out to recruit local farmers and retreating soldiers for transportation purposes'. There was also a problem with 'clothing for the soldiers' but this was to be settled 'by the night of 25th October'. The North Korean situation as a whole was bleak. 'We are in a bad position,' the soldier wrote. 'The time for overall counterplan is here . . . A new culture propaganda plan was established to change the tide of battle from defence to attack . . . Former staff members were replaced. Plans for assignment and reassignment of the culture staff members were completed.'

But the communist troops fighting to hold back the UN advance needed more than a new 'culture propaganda plan' to save them. Eight Australians were killed and 22 wounded at the Battle of the Broken Bridge, but the North Koreans lost more than ten times that number. Years later Muggleton took issue with a former platoon commander who described the Battle of the Broken Bridge as a skirmish. 'If you're looking down the barrel of a T-34 tank, I got news for him,' Muggleton said. 'It's not a skirmish.'

The 27th Brigade was now ordered to advance 30 kilometres to Chongju, where captured intelligence indicated that the North Korean 17th Brigade was establishing a new defensive line.

Leading off, the 1st Middlesex quickly ran into North Korean infantry supported by two tanks. An air strike knocked out the tanks, setting off explosions in a nearby village, where the North Koreans had been stockpiling ammunition. Beyond the village, the British troops were hit again by heavy small-arms, artillery and tank fire and were forced to withdraw while an air strike was called in. During the day, ten North Korean tanks were destroyed, the majority by aircraft.

The next day, 28 October, it was the Argylls' turn to lead the brigade. It had become clear to Brigadier Coad that the North Koreans were resisting more doggedly the nearer they were pushed to the Chinese border. Rapid advances by the 27th Brigade of 40 or 50 kilometres in a day were now a thing of the past. Thoroughness was more important than speed, and it became the responsibility of the leading battalion to clear all suspicious or likely defensive positions, rather than leave the job to the follow-up battalion.

Early on 28 October 3RAR, supported by a dozen Sherman tanks, began moving through the Argylls to lead the push towards Chongju. Diggers riding on the backs of tanks were frequently sent up into the hills to clear any enemy troops capable of threatening the line of advance. Around noon, Green was warned by a Mosquito spotter plane that well-camouflaged enemy infantry and four tanks were occupying a ridge about four kilometres ahead. Green requested an air strike, and for several hours American F-80s and F-51s bombarded the North Koreans, who fought back with 'mostly inaccurate' tank, mortar and small-arms fire.*

---

* The imbalance in air support available to each side is highlighted by a report in Keith Lewtas's typed journal of a night attack on Australian positions by a lone North Korean aircraft. 'Another weapon used against us,' Lewtas wrote, 'was the singular old type of a light plane nick-named "Bed check Charlie", which perilously flew around during the night at a very low altitude and hand-dropped small grenades wherever a camp fire was sighted, but we did not hear of anybody being injured as a result.'

By 2.30 p.m. the American pilots were optimistically reporting that nine T-34s and self-propelled guns had been knocked out. Meanwhile, Green had planned a two-company attack on an enemy force estimated at between 500 and 600 men dug in on the tree-covered ridgeline. The odds of a successful attack against well-entrenched opposition were not in the battalion's favour, and the North Koreans resisted fiercely before the diggers broke through. An enemy tank supposedly destroyed in the air strikes knocked out at least one American Sherman, but by 5.30 p.m. both D and A Companies had fought their way through to their objectives. The Australians put eleven T-34s and two self-propelled guns out of action with their 3.5-inch bazookas.

With night closing in, Green moved quickly to secure the battalion's position, bringing forward the two companies that had not taken part in the battle to form a compact defensive perimeter capable of fending off a counterattack.

It was dark when D Company, south of the road to Chongju, came under bombardment by North Korean artillery and mortars. A determined enemy assault by a battalion-strength force, supported by tanks and self-propelled guns, succeeded in working its way behind the forward positions and penetrating Green's HQ area before being driven off. The men of 10 Platoon, which had taken the heaviest casualties during the afternoon, again bore the brunt of the fighting, holding fire with their automatic weapons until the North Koreans were no more than a few metres away. Having failed to dislodge D Company in the initial assault, dozens of retreating North Koreans were cut down by the diggers who had stayed in their weapon pits.

A short lull followed before the North Koreans launched a second assault, this time against A Company on the north side of the road. Tom Muggleton recalled the North Koreans attacking in waves:

The Japanese used to charge forward calling out, 'Banzai, banzai.' Well, the North Koreans did this night. Mortar fire didn't seem to do any good with 'em and we had . . . what they call an artillery forward officer. He was an American and I said to him, 'How close can you get your artillery shells?' And he said, 'Well, how close do you want 'em?' I said, 'Well, drop a few and see where it lands,' and . . . it shook our teeth and . . . that stopped the banzai charges.

By 10.15 p.m. the diggers had repelled the attack. Sporadic artillery and mortar fire continued to land around the Australians throughout the night but the failure of the second attack put an end to North Korean efforts to evict the Australians from their positions. 'We knew that we'd killed a lot of people that night,' Muggleton recalled, 'but the next morning when the daylight came up not a body [was left], cause they'd taken their bodies with 'em.'

The Battle of Chongju cost the enemy 150 dead and as many as twenty destroyed tanks and self-propelled guns, while 3RAR's casualties were nine men killed and 30 wounded, many due to machine-gun fire from North Korean tanks. It was the Australians' toughest fight since their arrival in Korea.

General Hobart Gay of the US 1st Cavalry was so sceptical of the number of enemy tanks claimed to have been destroyed by 3RAR and its supporting American tank company that he reportedly insisted on being shown the evidence. Afterwards he sent a cable to Brigadier Coad:

Congratulations on your splendid and sensational drive into enemy territory. I know it is a proud day in your brigade's record and one which deserves the envy of all soldiers. I send my sincerest congratulations and commendations to you and all the officers and men of the Argyll and Sutherland Highlanders, the Middlesex Regiment and 3rd Battalion of the Royal Australian Regiment, who marched 31 miles [50 kilometres] in twelve hours to deal the enemy a disastrous blow.

Green himself was less effusive, but was obviously proud of the achievements, in attack and defence, of a battalion he had led for just seven weeks. In that time, according to Jack Gallaway, Green had not even had time to share a meal with his officers, yet during his brief period in charge he had inculcated lessons and habits whose value had been proved in three major attacks and countless skirmishes. 'They can send them on by divisions now,' Green reportedly said after Chongju. 'This battalion will accommodate them.'

The country ahead was difficult and mountainous, and the Commonwealth troops had to be constantly alert to the threat of attack by communist soldiers cut off by the UN advance. One patrol, sent up to reconnoitre high ground near Coad's headquarters, detected what sounded like enemy movement and without hesitation opened fire on what turned out to be a wild pig, which ended up in the brigade cooking pot.

Refugees continued to hamper the UN advance, although many Koreans refused to leave their homes. Diggers told Norman Bartlett about strangely worded placards and banners hung out to welcome them as the war took them up and down the peninsula: 'Kindly! Heartly love United Nations' and 'Victory Speed I pray, Unify', and sometimes simply 'Wellcome [sic] Victorious UN Army'. Bartlett had no doubt that communist troops were greeted with similar messages, written in North Korean or Chinese, when they retook the same villages and towns.

The orders for 3RAR were now to advance a short distance on foot to high ground overlooking the Talchon River, two kilometres short of Chongju, which was captured by the Argylls without opposition.

After securing the town, the brigade was due for a rest, its role in the vanguard of the UN advance to be taken by the US 21st Regimental Combat Team, whose task was to seize the undefended town of Sonchon, north-west of Chongju. Signals Sergeant

Gallaway, ever sensitive to slights, saw in 3RAR's orders a repeat of what had happened at Pyongyang, where the Commonwealth troops were taken out of the game to allow the Americans and their vainglorious commander to claim the victory for themselves.

At Talchon River, Colonel Green sited his battalion headquarters in an east–west gully, with C Company on a ridgeline to the west that faced the river. C Company was being fired at by a North Korean self-propelled gun, the occasional shell bouncing off the ridge and tumbling into the rice paddies below. Ben O'Dowd, the officer in charge of headquarters company, wanted to pitch Green's tent in the shade of a big tree, but the risk of a stray shell hitting the tree convinced him to move the tent further up the gully, to a spot as close to the ridge as possible. O'Dowd's own tent would be next to it.

Green had not slept for two days and was unhappy with the position of his tent, which would have caught the full glare of the morning sun. Green returned from his nightly visit to each of the four infantry companies and immediately 'demanded to know why he was in the sun while [Major Ferguson] had the shade', O'Dowd remembered.

I indicated the gun firing at C Coy and pointed out the odds about a shell landing on Ferg's tent as opposed to those applying to his. He accepted this, and went to rest. In no time, there was an explosion uncomfortably close, followed by a badly shaken batman bearing the news that the CO had been wounded.

According to the war diary, six high-velocity shells had burst over battalion HQ and the sixth 'struck a tree at the rear of C Company's position'. Of a thousand men in the area, the only one hit was Colonel Green. His batman, who was standing in Green's tent at the moment of the explosion, was unharmed.

Jack Gallaway quoted a signals platoon sergeant (presumably Gallaway himself) who saw the shell explode and laughed at the sight of a nearby wireless operator sprinting for cover.

[T]hen I heard yelling and saw Bennie O'Dowd and the adjutant racing toward Charlie's tent. Then I heard it: 'The CO's copped it.' I felt it physically, it was like being winded at football. I reckon every bloke in the battalion felt the same when he heard about it. There was only one Charlie Green.

Seriously wounded in the abdomen by shrapnel, Green was evacuated to a US Army surgical hospital, where he clung on for nearly 24 hours before succumbing to his injuries.

That fluke North Korean shellburst—it was the only one of the six to contain high explosive—robbed 3RAR of the commanding officer who would be remembered as the best they had ever had. Brigadier Coad, who later became a general, was reported to always keep a photograph of Green on his desk to remind him of the unflappable and brilliant soldier who, in less than two months, had transformed his battle-unready battalion into an awesome fighting unit.

The incident that robbed Green of his life also deprived him of the Distinguished Service Order (DSO) he had earnt through his leadership at the battles of the Apple Orchard, the Broken Bridge and Chongju. Coad and the commanders of the Argyll and Sutherland Highlanders and the 1st Middlesex battalion all received the DSO, an award that could not be made posthumously. General Gay was in no doubt, however, about Green's role in the offensive that took UN forces almost to the Manchurian border, describing him as 'the finest battalion commander I ever saw'.

General MacArthur awarded Green the Silver Star, commending his 'superb leadership, daring tactics and cool courage' in the Battle of the Apple Orchard – an action that, in the words of the citation, 'materially contributed to the successful prosecution of the campaign against the armed enemy of the United Nations and was in keeping with the highest traditions of the Military Service'.

13

I DID WHAT I WAS TOLD

The war could not stand still for Charlie Green or for anyone. As Green's second-in-command, Bruce Ferguson immediately took over, but his leadership did not last beyond lunchtime. The new commander of 3RAR was to be Lieutenant Colonel Walsh, who had led the battalion in Japan before being passed over for active command in Korea. Walsh was already on the spot, attached to the Eighth Army headquarters as an observer, and it was felt by some that putting him in charge would help mitigate any drop in morale caused by Green's death.

On the last day of October, the men of the 27th British Commonwealth Brigade were given their first day off since crossing the border into North Korea. For the past two weeks, except for three days south of Pyongyang, the brigade had been the spearhead of the UN advance. During that time, the Australians had lost a revered commander. In the words of the brigade diary, 'a rest and refit was in great need'.

Even so, the brigade had to be on its guard. Patrols were sent out to clear surrounding villages and destroy any arms and ammunition they found. All the evidence suggested that the victory at Chongju had been decisive and that North Korean resistance was crumbling. The news reaching MacArthur was uniformly good, with UN forces advancing on all fronts towards the Chinese border. So confident were the Americans of coasting to the border that instructions had been issued to all UN forces about how to behave when they got there:

a) No troops or vehicles will go beyond South Bank Yalu River.
b) No fire will be exchanged with, or air strikes requested on, forces north of South Bank Yalu River.
c) Rigid control of troop movements in vicinity of Korea will be exercised.
d) Damage, destruction or disturbance of service of power plants located at Sinuiju, Uiju and Supung-Dong will be avoided if practicable.
e) No personnel, military or civilian, will be permitted to enter or leave Korea via Manchurian border.

The instructions broadly followed the orders given to MacArthur by the joint chiefs when they authorised him to cross the 38th parallel in October, but they omitted MacArthur's undertaking to use only ROK troops in the border areas. The intent of the joint chiefs' orders had been to neutralise the risk of a wider war involving the Soviet Union, but the enemy troops already pouring across the Manchurian border were not Stalin's.

On the day the brigade was told that Charlie Green had died, the war diary recorded 'disquieting reports . . . about the presence of Chinese troops'. According to 'intelligence sources', some Chinese prisoners had already been taken.

In a cable dated two days later, Everett Drumright, the US chargé in Seoul, reported the capture of another Chinese, bringing the total number of Chinese prisoners seized in the Eighth Army's area to seventeen. 'Careful and repeated' interrogation of these prisoners indicated that there were two Chinese 'units'—designated the 55th and 56th 'units'—operating in the Eighth Army's sector of North Korea; they had been ordered from Manchuria to Pyongyang on 10 October and after 'various delays' had crossed the Yalu River 'in three groups on October 19, October 25 and 26'. There was confusion over the scale of the Chinese infiltration, with prisoners variously reporting the strength of each 'unit' as anything between 2500 men and 9000 men.

By the time Drumright's cable reached Washington, it had already been overtaken by news of the disaster at Unsan. The US 21st RCT, which had taken over the advance on the Yalu from the 27th Brigade, was now retreating as quickly as it had previously advanced. Since all available transport had been commandeered for the American withdrawal, 3RAR had to remain at Chongju—'immobile for the time being', in the understated words of the brigade diary, without artillery or tanks, and cut off from both the Americans and the rest of the brigade.

Orders were issued and then rescinded before the brigade was finally delivered by a fleet of American trucks to a new defensive position near the village of Pakchon, on the west side of the Taeryong River, where it was to provide cover for the retreating US and ROK divisions. The plan was to hold the bridgehead until a 'later date', when the UN force would resume its offensive.

Intelligence received by the brigade indicated there were now six Chinese divisions in Korea, all 'well trained in mountain warfare and in night fighting', whose tactics were to 'infiltrate through the hills, encircle and cut off and simultaneously attack frontally'. 3RAR's war diary put the number at sixteen divisions, but the diggers had yet to lay eyes on a single Chinese soldier. Air reconnaissance could find no evidence of the rumoured enemy divisions, although the ambush of a Middlesex patrol a few kilometres northeast of Pakchon was a sure sign that the Chinese were closing in.

An entry in the brigade diary for 4 November struck an ominous note:

A gap of five to six miles between the Brigade and [the US 19th Regimental Combat Team] is causing concern. Apparently no link up can be made as 19 RCT are fully committed for their tasks and no more troops are available to strengthen the bridgehead at the moment.

In the early hours of 5 November, PRC troops swept down behind the Commonwealth troops to attack a US Army artillery battery positioned astride a road that had been designated as the brigade's withdrawal route. Firing over open sights at almost point-blank range, the Americans were quickly overwhelmed. Not for the last time, they fled the battlefield, leaving their guns and casualties behind. A company of Argylls, with four tanks, drove the Chinese back to a ridge 500 metres east of the road, only to be forced to retreat when the enemy counterattacked. From their position on the high ground, the Chinese continued to threaten the brigade's line of withdrawal. With the brigade now in danger of being cut off, 3RAR was told to attack and retake the ridge.

The feature consisted of three crests, the two nearest of which were occupied by the enemy. Walsh ordered order A Company to take the first and B Company the second, but he left it to the two company commanders, captains Chitts and Laughlin, to work out how. Several factors complicated the task, including lack of artillery and the need to cross 500 metres of open rice paddies before assaulting the ridge. Two American Patton tanks were available to provide stationary fire but they would not join the advance. What the Australians did have was air support, provided this time not by the US Air Force but by Mustangs of the RAAF's No. 77 Squadron.

The start line for the attack was the road, and A Company began taking casualties from Chinese mortars the moment it crossed the road. While the diggers moved forward, the Mustangs swept the ridgeline with rockets, cannon and napalm. Scrambling up the slope, the Australians freed some Argylls, who had become trapped when the Chinese counterattacked the previous night. At the same time, B Company launched its assault on the second crest.

Stan Connelly was in B Company. He recalled advancing in three lines across the open paddy fields:

> We can't do much with our weapons there because we can't really see the enemy but he's sitting up there with his machine guns and he's trying to rake us . . . I remember clearly seeing the lines of bullets slicing into the mud across the line of advance where he's trying to get his range right. He'd be swinging his medium machine gun trying to mow down the troops. They only get a few . . . because we advance six feet apart and with, say, twelve feet between the ranks; it's pretty hard to pick up a single man even though you're using a heavy machine gun. Then you've got to climb up the hill and while you're struggling to get up he can sit up the top and try and pin you back . . . we lost a few people going across the open paddy fields and we lost a lot more when we hit the top of the hill.

One of those killed during the fighting at Pakchon was B Company's Lieutenant Larson. Connelly remembered how Larson 'charged up with his men with his pistol in his hand and got shot dead before he reached the crest'. Another casualty was Connelly's great mate Corporal 'Lofty' Goebel, shot down as he crossed the rice paddy. But by 3 p.m. the diggers had succeeded in pushing the Chinese off the ridge.

Walsh then ordered D Company to join them on the ridge, leaving Arch Denness's C Company to take up positions in the rice paddy between A Company and the road. On the other side of the road, O'Dowd put a group of newly arrived reinforcements to work digging weapon pits for the defence of Walsh's headquarters.

Walsh now began to have second thoughts about the site he had chosen for his HQ, which was close enough to his own mortar platoon to be vulnerable to retaliatory machine gun and mortar fire from the Chinese. Worried by the risk of an enemy counterattack during the night, Walsh ordered O'Dowd to shift the HQ to a safer location nearly a kilometre to the rear.

Captain Cyril Hall, who was in command of the support company defending headquarters, later told Gallaway that Walsh was more concerned with moving his HQ out of harm's way than with finding a suitable new location. Brigadier Coad consented to Walsh shifting his headquarters but gave strict instructions that the rifle companies on the ridge had to stay where they were.

The difficulty of moving a battalion headquarters in the dark, with all its communications equipment and with wounded men awaiting evacuation, meant that it was nearly 4 a.m. before the last vehicle departed. O'Dowd arrived at the new site to find anti-tank guns unmanned, trucks still loaded with equipment and casualties from the afternoon's fighting being treated on the roadside. He also learnt that Walsh, in defiance of Coad's instructions, had ordered the withdrawal of the three rifle companies on the ridge.

Sergeant Fred Rennie recalled hearing the order to withdraw and telling his mate, 'No, nobody withdraws troops in contact with the enemy in the dark. Take no notice of it.' But when the order was confirmed, Rennie had to pull back with the rest.

A Company had taken heavy casualties during the original attack; its commanding officer, Captain Bill Chitts, had been wounded and the company was now being led by a young lieutenant, Algy Clark. When he received Walsh's order to pull out, Clark obeyed. Recalling the incident later, he noted that the other two company commanders on the ridge were AIF veterans who had known Walsh when he commanded the battalion in Japan and 'were not very impressed by his competence'. Later, Clark was told that both had instructed their radio operators to turn their radios off and pretend not to have heard Walsh's withdrawal order. 'They stayed in position that night and received no casualties. But being a very young, inexperienced (aged 22) and I now believe a stupid officer temporarily in command of A Coy, I did exactly what I was told,' he said.

In fact, as Jack Gallaway confirmed, the other two companies did not remain in position on the crests, but both Captain Laughlin, in charge of B Company, and Major Walter Brown, in charge of D Company, took their time before acting on Walsh's order to withdraw. With enemy activity along the ridge dying down, D Company began moving at around 10.30 p.m. and B Company a short time afterwards.

Told that Walsh was pulling back his forces, Brigadier Coad ordered all three companies to return to their original positions. Already halfway down the slope, D Company had to turn around and go back, miraculously retaking the crest without making any contact with the enemy. For B Company, the order came too late: the Chinese had moved to reclaim the ridge and the diggers would have had to claw their way back up the slope in an improvised attack against a revitalised enemy. All Laughlin could do was continue the withdrawal. In the event, B Company got down with no casualties. A Company was not so lucky.

O'Dowd, at battalion headquarters, feared the worst. 'The only information on A Company came from stragglers and casualties,' he recalled, 'but this was all bad news, leading us to suspect that A Company was non-existent, or at best non-effective.'

According to Gallaway's account, both Algy Clark and Lieutenant Bill Keys queried Walsh's order, which went against conventional military wisdom that troops should never attempt to retreat while under enemy attack. Once the order was confirmed by Walsh, they had no choice but to comply. Keys' 1 Platoon, which had been kept in reserve during the assault and was therefore at full strength, was to pull back from its forward position on the ridge and set up an assembly area in the rear for the rest of the company. 'By removing his forward platoon,' Gallaway explained, 'Algy Clark left the front door open for an attack upon his unprotected Company Headquarters. The Chinese accepted the invitation.'

As 1 Platoon moved in the dark to take up its new position, Lieutenant Noel 'Chic' Charlesworth conducted a headcount. Soon he realised that he was counting Chinese as well as Australian heads: enemy soldiers had infiltrated the company HQ. Charlesworth scrambled for cover and started firing. Three diggers, including the company sergeant major, were killed. With battle raging on the ridge-line, Keys kept his platoon moving, eventually reaching the road with 45 men. By the time A Company had completed its withdrawal, barely 60 fit men remained of the 110 who had set off across the rice paddy the previous afternoon.

Ben O'Dowd, who would soon be given command of A Company, had no doubt where blame should lie for the ill-conceived withdrawal, which cost several diggers their lives:

The brigadier had instructed [Walsh] to defend on the features he had taken. He therefore had a right to expect that that was the forward defence of the brigade unless he authorised otherwise. The companies should have remained in position unless pushed off by the enemy or the brigadier had been consulted and agreed to their repositioning. In fact, Coad told Walsh he could move his HQ if it was being mortared, but . . . the companies must remain.

It is inscribed in letters of fire on any commander's heart that it is fatal to withdraw, retreat, bug out or whatever whilst under attack; to do so is to invite disaster. But in the dark, the rule is doubled and redoubled in spades. Withdrawal of a group from prepared defences is only on when more suitable ground has been selected. Where in hell were the companies supposed to go? How were the platoons and sections to be sited in the dark? . . . If Walsh was concerned about gaps requiring rearrangement of the companies, he should not have left it until after dark. I can see nothing in defence of Walsh's decision to move the companies when he did.

With the decision to withdraw the rifle companies, the battalion's 'spectacular success' in taking the ridge had been transformed, as O'Dowd put it, into a 'bad tactical joke'. A feature that had allowed the enemy to dominate the road had been captured, only to be given back a few hours later. A Company had been hammered, and while Captain Laughlin had skilfully extracted his men without taking further casualties, daylight found B Company and C Company dangerously exposed in a rice paddy, at the mercy of any enemy troops on the ridge. D Company, having begun to withdraw before being ordered back, was now alone, cut off from the rest of the battalion.* According to the war diary, 3RAR's casualties were twelve killed and 64 wounded.

Another casualty of the night of 5–6 November was Walsh's command. According to Len Opie, the 'officers' mafia' sent a spokesman to Brigade Headquarters to protest about Walsh's leadership. 'So he got on a pushbike and he rode down to Brigade Headquarters and he told the brigadier that the officers . . . wouldn't serve under Walsh.'

Whether Opie was right about the officers' mutiny or not, the fact is that the morning after the battle Walsh was sacked by Brigadier Coad, to be replaced as 3RAR's commanding officer by Major—soon to be Lieutenant Colonel—Bruce Ferguson. (Walsh would resume his position as an observer at Eighth Army HQ.)

Meanwhile, D Company, isolated on the ridgeline, was looking for a way out. Brown dispatched a patrol to reconnoitre the two

---

* D Company would eventually emerge from the battle unscathed, an extraordinary achievement in the circumstances. 'During the whole of the operation D Company did not make contact with the enemy,' the war diary noted.

adjacent crests taken and then relinquished by A Company and B Company. To their surprise, the diggers found that the Chinese had disappeared, probably having overstretched their supply lines. Sergeant Buck Buchanan recalled 'walk[ing] all over their objective . . . without having to fire a shot'.

It was clear from the number of Chinese dead and the amount of abandoned equipment that A Company and B Company had given the enemy a hiding—the first real defeat inflicted on the Chinese in Korea by any UN unit. Before Pakchon, bugging out had been the norm, with both the Americans and the ROK army panicking in the face of Chinese 'human wave' attacks carried out without artillery or air support. At Pakchon, 3RAR showed that the Chinese were not invincible: the battalion had taken and held its objectives in the face of a numerically superior force, only ceding ground when ordered to do so. But the cost had been high. Since arriving at Pusan, the battalion had suffered more than 150 casualties, including more than a third of its frontline fighting strength.

Given the scale of its losses, Ferguson gave priority to A Company for reinforcements. The company had lost most of the original men brought to Korea earlier that year, either killed or wounded. O'Dowd found himself in charge of a company reduced to one officer (Algy Clark), no company sergeant major, one platoon sergeant and not enough other ranks for an effective fighting unit. All of its reinforcements would be K Force volunteers.

'K Force soldiers were an adventurous breed who volunteered for service in Korea only,' O'Dowd wrote later.

These men were imbued with the AIF spirit, they enlisted for the hell of it but, having been there before, had no illusions about the consequences of battle. From experience they understood that survival depended on that form of discipline peculiar to the AIF volunteer and so puzzling to British officers. They could be difficult at times in rear areas but never lacking when the chips were down. In addition, based on a national characteristic of mateship, they easily developed the team spirit so essential in difficult situations.

Despite their losses, there would be no rest for the diggers. Clearing patrols were sent out at sunrise on 7 November, killing seven enemy soldiers. A few Chinese from the battle for the ridge were found hiding in villages and taken prisoner. As MacArthur's forces moved to expand the bridgehead, the 27th Brigade—now under the command of the US 24th Infantry Division—reprised its role as vanguard of the advancing left flank of Walker's Eighth Army.

Intensive patrolling over the following days resulted in the capture and interrogation of more prisoners, including a North Korean NCO who confirmed that his battalion had arrived in the Pakchon area with orders to attack on the night of 7–8 November, a plan thwarted by the brigade's advance. In order to protect themselves from UN air strikes, enemy troops were now putting on civilian clothes and living by day in villages, emerging again at night as soldiers. To combat this, UN aircraft started hitting villages, targeting any building that might be harbouring enemy soldiers. An entry in the brigade diary noted, 'When planes are in the area and cannot find a target they are to attack any likely-looking village.'

Ever-deeper patrolling by 3RAR—as far as 4000 and 6000 metres—revealed further signs of hasty Chinese withdrawal, including unburied dead, but found no trace of Beijing's phantom divisions. 'It is obvious that the enemy have broken contact and have withdrawn to the North,' the brigade diary reported on 13 November 1950. 'Their limited attempt to break through to the Chongchon River failed and it appears that they are not in a position and do not wish to resume the offensive.'

With the communists seemingly beaten, it looked as though the diggers' biggest worry would be the Korean winter.

14

THAT AWFUL GODDAMN TRAP

The Chinese offensive that began in the last days of October 1950 and was broken off around ten days later only deepened the mystery surrounding Beijing's intentions in Korea. In the immediate aftermath of the offensive, the CIA reported that 30,000 to 40,000 Chinese communist troops had entered Korea and were fighting UN forces 'at various points' south of the Korean–Manchurian border, while Russian-built jet fighters had also engaged US aircraft over Korea. It estimated that another 700,000 Chinese troops were stationed just across the border in Manchuria, giving Beijing the capability either to block further UN advances northwards through 'piecemeal commitment of troops' or to force UN withdrawal to defensive positions further south by what it termed 'a powerful assault'.

Beijing's objective appeared to be twofold: to halt the advance of UN forces in Korea and to maintain a communist regime on Korean soil. Accomplishing both would avert the psychological and political consequences of a 'disastrous outcome', and keep UN forces away from the Chinese and Soviet frontiers, while retaining a Korean base for military and guerrilla operations and tying down

UN (and especially US) forces 'indefinitely' in Korea. The CIA also raised the possibility of another motive for the Chinese intervention: the protection of hydroelectric stations along the Yalu River, which supplied power to the Manchurian industrial area.

> The Chinese Communists appreciate that in intervening in Korea they have incurred grave risks of retaliation and general war, but have accepted the risk. They would probably ignore a UN ultimatum requiring their withdrawal. If Chinese territory were to be attacked, they could and probably would enter Korea in full force, with the purpose of expelling UN forces altogether.

On the ground, the situation seemed a good deal more encouraging for the UN side. The North Korean army had been out-thought and outfought, its battered survivors retreating into the mountains to fight as guerrillas or fleeing north to the sanctuary of Manchuria. General Walker's Eighth Army had built a dominant position on the Chongchon River, halfway between the 38th parallel and the Manchurian border. While the 8th Cavalry Regiment had been badly mauled at Unsan, the 5th and 7th Cavalry Regiments were both intact. The 24th and 25th Infantry Divisions were in reasonable shape too. The reluctance of South Korean commanders to move forward in strength had hamstrung Walker's advance, but the two ROK divisions on Eighth Army's right flank would have the support of the US 2nd Infantry Division. Almond's X Corps, with the full-strength 1st Marine Division, had made good progress up the east of the peninsula. Total UN combat strength was around 425,000 ground troops, including nearly 180,000 Americans— more than a match for the scattered remnants of Kim's army. There appeared every reason for UN troops to be confident of reaching the Yalu and winning the war by year's end, just as their commander-in-chief had promised.

The Chinese forces that had routed the 8th Cavalry at Unsan and threatened to overrun the 27th Brigade at Pakchon had not been seen since 6 November. In his official army history, Appleman recounted how one Chinese army of three divisions marched 460 kilometres on foot from An-tung, in Manchuria, to its assembly area in North Korea. Marching over rough mountain roads, one division averaged nearly 30 kilometres a night for eighteen nights, each night's march starting at 7 p.m. and ending at 3 a.m. Every man, animal and piece of equipment was camouflaged and hidden during the daylight, with only scouting parties walking ahead to find the next day's bivouac area. Spotter planes sent up to find the Chinese returned without having sighted a single soldier. The Chinese wore white parkas to blend in with the snow, and on the rare occasions that the planes flew over Chinese soldiers, they would lie down and not move. According to Appleman, officers were authorised to shoot any soldier who violated this order.

An American reconnaissance patrol consisting of infantry and tanks reported entering a valley and hearing strange music, just as the diggers had heard music before the Chinese counterattacked at Pakchon, but on this occasion there was no attack. The same patrol captured an enemy soldier wearing a Chinese uniform and what was thought to be an officer's blouse under his Korean uniform. Eighth Army intelligence showed little interest.

The failure by the Chinese to follow up their successful surprise attacks seemed to validate MacArthur's belief that the attacks were the work of small 'volunteer' units and not Chinese regulars. His intelligence chief, Willoughby, was convinced that only battalion-sized elements had intervened.* Asked by General Almond what had happened to the 8th Cavalry Regiment, Willoughby more

---

* The Chinese disguised their fighting strength by using misleading code names. For example, they designated divisions as battalions. When Chinese prisoners gave interrogators the proper names of their units, they were not believed.

or less accused the regiment of having been unable to fight in the dark.

Yet as far back as July, the US Armed Forces Security Agency (AFSA) had been circulating intelligence obtained from intercepted Chinese and North Korean signals traffic about the massing of Chinese divisions on the Manchurian border. This intelligence had been made available to the Joint Chiefs of Staff, the White House and General MacArthur. By September, AFSA was able to name six of the nine field armies (the elite combat units of the People's Liberation Army) that Mao would send to fight in North Korea, and to place them close to the border in Manchuria.

The signs of a looming Chinese attack increased even as Peng's army melted away after Unsan: during the first half of November, Chinese civil communications revealed that Beijing was in a state of emergency, with authorities encouraging street protests calling for military intervention, bolstering air defences and urging officers and soldiers to volunteer for the war in Korea. While there is no proof that MacArthur personally read the reports of Chinese armies deploying to Manchuria, the information was certainly received by his intelligence staff in Tokyo.

The decision by the Chinese to break off their first offensive and withdraw into the mountains baffled American military and intelligence officials. Two weeks after the apparent disappearance of Peng's army, CIA officials were still puzzling over the 'lack of aggressiveness' of the Chinese forces. The Joint Indications Intelligence Committee, chaired by the army's G-2 intelligence section, was convinced that the Chinese had made only 'piecemeal commitments of small forces . . . from various divisions of three different armies', and concluded that Beijing wanted to promote 'the fiction of volunteer forces but also . . . to create the impression of greater strength than was actually present'.

On 21 November forward elements of General Almond's X Corps reached the Yalu. Although it was no more than a reconnaissance in force, MacArthur was euphoric. Lieutenant General Matt Ridgway, a renowned airborne commander from World War II who was then serving on the army staff at the Pentagon, would later compare him with Custer at the Little Bighorn, writing that MacArthur 'had neither eyes nor ears' for information that might interfere with his plans. Bill Train's recollection was more sombre. It was, he told Halberstam, 'the saddest thing I was ever associated with because you could almost see it coming, almost know what happened was going to happen, those young men moving into that awful goddamn trap'.

The trap was four days from closing, and there was still no sign of the Chinese army that had ambushed the 8th Cavalry at Unsan.

The mystery surrounding Chinese intentions deepened with the unexpected release of 27 wounded US prisoners of war. In his 23 November cable to the secretary of state, Ambassador Muccio reported that the soldiers from the 8th Cavalry Regiment had 'appeared in US lines' on the evening of 21 November—an event he termed the 'most significant development' of the past few days.

Apparently the men had been part of a group captured on 3 November. Details reaching Seoul were still sketchy, but according to Muccio's cable the men were 'taken overland to the town of Pyoktong on Yalu River where they were kept in schoolhouse. They were treated well, not even their valuables being taken from them, and they were interrogated, but the questions related mainly to their political ideas and beliefs, not military matters.'

After being held captive for sixteen days, 27 enlisted men were selected and put on trucks. They travelled south for two nights, sheltering in a village during the daytime. When they were within seven kilometres of the UN lines, their Chinese captors 'patted POWs on back and shook hands with them and directed they return to own units'.* On reaching their own lines, the released prisoners reported that about 300 American and 600 ROK prisoners of war were still being held at Pyoktong. Spotter planes were immediately sent up to try to locate the remaining prisoners but could find no trace of them.

The recovered POWs were carefully interrogated by military intelligence but they could not explain their release. Muccio noted, however, that during the Sino-Japanese War, Chinese communist units had occasionally released Japanese POWs after subjecting them to political indoctrination, in the hope that they would be able to influence the Japanese to stop fighting.

Sightings of Chinese soldiers on the ground remained rare. 'Contact with Chinese Communist [in] X Corps areas North Korea continued negligible yesterday,' Everett Drumright advised Acheson on 18 November. 'Only four Chinese stragglers were made prisoners, two from Chinese Communist 39th Army and two from Chinese Communist 40th Army.' Five days later, Muccio reiterated that 'contact with Chinese both on ground and in air has been virtually negligible last three days'.

On the basis of information supplied by Eighth Army intelligence, Drumright concluded that the Chinese were fighting a 'delaying action' and were 'not committed to all-out intervention'.

---

* By the time Ambassador Muccio was able to confirm the interrogation reports, the story had changed. The 27 POWs were captured on the night of 2 November and taken to a central assembly area. It took some men eight days to reach their destination, during which they 'received hard treatment' and some personal items were stolen from them. On arriving at the central assembly point, American POWs were separated from other UN POWs. Interrogation was mostly political, with questions such as 'Why fight in Korea?' and 'Why aiding American imperialists and Wall Street tycoons?'. The Americans were billeted in farm houses and given millet to eat, although later they were also given rice and fish. Although the POWs themselves could offer no reason for their release, the US intelligence officer who questioned them suspected that the decision 'must have been made on [a] high level'.

He admitted, however, that the reasons for a delaying action, 'if it indeed be that, are not clear'.

Almond's X Corps was equally sure that the Chinese would not intervene in force. On 22 November, X Corps intelligence reported that there was 'no evidence to indicate any considerable number of CCF [Chinese communist force] units have crossed the border since the initial reinforcement'.

A secret CIA memorandum, based on information available on 21 November, asserted that Beijing would use 'intimidation and diplomatic means' in an attempt to obtain a UN withdrawal from Korea. If this failed, the Chinese would ramp up their military intervention.

> At a minimum, the Chinese will conduct, on an increasing scale, unacknowledged operations designed to immobilize UN forces in Korea, to subject them to prolonged attrition, and to maintain the semblance of a North Korean state . . . Available evidence is not conclusive as to whether or not the Chinese communists are as yet committed to a full-scale offensive effort . . . It is estimated they do not have the military capability of driving the UN forces from the peninsula, but that they do have the capability of forcing them to withdraw to defensive positions for prolonged and inconclusive operations which, the Communists might calculate, would lead to eventual UN withdrawal from Korea.

The intelligence agencies of the departments of State, the Army, the Navy and the Air Force all 'concurred in' the CIA's assessment that while military preparations being carried out in Manchuria were capable of supporting 'major operations of prolonged duration', military activity by Chinese troops in Korea to date was 'not . . . sufficient to demonstrate the existence of a plan for major offensive operations'.

The four-year post-war occupation of Japan left 3RAR far from battle-ready when the Korean War broke out. Intensive training knocked the Diggers into shape before they left for Korea. *SLV*

3RAR arrived in Korea two weeks after the successful amphibious assault by US and South Korean forces at Inchon. Here a US Marine watches as naked North Korean prisoners are marched to the rear. *SLV*

Lieutenant Colonel Charles Hercules Green (*left*) took command of 3RAR at midnight on 12 September 1950. General Gay of the 1st US Cavalry Division described him as 'the finest battalion commander I ever saw'. *Lloyd Brown/AWM*

The 1st Battalion, the Argyll and Sutherland Highlanders, here marching to bagpipes, fought alongside the 1st Battalion, the Middlesex Regiment ('the Diehards') and 3RAR in the 27th British Commonwealth Brigade. *A. Gulliver/SLV*

In January 1951 the gunners of the 16th New Zealand Field Regiment arrived in Korea to reinforce the 27th British Commonwealth Brigade. Their support would prove critical at the Battle of Kapyong. *SLV*

An Australian soldier fires his Sten gun at portraits of Stalin and the North Korean leader, Kim Il Sung, during the UN drive on Pyongyang. *SLV*

Korean refugees stream south to escape the fighting. North Korean and Chinese soldiers often mingled with refugees to infiltrate UN positions. *A. Gulliver/SLV*

Diggers inspect a Type 50 sub-machine gun, a locally made version of a Soviet weapon dubbed the 'burp' gun because of the sound it made when fired. *A. Gulliver/SLV*

A wounded North Korean prisoner being led by South Korean soldier. *A. Gulliver/SLV*

An elderly Korean man struggles south with his possessions while American soldiers head north towards the front line. *SLV*

Koreans employed as porters trudge uphill with rations for Australian troops. Working for the Diggers offered some protection against ROK army recruitment squads. *Phillip Oliver Hobson/ AWM*

Australian soldiers interrogate two North Korean prisoners. Captured Chinese soldiers were usually more forthcoming than North Koreans. *SLV*

A wounded American paratrooper receives blood plasma, using a captured Russian rifle as a stand for the plasma bottle. *A. Gulliver/SLV*

A mortar crew in action during an Australian attack on a North Korean position, with an American Sherman tank in support. *SLV*

A Russian-made T-34 tank knocked out by a napalm bomb. The T-34's initial aura of invincibility wore off in the face of UN air power and improved anti-tank weapons. *A. Gulliver/SLV*

An elderly Korean woman bows to the crew of an Australian Bren gun carrier. Towns and villages constantly changed hands during the first year of the war, so civilians learnt to greet both sides. *A. Gulliver/SLV*

A British Bren gun carrier with a burning village in the background. Communist troops often hid in villages during daylight to avoid UN reconnaissance planes. *A. Gulliver/SLV*

An old North Korean man points out a sniper's position to a British soldier. *A. Gulliver/SLV*

Soldiers from A Company, 3RAR, move through a paddy field near Pyongyang. Unlike the Americans, the Diggers took patrolling seriously, clearing country ahead of an advance to avoid ambushes. *A. Gulliver/SLV*

Australian machine-gunners watch as napalm bombs are dropped on a communist position. At Kapyong napalm was mistakenly dropped on Australian troops. *SLV*

An American tank carrier off the road in the mountains of North Korea. Steep winding roads made it hard for UN forces to exploit their advantage in heavy armour. *A. Gulliver/SLV*

Lieutenant Colonel Bruce Ferguson took over command of 3RAR after the death of Charles Green. Ferguson would receive the Distinguished Service Order for his leadership in the Battle of Kapyong. *Claude Rudolph Holzheimer/AWM*

An American chopper sets down in a frozen paddy field to receive wounded Australian soldiers. During the Korean winter of 1950–51 temperatures plunged to 30 degrees below zero. *SLV*

Private Harry Power and Lance Corporal Fred Murphy enjoy some tinned rations while covering the road below. Soldiers often had to carve the food out of its can with a bayonet. *A. Gulliver/SLV*

Mustangs from the RAAF's No. 77 Squadron provided vital air support for infantry operations. Here two ground crew take time off for a brew. *SLV*

Australian soldiers in a two-man tent celebrate Christmas with their mates. Keeping their beer from freezing called for all the Diggers' ingenuity. *SLV*

Australian soldiers patrolling in deep snow 20 kilometres into enemy territory. Many returned from patrols suffering from acute snow glare. *A. Gulliver/SLV*

Australian soldiers carry artillery pieces by hand across a muddy field. *SLV*

Padre A.W. Laing of Bathurst, New South Wales (*left*) conducts a Sunday service in the snow for members of 3RAR. *Phillip Oliver Hobson/AWM*

Members of 3RAR's Field Ambulance Section carry a wounded digger near Pakchon, North Korea. *SLV*

Soldiers from A Company, 3RAR, with full gear on their backs, move along the track to begin their attack on Hill Sardine.

A well-camouflaged Chinese dugout, roofed with logs and with walls of rock, hay and matting, discovered when 3RAR attacked and captured Hill Sardine.
Ian Robertson/AWM

Snipers from 3RAR in a shallow trench they have just captured from the Chinese on Hill Salmon.

A Sherman tank of the 72nd US Tank Battalion drives onto the low section of the Island feature in the Kapyong Valley defended by B Company, 3RAR. Chinese troops poured along the road (*centre of picture*) on the night of 23–24 April. A, D and C Companies occupied the high ground beyond the road.

Members of a US tank crew camouflage their Sherman tank with foliage in the hours before the Chinese attack at Kapyong.

Australian soldiers stand guard over Chinese prisoners after the Battle of Kapyong.

During the battle Lieutenant Len Montgomerie MC (*front row, centre*) led 4 Platoon, B Company, in desperate hand-to-hand fighting to clear the Honeycomb feature against 'fanatical' Chinese resistance.

General Van Fleet, commander of the US Eighth Army, inspects 3RAR when presenting the battalion with a Presidential Unit Citation for halting the Chinese at Kapyong. *Phillip Oliver Hobson/AWM*

Intercepted Chinese communications, however, were telling a different story.

According to a declassified paper by Guy Vanderpool, a former intelligence analyst for the US National Security Agency, communications intercepted between 9 and 22 November 1950 revealed that 30,000 maps of Korea were being sent to cities on the Chinese–Korean border. The first message stated that Shanghai was sending 'at least 10,000 maps' to Shenyang, just over an hour by train from the border. When told of this, Willoughby's intelligence team estimated that China might allocate 1000 maps to a division—in other words, one map between ten men. While those 10,000 maps 'might' have been intended to supply ten Chinese divisions, Willoughby's staff thought it more likely they were intended for the 75,000 Chinese 'volunteers' they now conceded to be in North Korea. On 18 November another 20,000 maps of Korea were reported to have been sent to Shenyang. According to the original calculation by Willoughby's staff, that number of maps was enough to furnish 30 Chinese divisions—exactly the number General Peng would deploy in his second-phase offensive.

On 22 November the medical HQ of the 4th Field Army 'urgently' ordered PRC troops in Manchuria to be inoculated against smallpox, cholera and typhoid—diseases that were common in North Korea.

MacArthur had guaranteed President Truman and the joint chiefs that China would not enter the war, and they in turn had gambled everything on his plan for a unified, democratic Korea. But not everyone trusted MacArthur to stick by the terms laid down by the joint chiefs—in particular, their warning against any action near the Manchurian border that might provoke Chinese intervention. 'Mr Broustra [a French delegate to the United Nations] last night told me in strictest confidence that the French were considerably worried over what General MacArthur might do,' an adviser to the US delegation wrote in a memorandum dated 24 November.

'Broustra said the French knew the ways of successful generals and also of course had heard of General MacArthur's reputation for independence. I attempted to assure Broustra that the General was under the strictest orders not to violate the frontier in any way.'

With tension mounting at the United Nations, the secretaries of state and defense and the Joint Chiefs of Staff met in Washington on 22 November. Two days later, in a cable marked 'top secret—operational immediate', General Collins warned MacArthur of 'growing concern' among UN members over the 'possibilities of bringing on a general conflict should a major clash develop with Chinese Communist forces as a result of your forces advancing squarely against the entire boundary between Korea and Manchuria-USSR'.

On the 'assumption' that MacArthur's coming attack would be 'successful', Collins outlined some 'military measures' aimed at reducing the risk of Chinese intervention. These included halting his forces south of the Yalu River and using 'principally ROK troops' to hold the area; and making 'every effort' to avoid destroying the hydroelectric stations on the Yalu. While they might 'leave much to be desired' from a military point of view, Collins believed that such measures would 'not seriously affect' the outcome of MacArthur's mission and 'might well provide an out for the Chinese Communists to withdraw into Manchuria without loss of face'.

MacArthur rejected the suggestions out of hand. Calling on his own 'personal reconnaissance' of the Yalu River line, MacArthur told the joint chiefs that it was 'utterly impossible' for him to stop his forces south of the river and retain control of the line of advance into North Korea. Any failure by the United Nations to prosecute the military campaign through to its public and oft-repeated objective of 'destroying all enemy forces south of Korea's northern boundary' would be fraught with disastrous consequences. 'It would be regarded by the Korean people as a betrayal of their sovereign and territorial integrity . . . and by the Chinese and all other peoples of Asia as weakness reflected from the appeasement of Communist aggression.'

Emphasising that his forces were 'committed to seize the entire border area', MacArthur pointed out that X Corps had already occupied a sector of the Yalu River with 'no noticeable political or military . . . reaction' from the Chinese.

Nobody would have been less surprised by MacArthur's dismissive response to the joint chiefs' suggestions than Mao, who believed that MacArthur was both too arrogant and too complacent to realise the significance of the intelligence he was receiving about Chinese preparations for a massive strike against his forces. Nearly four months earlier, while UN troops were penned inside the Pusan Perimeter, Mao had asked his staffer Lei Yingfu to go away and think about what MacArthur's next move would be. Lei correctly predicted the Inchon landing. (The information was given to Kim Il Sung, who failed to act on it.) Lei also undertook an analysis of MacArthur's personality and his tactics during the Pacific War.

Mao knew that MacArthur had underestimated the strength of the Chinese units inside Korea. According to Guy Vanderpool, Mao told the commander of the 13th Army Group on 18 November that 'MacArthur believed there were only 60,000 to 70,000 PRC troops in North Korea', and that this misconception 'would help the PRC destroy "tens of thousands" in MacArthur's army'.

At 10 a.m. on 24 November 1950, the US Eighth Army, supported by Commonwealth, ROK and Turkish troops, launched an offensive intended to make contact with and destroy any remaining North Korean forces and Chinese 'volunteer' units. Three corps were to advance side by side: in the west, I Corps (including the 27th British Commonwealth Brigade); in the centre, IX Corps; and in the east, guarding its right flank, the ROK II Corps. Identified by the Chinese as the weakest link in Walker's army, the ROK II Corps was doubly disadvantaged, lacking the heavy weaponry of an American corps and assigned the most awkward terrain. The 1st

Cavalry Division, barely recovered from the beating it had suffered at Unsan, was in reserve, tasked with protecting vital transport hubs at Kunu-ri, just below the Chongchon River in the IX Corps zone, and fifteen kilometres further south at Sukchon, behind I Corps.

The 27th Brigade's war diary celebrated 'the opening day of the offensive which it is hoped [will] reach the Manchurian border and finish the Korean War'.

The same day—which happened to be Thanksgiving—General MacArthur made one of his rare flying visits from Tokyo to 'direct' the start of the operation. Under the headline, 'MacArthur to see the knockout', Australian newspapers reported his announcement that a general assault 'to end the war' had begun in north-west Korea. MacArthur repeated his promise to get the troops home by Christmas, telling the IX Corps commander, 'You can tell them that when they get up to the Yalu . . . they can all come home.'

According to Appleman, the Eighth Army had three and a half times the firepower of the opposing Chinese and North Korean forces. Owing to the enemy's lack of anti-aircraft weapons, Walker could also rely on the near-total air superiority of the US Fifth Air Force, which would support his troops with ground attacks.

Replete from their Thanksgiving turkey dinner, and expecting to be home by Christmas, some American soldiers abandoned their equipment and ammunition before the offensive got underway. The men in one rifle company reportedly threw away their helmets and bayonets and headed north with an average of one grenade and a few dozen rounds of ammunition each. Despite the bitter cold—on the day forward elements of X Corps reached the Yalu the temperature hit 30 degrees below zero—many of Walker's troops were still wearing summer-weight uniforms.

On the east coast, X Corps was counting down the hours before its own offensive, due to start on 27 November. Almond, like Walker, shared the view of MacArthur's Far East Command that the Chinese were only interested in fighting a delaying defensive action.

On the eve of the attack, X Corps believed that not more than one or two divisions of Chinese infantry stood between it and the border: the true figure was twelve divisions (120,000 men).

Mistaking the enemy's withdrawal as a sign of weakness, MacArthur and his commanders failed to recognise a stratagem developed by Mao Zedong in his war against the Japanese. The purpose of the Chinese disengagement, as Billy Mossman pointed out in the second volume of the official army history, was not to establish a defensive position but rather to gather strength before renewing the offensive begun at Unsan.

After breaking contact on 6 November, the Chinese commander of the 13th Army Group sent out a skeleton force as a screen for the bulk of his troops, who were concentrated much further north. By 23 November, as the Americans prepared for Thanksgiving, the group's six armies—a total of around 180,000 men[*]—were positioned up to 25 kilometres north of the Eighth Army front, with two armies facing each of I and IX Corps and the ROK II Corps. In the east, three more Chinese armies were in place to stop Almond's X Corps from rolling west to link up with the Eighth Army. The disposition of the Chinese forces on the eve of MacArthur's 'home by Christmas' offensive conformed precisely to the doctrine laid out by Mao twelve years earlier in a series of speeches entitled 'On the Protracted War'. Mossman quoted a key passage in his official history:

> To achieve quick decision we should generally attack, not an enemy force holding a position, but one on the move. We should have concentrated, beforehand under cover, a big force

---

[*] In his contribution to *In from the Cold: Reflections on Australia's Korean War*, Xiaobing Li put the number of Chinese troops significantly higher. General Peng, he wrote, 'had 230,000 men on the western front against 130,000 UN troops, and 150,000 men on the eastern front against 90,000 UN troops, a ratio of nearly two to one'. The official army history, however, put the combat strength of UN ground forces at 425,000 men.

along the route through which the enemy is sure to pass, suddenly descend on him while he is moving, encircle and attack him before he knows what is happening, and conclude the fighting with all speed. If the battle is well fought, we may annihilate the entire enemy force or the greater part or a part of it. Even if the battle is not well fought, we may still inflict heavy casualties.

Unaware of the vast enemy force lying in wait, Walker's Eighth Army easily reached its first-day objectives, along the way picking up another 30 survivors of the 8th Cavalry's defeat at Unsan, men who had been captured and then released by the Chinese.

The second day of the advance was more difficult, with ROK units in particular meeting tougher opposition, but there was nothing serious enough to cause Walker to have second thoughts about the offensive. Most importantly, there was no intelligence to suggest that the PRC armies in Manchuria had moved into Korea; a report for 25 November put the number of Chinese facing the Eighth Army at just 54,000.

Peng's armies struck before midnight, a symphony of bugles and whistles heralding human wave attacks along the length of the Eighth Army front. The 9th and 38th Regiments of the US 2nd Infantry Division were among the first to be hit, the Chinese attacking with grenades and small arms as they probed for gaps that would allow them to reach the rear areas and assault the flanks. Terrified GIs fled, many wading waist-deep through the icy Chongchon River. A battery of the 61st Field Artillery Battalion, having seen its commander killed and every other officer wounded, abandoned its guns and vehicles. By the end of the first day, the 2nd Infantry Division had been driven back several kilometres.

The ROK II Corps on its right fared even worse. Penetrated by the Chinese in numerous places and with its escape route blocked, the entire corps disintegrated, its three divisions falling back in disarray, exposing the entire Eighth Army flank and opening a 120-kilometre hole between the Eighth Army and X Corps. With his whole army at risk of being enveloped, General Walker ordered the 1st Cavalry Division and the Turkish Brigade forward to deny the enemy the use of the key road between Kunu-ri and Sunchon. I Corps, in the western sector, got off lightly by comparison, although the threat of encirclement by the Chinese put an end to the advance on the Yalu.

In less than 24 hours, the Chinese had brought the UN offensive to a halt and nearly destroyed the ROK II Corps as a fighting unit.

Even now, Walker failed to recognise this as the start of a major Chinese offensive. While nearly doubling its estimate of Chinese troops in the area (from 54,000 to 101,000), Eighth Army intelligence still believed that the enemy would maintain an 'active defence in depth along present line employing strong local counterattack'. Far East Command in Tokyo seemed untroubled by the day's events, Willoughby advising Washington around noon on 26 November that if the enemy attacks continued, 'a slowing down of the United Nations offensive may result'.

That night the Chinese tried again to capitalise on the collapse of the ROK II Corps, throwing five field armies at the Eighth Army's vulnerable right flank and sending another into the I Corps sector to contain the 24th Division. It took until early evening on 27 November for Walker to stabilise his forces, but by then it had become clear that the situation of the Eighth Army was irretrievable.

Ambassador Muccio's cable to Secretary Acheson the following day perpetuated the fiction of a Chinese counterattack: 'Yesterday UN elements in Eighth Army ran into heavy enemy opposition except on west flank . . . Both Chinese and North Korean elements appear involved in counter-attacks . . . Enemy counter-attacking forces were well-equipped with artillery, mortar and executed skillful infiltrating movements.'

By nightfall on 27 November it was clear that the Eighth Army was not facing a series of coordinated Chinese counterattacks but a major offensive—a mirror image, almost, of the UN offensive begun just three days earlier. Two PRC armies were surging through the gaping hole left by the collapse of the ROK II Corps. There was every chance that they would capture the key road hubs of Kunu-ri and Sunchon. Once that happened, there would be little to prevent them from pushing deep into the Eighth Army's rear and ultimately encircling it.

Just hours earlier Walker had dared to believe that he could turn back the Chinese and resume his own offensive. Now that dream was in tatters. Withdrawal was his only hope—and not a tactical withdrawal, but a deep and humiliating retreat that would put his forces beyond reach of the Chinese bearing down from the east.

Far East Command could no longer deny the truth of what was happening. At 4.45 p.m. on 28 November, MacArthur cabled the Joint Chiefs of Staff with news of the catastrophe:

> The Chinese military forces are committed in North Korea in great and ever increasing strength. No pretext of minor support under the guise of volunteerism or other subterfuge now has the slightest validity. We face an entirely new war . . . our present strength of force is not sufficient to meet this undeclared war by the Chinese . . . This command has done everything humanly possible within its capabilities but is now faced with conditions beyond its control and its strength.

15

DANGEROUS TO TOUCH

The diggers had been trained to live and fight in Middle Eastern deserts and in the jungles of New Guinea and South-East Asia; nothing had prepared them for the brutal Korean winter.

'We went over there with our service dress, the little frock coat, serge uniform—suitable for a Melbourne winter, totally inadequate for a Korean winter,' Sergeant Ron Perkins recalled.

When the temperature got down to 27 below zero, as it did with the bitterly cold winds blowing down from Manchuria, then it really affected everybody. Trying to sleep at night on frozen ground with one thin blanket and this rubber-ised . . . groundsheet over you, not the best . . . the older fellows, they really felt it. It affected their bones, backs and everything.

Reginald Thompson, a British war correspondent, felt that the diggers suffered more than most from the cold:

143

[T]hey were the toughest and most experienced soldiers, but many of them were over 35 years of age and some, having cheated on their age, were now over 40. The cold was beginning to find them out and the doctors were working hard, examining men doubled up with lumbago and kidney trouble. But the men were remarkably cheerful and making themselves snug in rice-straw.

The winter of 1950 started in the middle of November, several weeks earlier than expected. The first cold snap arrived on 10 November, with the battalion diary reporting heavy frost at night. On 14 November the diary noted 'cold and gusty winds' during the day. The next day the battalion was issued with US Army field jackets and shoe packs, but not the warm pile linings and pile caps the diggers had been hoping for. By the following week the weather had worsened, with frequent falls of snow and icy winds.

Caught out by the plummeting temperatures, the diggers had to learn quickly how to maintain and fire their weapons in subzero conditions. If a rifleman touched the freezing metal of his rifle with bare hands, his fingers would stick to it. 'Everything had to be done with gloves on,' Jack Gallaway recalled.

The gloves that we wore were . . . big leather mittens with trigger fingers in them where you could slip your finger into the special space in the mitten, allowing you to pull the trigger of a rifle. It didn't give you much of a grip on the rifle which meant you couldn't shoot as straight as you'd want to. Everything that was metal was dangerous to touch.

The diggers got used to sleeping with their automatic weapons to stop the moving parts from freezing. Private Kenneth Travers remembered men writing home for sardines so they could smear the oil on their rifle bolts. Some soldiers kept grenades inside their clothing to stop frost from building up on the detonators.

In his book *With the Australians in Korea*, published by the Australian War Memorial just a year after the war ended, Norman Bartlett recounted a joke that old Korea hands would tell to newcomers about the 'Kur-kur bird . . . the only bird that stays in Korea for the winter'.

> Just listen when you're out there tonight, sport, you'll hear the Kur-kur bird all right. It flies around the corners of the mountains and across the paddy fields with a harsh cackle, like this: Kur-kur-kur-Christ it's cold.

As a signaller, it was Jack Gallaway's job to lay and repair telephone lines. A simple operation like tying a reef knot in the wire inside a telephone cable, a job that took 30 seconds in normal temperatures and could not be done wearing gloves, could take two signallers as long as five minutes. 'Your hands started to freeze almost as soon as you took your gloves off,' Gallaway said.

'Personal hygiene amounted to nothing much more than washing the face and the hands and a shave,' Private Stan Connelly recalled.

> We never washed or showered . . . Never changed our underwear, usually had constipation from being too cold to take a crap . . . We shaved every day, there was never any breakdown in that sort of discipline. Usually with melted snow, a handful of snow in an empty food can. Put it on the fire, get a little bit of warm water and away you go.

Gallaway remembered the mornings being so cold in Korea that the soapy lather would freeze on his face. Luckily for his mates in the signals platoon, Gallaway had made friends in some American units through scrounging for such things as signal wire and radio batteries, and was able to get hold of cartons of American-made Gillette razor blades and brushless shaving cream.

Australian soldiers each carried half of a tent, which enabled two men to put up a small shelter in their weapon pit. The diggers, Gallaway recalled, 'were always on the move, always digging holes in frosted ground. An axe was the only implement able to deal properly with the first layer of topsoil, frozen, sometimes, to a depth of 30 centimetres or more.'

'The yanks would pull up in a truck,' Raymon Wilson recalled. 'The first thing they would do is get a jerrycan of petrol, pour it on the ground and throw a light on it, "bang!" and everybody would see it for miles and miles around, but even that would not soften the ground.'

It could take half an hour, Joe Vezgoff recalled, just to dig a hole the size of a milk bottle. After penetrating the layer of permafrost you had to scrape away at the sides of the hole and then crack the overhanging layer until eventually you had a foxhole. The whole job could take a man as much as four hours. 'You'd do that and then [an officer] says, "Okay, move." That was the worst part.'

'We dug in every night,' Corporal Len Opie recalled. 'I dug a hole every night for seven or eight months.'

Although the battalion had been issued with American sleeping bags, they came without the warm inner lining. As the temperature plunged during November 1950, the diggers were forced to carry heavy blankets in their packs.

'They sent us to Korea with a blanket that you used to wear as a roll on your back,' Tom Muggleton recalled, 'and when your blanket got wet . . . it was wet for days because you couldn't get it dry.' Some diggers took sleeping bags from US soldiers killed in ambushes. 'We would knock off the sleeping bags and, well, [it was] one way of getting them,' Muggleton said.

At night it was too cold to undress, and the risk of an enemy attack meant the diggers nearly always slept in their boots. Stan Connelly recalled taking his boots off one night during the advance to the Manchurian border. The next morning some diggers had a fire going on the far side of the hill but Connelly's hands were so cold that he could not get his boots on.

> I was almost in tears with the frustration of needing to get these boots on and trying to and [I] couldn't . . . Eventually I just had to grit my teeth and jump out of the trench barefoot and charge through the snow before my feet could freeze and over the hill to safety by the fire. Dry out the boots and warm up the feet and get it all together again.

Rations froze. 'If you got a tin of rations, the best thing you could do was kick a dent in the can if you could, throw it on the fire and when the dent pops out, hook it out of the fire and open it as quick as you can,' Ron Perkins recalled. 'You were just as likely to find that the outside was burnt to a cinder and the rest was still frozen solid in the middle.'

It was not only the Australian Army that was caught napping by the deteriorating weather. Historian Karl Warner described American troops losing fingers, toes and ears as they sat on frozen outposts waiting for winter clothing to be supplied from the south. Soldiers in artillery units turned empty 105-millimetre shell casings into makeshift heaters by filling them with petrol. Troops used whatever they could find as fuel for campfires, including the rice stooks farmers left beside their rice paddies—a practice that stopped when enemy troops began booby-trapping the stooks with grenades.

Eventually the diggers got the pile liners for their American jackets, along with warm caps complete with earflaps; they were quickly banned from wearing these, as the flaps made it difficult to hear orders unless they were shouted.

The battalion was encamped north of Pakchon when news began to come through of the unfolding disaster of MacArthur's offensive. The 27th Brigade had been assigned the role of reserve for I Corps on the Eighth Army's west wing, but it was IX Corps, in the centre, that was now in trouble. The main thrust of the enemy attacks was against the road and rail centre of Kunu-ri, around 50 kilometres east of Pakchon. The Commonwealth troops were immediately transferred from I Corps to IX Corps and sent to Kunu-ri, arriving around midday and making camp in a creek bed a kilometre south of the town.

The confusion, verging on panic, in Eighth Army command meant that orders were sometimes revised or rescinded before they could be acted on. During the evening of 26 November, the 1st Middlesex battalion was put on two hours' notice to plug a hole on the brigade's west flank that had opened up when the US 5th Regimental Combat Team was rushed up to support a vulnerable ROK regiment. At 11.15 p.m., as reports confirmed the disintegration of the IX Corps front, the brigade was told it would be moving 'without delay' the following morning. By 3 p.m. on 27 November the brigade had been delivered by truck to a concentration area as IX Corps' reserve.

That evening, Coad received orders to be ready to move 'at a moment's notice' to new defensive positions. ROK units on both the west and east of IX Corps had collapsed, leaving both its flanks exposed. A battalion of the Turkish Regiment, hurriedly thrown in to replace the South Koreans, was encircled and was trying to break out. In the rush to shore up the Eighth Army's desperate position, little thought was given to the difficulties of moving the 27th Brigade and all its heavy equipment at night, or to the need for reconnaissance once it arrived. Coad refused to move his brigade without its artillery and without information about the whereabouts of both enemy and friendly forces. In the end, the decision was taken to postpone the brigade's move until 6 a.m., 'according to the situation as known at that time'.

With the Eighth Army's plight worsening by the hour, and the possibility of a general withdrawal being 'openly discussed' at IX Corps headquarters, the 27th Brigade was put on an hour's notice to move.

At 5 a.m. the situation was described by IX Corps HQ as 'critical'. The US 2nd Infantry Division had been 'completely routed', contact had been lost with the ROK II Corps, and the ROK 1st Division on IX Corps' left had been driven back. Coad was now ordered to take his brigade nearly 60 kilometres south, where they would remain in corps reserve and be responsible for patrolling and keeping open the Kaechon–Sunchon road, which ran south towards Pyongyang and was a critical withdrawal route for the Eighth Army.

The orders for 3RAR were to hold the Taedong River ferry crossing at Chasan, eight kilometres south of Sunchon. No American transport was available, so the Australians had to make do with what they had. While B Company and D Company started marching, stores were offloaded from the battalion's trucks to make room for A Company and C Company, as well as for the battalion's headquarters and support. With refugees crowding the roads, the journey took six hours. On arrival, the trucks were turned around and sent back to pick up the footsore diggers from B Company and D Company, as well as troops from the Middlesex Regiment and the Argylls. The shuttle service ran until two in the morning. After every soldier had been withdrawn, the trucks went back yet again to fetch the offloaded stores. By then Kunu-ri was in enemy hands.

General Walker still hoped to be able to withdraw his Eighth Army to a new line across the waist of the peninsula, near Pyongyang. On the east coast, however, General Almond continued to drive X Corps north along increasingly difficult mountain tracks, convinced he could carry out MacArthur's grand (some said deranged) plan for a link-up between the two UN forces.

The most exposed unit of Walker's army was General 'Dutch' Keiser's 2nd Infantry Division. Isolated at the tip of IX Corps while other American units hurried south, the 2nd Division was in danger of being cut off by the Chinese and destroyed. On 29 November,

IX Corps HQ finally gave Keiser permission to break out. His with-drawal route would be the road to Sunchon, which wound between arid slopes as it climbed towards a narrow 400-metre pass walled by steep 50-metre embankments.

Keiser knew there were Chinese behind him, but not where or how many. American tanks patrolling the road had been fired at that day but there were no reports of roadblocks. After learning that a relief column of Turks had been ambushed on its way north, Keiser decided that the Sunchon Road was too dangerous, but his request to use an alternative route fell on deaf ears. Instead, staff at IX Corps HQ reassured him that the Middlesex battalion was fighting its way north and would link up with him a couple of kilo-metres down the road.

Around midday on 29 November, the Middlesex battalion reached its destination and seized the foothills around 1000 metres short of the high ground guarding the pass. Straightaway it came under mortar attack by the Chinese in the hills. In the absence of tank and artillery support, the battalion's efforts to drive the enemy off the heights failed. In the words of the brigade diary, 'the CO decided that the task was too much and called it off'. Aware that the Chinese were attempting to get around behind them, the Middlesex battalion withdrew, leaving the road under enemy control.

By the night of 29 November, as many as six Chinese divisions were converging on the 2nd Division. Two of Keiser's three regi-ments were no longer capable of fighting effectively. Retreat was the only option if the 2nd Division was to avoid being surrounded.

General Keiser's orders were to head south on the Sunchon road, regardless of the presence of Chinese troops. But there was another route out of Kunu-ri: west to Anju, on a road largely constructed by US Army engineers as a fallback in case all other escape routes were blocked. With the condition of the Sunchon road unclear, but almost certainly hazardous, the road to Anju seemed a safer bet.

The commander of I Corps, Major General Frank Milburn, called Keiser sometime during the night of 29 November and was told that Chinese mortars were hitting 2nd Division headquarters. Milburn and Keiser were friends. Milburn's advice was to 'come on out my way', meaning the road to Anju. But without approval from IX Corps headquarters, Keiser could not move.

While headquarters prevaricated, the 2nd Infantry Division's last chance to save itself ebbed away. The Sunchon Road, already bristling with Chinese soldiers, was now choked with burnt-out vehicles left behind by the Turks.

In the early hours of 30 November, Keiser again asked for permission to withdraw west, although neither he nor anyone at Corps HQ knew whether the road was open. Again permission was denied. Corps had sent an aircraft over the Sunchon road and was now satisfied that the Chinese were not there in sufficient strength to stop Keiser's troops from breaking through. Thus the fateful decision was made to order the 2nd Infantry Division into the jaws of a Chinese ambush.

At around 10.30 a.m. on 30 November, the Middlesex battalion, dug in just south of the pass with orders to keep the road open to the rear and provide whatever support it could to the retreating 2nd Division, observed signs of a battle in progress. Soon afterwards, five American tanks rumbled into view, followed by several jeeps. Dead and wounded infantrymen were hanging out of the trucks, evidence of a bloodbath taking place behind them.

The cause soon became apparent. Rather than sweeping along both ridges to clear the enemy off the high ground, the 2nd Division was moving in convoy along the road. As they entered the pass, the Americans became sitting ducks for the disciplined Chinese troops waiting for them with mortars and machine guns.

The road was soon jammed with twisted and burning vehicles. Survivors leaping from disabled tanks and trucks were shot down as they tried to run the gauntlet. Bullets fired at the ridges by

UN aircraft ricocheted off the rocky embankments and burning napalm spilt onto the road, while vehicles still capable of moving ran over the bodies of dead and wounded men as their drivers attempted to smash their way through.

Command and discipline broke down as officers and men stumbled blindly through the wreckage. General Keiser's own jeep was stopped in the pass, and his bodyguard killed, but Keiser made it out, only to be relieved of his command four days later. In his book *Scorched Earth, Black Snow*, Andrew Salmon quoted the words of Major John Willoughby, who witnessed the carnage from a distance as a company commander in the Middlesex battalion:

> A long stream of survivors now started to reach us from below the pass, first in twos and threes, then a steady stream, many wounded, utterly forsaken and in tears . . . solitary refugees hoping for sanctuary . . . many were wounded and dragging themselves along, but never did I see a comrade helping another . . . I don't believe this was lack of humanity, but total bewilderment.

The 'bewilderment' of the Americans who survived the massacre is confirmed by the entry for 30 November in the 27th Brigade's war diary:

> Almost all vestige of control and leadership of the men who came through appeared to have been lost. Despite being told by an officer . . . that they were now in friendly hands, in some cases men in vehicles continued to shoot at random and were responsible for causing casualties amongst our own troops.

By around 4 p.m. the pass had fallen quiet; no more men were coming out, although it turned out to be a pause between sections of the convoy. But PRC units were coming down off the hills and probing for gaps in the Middlesex battalion's defensive perimeter. A Chinese attack on its tactical headquarters was driven off with rifles and bayonets. Given orders to disengage, the battalion pulled out, its trucks packed with American wounded.

One unit managed to escape the carnage on the Sunchon road. The US 23rd Regimental Combat Team had been left behind as a rearguard to protect the retreat from the Chinese forces bearing down on Kunu-ri. Cut off from Division HQ, Colonel Paul Freeman relied on artillery spotter planes for information on what was happening on the road south. Their reports convinced him that it would be suicide to follow the rest of the division down the Sunchon road.

With Keiser unreachable and the Chinese preparing to attack as soon as darkness fell, headquarters gave Freeman permission to follow his own judgement about how to save his regiment. He decided to head west, along the road to Anju. Before breaking out, he pointed the regiment's eighteen howitzers at the Chinese and ordered his artillerymen to fire off every shell they had. The devastating barrage stopped the Chinese in their tracks and bought enough time for the 23rd RCT to get away. The road to Anju turned out to be open, with hardly an enemy soldier in sight.

Meanwhile, the Eighth Army staggered south in what would turn into the longest retreat in US military history. The Turkish Brigade commander, enraged by the inept American leadership that had cost so many Turkish lives, was heard telling 27th Brigade HQ that he would never again fight under US command.

Keith Lewtas saw with his own eyes the anger and disillusionment of ordinary Turkish soldiers caught up in the Eighth Army's humiliating retreat:

One [Turkish] officer, who spoke a little English, halted our three-tonner, pointed his sub-machine gun in the face of our driver whilst his men scrambled over the tail-board and challenged us with their weapons.

'Why is everybody going this way?' he demanded. 'The enemy are that way.' We heard later that the officer and his men were the shocked remnants of a force which earlier in the day had almost been cut to ribbons.

'I don't know,' replied the tired driver.

'You will turn around and take my men to fight the enemy,' the Turkish officer ordered.

'I am going this way because I am ordered to. Now, if you want a ride, get in, but if you don't, don't just hold us up,' the driver replied.

As panicked American units swarmed south—sometimes under the flimsy pretext of having 'sighted' enemy troops nearby—3RAR was sent to secure a newly constructed bridge over the Taedong River. Its orders were to hold the bridge until it had been crossed by retreating US forces. Apart from a brief skirmish and some random mortar and artillery fire after dark, the Australians were left alone, although the sound of Chinese bugles during the night left no doubt that the enemy knew they were there.

Sergeant Fred Rennie recalled being dug in on a hill overlooking the river when US Air Force Boston bombers flew over:

> They circled over us, and they came down . . . Harry Gleeson was running across the flat for something and this Boston aimed at him and . . . let go of napalm. The napalm wandered all over the sky, but Harry managed to get into a hole and the napalm, luckily, was a dud.

In the end the retreating Americans, spooked by the Chinese presence, chose a different route.

After the diggers withdrew, the bridge was demolished—a probably needless act of destruction, as Captain Ben O'Dowd observed, since the Taedong was already freezing over and it would soon be possible to drive even heavy trucks across the ice. O'Dowd was not the only one left wondering why the Chinese, who must have realised what the diggers were up to, allowed them to pull out without firing a shot.

The next day, Coad was given orders to move the brigade nearly 150 kilometres south to Hayu-ri, via Pyongyang. Due to the traffic clogging the roads, the journey took more than twelve hours, partly due to the Americans' habit of blocking the road behind them with semi-trailers to facilitate their own retreat. Australian morale was 'pretty low', Len Opie recalled. 'We were alright because we hadn't really got into a fight. Every fight we got into we won but we weren't very happy because we were freezing cold.'

Raymon Wilson recalled the diggers finding their long retreat 'very traumatic'. They caught a ride on any transport they could find. Wilson himself spent the whole time on the seat of a 155-millimetre artillery piece towed by a truck crawling south at just a few kilometres an hour through icy winds and snow. By the end of the journey he was frozen stiff and had to be lifted off the gun seat.

It was a 'most miserable and cruel trip due to the intense cold', the war diary reported, 'and will most likely be recalled as the battalion's bleakest day in Korea'.

According to Mossman's official history, the 2nd Infantry Division suffered around 4500 casualties—nearly a third of its authorised strength—between 25 November and 1 December, and lost scores of artillery pieces, hundreds of trucks and trailers, and virtually all of its engineer equipment. So traumatised were the survivors of the Sunchon road massacre that the 2nd Division had to be taken out of the line and was not committed again until February 1951.

16

LAUNDRYMEN

MacArthur's 'entirely new war' was spinning out of control, or at least out of American control. 'We can't defeat the Chinese in Korea; they can put in more than we can,' Secretary of State Acheson told a crisis meeting of the National Security Council on 28 November. What was imperative now, Acheson told the president and his advisers, was to 'find a line that we can hold, and hold it . . . We should know what line MacArthur thinks he can hold . . . We should not say that we must push forward. We should hold the line and turn it over to the ROK as soon as we can.'*

The consensus in Washington was that the Chinese had been pushed into the war by Stalin, but that this could not be said publicly for fear of upsetting America's allies. The crucial thing now was to avoid being drawn into a general war with the PRC. 'To do so would be to fall into a carefully laid Russian trap,' Secretary of Defense General George Marshall warned the meeting. 'We should

---

* Comments made at the White House meeting of the National Security Council on 28 November 1950 were recorded in a top-secret 'memorandum of conversation' by the US ambassador at large, Philip Jessup.

use all available political, economic and psychological action to limit the war ... We should not go into Chinese Communist territory and we should not use Chinese Nationalist forces. To do either of these things would increase the danger of war with the Chinese.'

As the National Security Council met in Washington, the second pincer in MacArthur's 'home by Christmas' offensive, General Almond's X Corps, was facing annihilation in the north-east. Late on 27 November, two days after the Chinese launched their assault against the Eighth Army, twelve divisions of the elite Chinese 9th Army Group attacked UN troops on both sides of the frozen Chosin Reservoir, effectively splicing the 1st Marine Division, on the reservoir's western edge, from the army's 31st Regimental Combat Team, on the east.

Almond's plan, hatched by MacArthur in Tokyo and described by Almond's own chief of staff as 'insane', was for the marines to drive west, cutting Chinese supply routes and encircling any Chinese units in the area, before linking up with the Eighth Army on the Yalu River. Instead, it was the UN forces that were cut off and cornered.

Between 27 November and 13 December, as many as 120,000 Chinese soldiers attempted to close the trap on Almond's force of around 30,000 American and ROK troops. Like MacArthur and his intelligence chief, Willoughby, Almond convinced himself that the enemy force consisted of nothing but small groups fleeing north after the Battle of Unsan. 'We're still attacking and we're going all the way to the Yalu,' he reportedly told one of his battalion commanders. 'Don't let a bunch of goddamn Chinese laundrymen stop you!'

The brutal weather was some of the harshest of the war, causing thousands of inadequately clothed Chinese soldiers to succumb to frostbite. The road south, often a single gravel track with steep slopes and vertiginous drops, was virtually impassable in places due to blown bridges. Only the effectiveness of UN air support, together with supply drops from US Air Force planes based in Japan, enabled X Corps to hold on and eventually break out, although at the cost of a thousand soldiers killed and total battle and non-battle casualties of nearly 18,000. According to Appleman, the 1st Marine Division alone suffered more than 7000 non-battle casualties, mostly frost-bite. Total Chinese casualties were closer to 50,000.

The marines, at least, remained a cohesive unit, fighting their way back to the east-coast port of Hamhung with the bulk of their transport and heavy equipment intact, and with their dead in tow. Senior officers were confident of being able to hold the perimeter around the port through the winter, enabling the UN army to retain a stronghold in North Korean territory, but Almond's orders were to evacuate the whole of X Corps to Pusan.

As well as putting an end to MacArthur's ill-conceived offensive, the catastrophic defeats suffered by X Corps and the Eighth Army convinced Washington that the war could no longer be won. MacArthur's military judgement was compromised and his position as supreme commander fatally undermined. His promise to get the troops home by Christmas was, in General Marshall's words, 'an embarrassment which we must get around in some manner'. For the time being, however, President Truman had no choice but to leave MacArthur in charge.

The burning question in the minds of the Joint Chiefs of Staff in the days following the Chinese strike was this: how far south would the UN forces have to retreat?

General MacArthur did not visit Korea until 11 December. His cables to Washington veered from the apocalyptic to the delusional. With no substantial American reinforcements available, he asked on 29 November for permission to use Chinese Nationalist troops—a move that would not only have horrified Commonwealth allies, including Australia, and left America isolated at the United Nations, but also risked extending the war to Formosa (now Taiwan).

He flirted publicly with the idea of dropping atomic bombs on North Korea and even on China.*

On 30 November, with Almond's troops facing destruction in the frozen hills above the Chosin Reservoir, MacArthur chose to focus instead on the 'threat' X Corps posed to the supply lines of enemy forces menacing the right flank of the Eighth Army. Rejecting the possibility of Almond's dangerously spread-out forces becoming isolated and trapped, MacArthur assured the joint chiefs that while Almond's forces 'seem to be well extended, the actual conditions of terrain make it extremely difficult for an enemy to take any material advantage thereof'.** Lieutenant General Matthew Ridgway would later say that when messages like that arrived at the Pentagon, 'it was as if the madness were in the room'. Meanwhile, preparations were made for the possible evacuation of UN forces from the peninsula.

On the same day, 30 November, Dean Rusk fronted a delegation from Commonwealth countries and others contributing to the UN forces in Korea. Australia's ambassador in Washington, Norman Makin, said he was 'puzzled' by the disparity between

---

*   On 30 November, President Truman told reporters that there had 'always been active consideration' of the use of the atomic bomb, while adding that it was a 'terrible weapon' that should not be used on 'innocent men, women and children'. The British, wrongly taking this to mean that MacArthur would make the decision on whether or not to use atomic weapons, were aghast, others perhaps less so. Walking to the elevator after a meeting with Dean Rusk, the Belgian ambassador, Baron Silvercruys, reportedly 'stated that if we were to use the atomic bomb, he could not see any particular value to using it against Chinese cities. Why not go a little further and destroy the Soviet facilities for manufacturing atom bombs which, according to the Ambassador, were not located at too great an air distance from the scene of our present operations.'

** Delusion also reigned on the west of the peninsula. Salmon quoted an Eighth Army communiqué from 29 November: 'The assault launched by Eighth Army five days ago probably saved our army from a trap which might well have destroyed them. Had we waited passively in place . . . from beyond the Yalu, [the enemy] would have undoubtedly brought the 200,000 troops known to be assembled there . . . The timing of our attack was indeed most fortunate.'

MacArthur's comments at the start of the offensive indicating the war was nearly over and the discovery of 'large Chinese forces' in North Korea. According to a memorandum of conversation, Makin 'wondered what had happened to the UN intelligence'. The Dutch minister plenipotentiary, Jacobus de Beus, also 'wondered why the surprise', given that a report had been received 'several weeks ago' from Beijing indicating that there were 'about 160,000 Chinese Red soldiers in Korea ready to go'.

Admitting that the intelligence was 'of course' faulty, Rusk could only reply that the report from Beijing was one of 'hundreds, each one different', and that it was impossible to tell in advance which one was right. 'There were so many reports,' Rusk explained, that one of them 'was bound to be right'.

The joint chiefs urged MacArthur to unite his forces, combining X Corps with the Eighth Army to prevent large enemy forces from 'passing between or outflanking them'. They suggested falling back to a line across the narrow waist of Korea. MacArthur refused, citing the 'numerical weakness' of his forces and the logistical problems caused by the mountains that ran down the spine of the peninsula.

The joint chiefs' suggestion had, in any case, been overtaken by events. Walker was now convinced that he could not hold a line near Pyongyang and that his army would be forced all the way back to Seoul. 'This small command . . . under present conditions is facing the entire Chinese nation in an undeclared war,' MacArthur cabled the joint chiefs on 3 December, 'and unless some positive and immediate action is taken, hope for success cannot be justified and steady attrition leading to final destruction can reasonably be contemplated.'

Given the adverse terrain and weather conditions, Ridgway wondered whether X Corps was capable of withdrawing at all. He was not confident that either X Corps or the Eighth Army could outrun the Chinese and reach Seoul, and instead suggested occupying a series of beachheads that could be held 'until a decision is made on the question of evacuation'.

How to respond to the Chinese onslaught had long ceased to be a purely military decision. American prestige was at stake, not just in the Far East but in the whole world. If American soldiers were to be evacuated, what would become of the ROK troops? Would they be left to the mercy of the North Koreans? Or would they too be evacuated to Japan?

If evacuation became necessary, it was far from certain that the Americans would even be able to take their equipment. Admiral Sherman, probably the most hawkish of the joint chiefs, told Acheson that the navy could evacuate 60,000 troops minus their equipment in one day but that it would take six days to evacuate a single American division with all its equipment. Asked whether the equipment was 'vital', General Omar Bradley replied that it could not be considered 'vital' but conceded that the army had 'nothing else'.*

While Truman and the joint chiefs talked, the Eighth Army continued its humiliating retreat, leaving wounded as well as dead soldiers behind in its desperation to outrun an enemy that, by now, had largely given up the chase. The ability of the Chinese to maintain their troops fell sharply the further south they advanced. Exhausted frontline units lost contact not only with the retreating UN forces but with their own command. Poor radio communications and a lack of motorised transport, which together made

---

* With MacArthur refusing to impose censorship, American war correspondents were free to broadcast details about American troop strength and troop movements. After the war, Chinese officials admitted to having obtained valuable information from Western press and radio. Monitoring agency wire services enabled them to have advance warning of the Inchon landings and deployment of new F-86 Sabre jet fighters to counter their Russian MIGs. Worried about the consequences of UN evacuation plans being leaked to the enemy, Acheson reminded the joint chiefs that during the American Civil War General Sherman used to tell the correspondents all his plans 'and then lock them up in jail'.

it impossible to coordinate large-scale attacks, cost the Chinese their chance to destroy Walker's broken army. The same was true on the east coast, where primitive communications, inadequate clothing and limited firepower all hampered the ability of Chinese commanders to exploit their superior troop numbers.

In ten days the Eighth Army retreated nearly 200 kilometres. Staff at the 27th Brigade were appalled by the chaotic nature of the retreat and by the abandonment and destruction of valuable military equipment. They suspected that some enemy sightings were being fabricated in order to justify the exodus. In the words of the war diary, 'It is the opinion that certain units are giving false infor-mation in order to extract from commands and staffs permission or even orders for premature and quite unjustifiable withdrawals. It was just this type of excitable dishonesty which caused some unnec-essary and expensive withdrawals in France in 1940.'

Ben O'Dowd's A Company was sent to the aid of an American column that had been ambushed by guerrillas. By the time the diggers arrived to clear the high ground overlooking the road, the guerillas had fled, and so had the Americans. 'A Company's efforts were not unrewarded,' the battalion diary recorded. 'The Americans had abandoned some vehicles and winter clothing.'*

News that Pyongyang was to be evacuated and that the Eighth Army was to withdraw all the way to Seoul was met with incre-dulity, officers and men both 'amaz[ed]', as the diary put it, 'that so much ground was to be given up without a fight and at a time when there was no contact with the enemy'.

---

*   It was not only the diggers who were able to keep warm at American expense. Li Xiu, a regimental propaganda officer with the Chinese 27th Corps, told Max Hastings that without weapons, clothing and supplies captured from the Americans, the communists would have struggled to sustain their advance beyond the end of 1950. American sleeping bags and overcoats were especially prized in an army that suffered twice as many casualties from the cold as it did from combat.

The British, too, were dismayed. General Sir Robert Mansergh bemoaned the Americans' 'lack of determination and their inability . . . to stand and fight'. Brigadier Coad reported to his superiors that American soldiers '[do] not like being attacked, especially at night, and with exceptions will not stand and fight'. The attitude of British soldiers to the American infantry, Coad wrote, was 'largely one of contempt'.

Nobody in Washington now believed that it was possible to achieve a unified, democratic Korea. Nor, it seemed, was there any prospect of China, given its stunning success on the battlefield, agreeing to a peace proposal based on a return to the pre-war status quo, with a two-state Korea divided at the 38th parallel. For the same reason, it now appeared unlikely that China would agree to a ceasefire, except on terms that the Truman administration would find impossible to accept.*

On 8 December, General Collins, chief of staff of the army, returned from a five-day trip to Korea, during which he visited both the western and eastern fronts. Collins' conversations with Walker and Almond convinced him that the UN army could, after all, hold on. The Eighth Army, he declared at a White House meeting between President Truman and Britain's Prime Minister Clement Attlee, was 'not in danger'. The situation in the east was more precarious, with bad weather preventing the air force from supporting the marines in their perilous retreat from the Chosin plateau, but provided the weather improved, Collins believed they had a 'good chance' of getting back. Overall, he concluded that the UN army was 'not in a critical condition' and that a bridgehead at Pusan could be held 'indefinitely'. Collins' upbeat assessment delivered a timely boost to morale and, according to the minutes of

---

* As well as insisting on the removal of all US and UN troops from Korea, China demanded the withdrawal of US forces from Taiwan, the admission of the PRC at the United Nations and the simultaneous dismissal of Taiwan's representative.

the meeting, prompted President Truman to remark that he 'did not think we were going to be kicked out of Korea'.*

Encouraged by Collins' battlefield report and not wanting to negotiate from a position of weakness, Truman resisted pressure from the British and others for a ceasefire. At the same time, he could not let the United States, which claimed to have gone to war to repel North Korean aggression, be seen by the rest of the world as standing in the way of peace. Gambling on the Chinese rejecting a UN demand for an immediate ceasefire, Washington supported the resolution and was duly rewarded when it was spurned by Beijing. Further attempts by a specially convened UN committee to bring China to the negotiating table proved futile.

There was a reason why China's leaders had no interest in negotiating for peace in the final weeks of 1950: they now believed they could win the war.

---

* Attlee was less optimistic. According to the minutes, his guarded response to Truman's comment was that 'we must take a stand and see what happens'.

17

CHAOS AND CONFUSION

On 6 December 3RAR, now under the command of the US 1st Cavalry Division, retreated another 30 kilometres. Two days later the battalion fell back a further 30 kilometres. The central part of Korea, both north and south of the 38th parallel, had never been properly cleared of enemy fighters and 3RAR received a flurry of reports—not all reliable—about communist guerrilla activity in the area. The guerrillas' intention appeared to be to cut the Eighth Army's line of communications, raid smaller units and generally cause trouble in the rear areas. There was no sign of the Chinese divisions, who were believed to be at the limit of their supply lines and attempting to regroup north and north-east of Pyongyang.

After yet another retreat—this time in American trucks to Uijongbu, twenty kilometres north of Seoul—the battalion had withdrawn a total of 400 kilometres in a fortnight. The UN army had given up virtually all the ground it had taken in North Korea and was preparing to defend a new line along the 38th parallel. The brigade diary reported no contact with Chinese forces along the whole length of the front, the only actions being against guerrilla groups operating north of the parallel.

Since arriving in Korea, 3RAR had never spent more than three nights in one place, but the Australians now enjoyed three relatively untroubled weeks at Uijongbu, although always on half an hour's notice to move. The Chinese were coming, they knew that, but for the time being all they had to worry about were North Korean guerrillas who emerged at night to raid villages and police posts and hid by day in the snow-covered hills.

Jack Gallaway remembered those three weeks as a happy time. Each digger received a Christmas parcel from the Returned and Services League containing a bottle of Foster's beer, while a lucky few got five days' R&R leave in Tokyo. Officers in the rifle companies were entitled to spirits but Ben O'Dowd recalled buying up all A Company's allocation and storing it in his trailer until he judged the operational conditions to be safe.

Like nearly every other Australian soldier at Uijongbu, Stan Connelly was part of a poker school, playing for BAFs, the British Armed Forces currency issued to diggers in the Japanese occupation force. Connelly ended up winning the equivalent of around £500—'a fortune in those days but . . . there was nothing that you could do with it'.

Uijongbu was colder than any place they had been. Deep patrolling, sometimes in trucks to a radius of more than 30 kilometres, was 'most unpleasant', the battalion diary noted, due to the freezing winds. Men on watch duty at night froze almost rigid in their foxholes and had to be hoisted out and revived by their mates.

Routine Order No. 4 was a warning to any digger tempted to use the local rotgut to fend off the cold: 'One case of moderately severe visual disturbance has occurred as a result of drinking a local spirituous liquor. All personnel are warned that blindness, insanity, muscular paralysis and other disorders may result from this practice and that the severity therof need bear no relation to the quantity consumed.'

At a village near Uijongbu, Private Joe Vezgoff and his mates pulled down a two-storey timber schoolhouse, carrying off the walls and everything inside, including blackboards and chairs, to burn for warmth. Vezgoff often wondered what the villagers felt when they found their school demolished, but without fuel for their fires he believed the diggers 'wouldn't have survived' the winter.

On 13 December B Company lost one man killed and another wounded after running into enemy soldiers on the peak of a 1000-metre mountain that commanded the approaches to Seoul.

Heavy snow made movement difficult and patrols sent out to investigate reports of guerrilla activity often found themselves chasing shadows. Some patrols went out solely for the purpose of contacting other friendly units in the brigade's designated area and finding out what they were up to. With large numbers of retreating ROK troops arriving in the area, Brigadier Coad became worried about the risk of an accidental firefight breaking out with friendly units. At the village of Sopa, diggers from B Company, supported by a mortar platoon, were met by civilian police, ROK soldiers and patrols from the US 5th Regimental Combat Team and the 1st Cavalry. Another patrol narrowly missed being hit by artillery from the 1st Cavalry, while another, sent to investigate reports ('by an officer') of '75–100 enemy ... changing from civilian clothes into uniform', arrived to find counterintelligence officers searching refugees.

'[I]t is hard for troops to understand why they are sent long distances under unpleasant weather conditions to patrol areas already patrolled by various other friendly formations,' Coad protested to the commander of IX Corps, 'and ... extremely hard to avoid the resultant drop in interest in tasks given—and even in morale.'

To avert potentially fatal mishaps, Coad decided in future to send out contact patrols only, warning them in advance about the probability of running into ROK troops. He put a stop to fighting patrols until he could be guaranteed that they would be able to engage any forces they encountered without fear of their being friendly troops, without risk of running into friendly training fire and without feeling that the area was already being patrolled by others.

The presence of ROK troops in the brigade's area posed a threat to Korean civilians employed by the diggers as porters and kitchen hands. These civilians were happy to work in return for regular meals and protection from the ROK army recruitment squads, which went from village to village rounding up males aged between fifteen and 60. The fittest men were sent to fight while the rest were assigned to labour units. When word got out that A Company's cooks had two Koreans working for them, a party of ROK soldiers arrived to drag them off. 'Our gallant cooks, each ramming a round into the breach of his rifle, confronted them,' O'Dowd recalled. 'They declared that the lads were executing their war service as part of the Australian Army and that there would be blood on the ground if any attempt were made to remove them.' On this occasion the ROK soldiers backed off.

With reports coming in of Chinese troops moving down to the 38th parallel, tentative plans were made to evacuate Seoul and retreat to a new line behind the Han River, which ran through the capital. As usual, the 27th Brigade would act as rearguard for the withdrawal of US and ROK units. The Commonwealth troops were to dig in north of the river, while IX Corps crossed via a floating bridge, footbridges and amphibious vehicles. When the last American soldier had crossed the river, the 27th Brigade would then follow with all its vehicles. If the Chinese could be held back long enough, engineers would dismantle and salvage the floating bridge; if not, Coad had orders to blow it up.

Four days before Christmas, the Chinese attacked north-east of Seoul, forcing an ROK regiment to withdraw nearly ten kilometres before the South Koreans recovered some ground in a counterattack. They attacked again the following day, with similar results. The signs of a looming enemy offensive were becoming harder to ignore, but the diggers, long accustomed to being on a half-hour's notice to move, were in no mood to let the Chinese Army disturb their festivities. According to Sergeant Jack Gallaway, their main concern was how to store their Christmas beer without it freezing in the bottle.

During the next 48 hours there were clashes with Chinese troops right across the front line. Intelligence reports indicated that the Chinese were taking over from the North Koreans in the west and central sectors of Korea and that North Korean units were moving into the eastern sector. But when the big attack finally came, the commander who had presided over the US Army's longest-ever retreat was not alive to see it.

On 23 December 1950 the South Korean leader, Syngman Rhee, was due to present the 27th Brigade with a Presidential Unit Citation for its performance during the advance into North Korea. The Eighth Army commander, General Walker, was on his way to the ceremony when his jeep was flipped by an ROK army truck that swung across its path. The driver and two other passengers survived but Walker was killed.

Walker's death overshadowed the 27th Brigade's Christmas cele-brations, which nevertheless went ahead, with officers and sergeants honouring army tradition by serving Christmas turkey and plum pudding to the men. The diggers received gift parcels from the Rose Bay sub-branch of the RSL and the Queensland Patriotic Fund. All Joe Vezgoff remembered about that Christmas in Uijongbu was that his beer froze.

On Boxing Day, 56-year-old Lieutenant General Matthew Ridgway took over as Eighth Army commander. Ridgway was profoundly shocked by the poor morale of American troops, writing later that 'our forces were simply not mentally and spiritually ready for the sort of action I had been planning'.

In his analysis of the Eighth Army's performance, Ridgway identified errors that had long been apparent to British and Australian commanders, chief among them the reluctance of American forces to leave the roads and their failure to take and hold the high ground. Both had been critical factors in the massacre at Kunu-ri.

Well aware that he would never be able to match the Chinese in manpower, Ridgway was determined to maximise America's superiority in heavy weapons. He ordered in more artillery battalions equipped with long-range guns and reorganised the command structure to sideline commanders he considered insufficiently aggressive. (Almond would hold on to X Corps but would not continue as MacArthur's chief of staff.) From now on, success would be measured in casualties, not territory: Ridgway's aim was to inflict losses that not even the Chinese could bear.

Ridgway knew that the forces under his command were not strong enough to destroy the Chinese and North Korean armies in the field. What he could do was launch a series of limited offensive operations capable of inflicting casualties on the communists that far outweighed his own, pausing when it suited him to allow the Chinese to exhaust themselves attacking strongly held UN defensive positions. Taking and holding high ground might be advantageous but by itself it would not decide the outcome of the war. The success of Ridgway's strategy depended, in Robert O'Neill's words, on 'convincing his subordinate commanders to be very economical in spending the lives of their own men while causing the maximum casualties to their enemies'.

Under Ridgway, there would be no more discussion of evacuating the Korean Peninsula. If enemy pressure proved too great, he told Brigadier Coad and other senior officers on 28 December, then he was prepared to withdraw to a new defensive line further south, but the new line would be 'held against all comers'.

Ridgway had arrived in Korea with high hopes of being able to launch a rapid counterattack, but events on the battlefield soon disabused him. On the night of 31 December the Chinese launched a major attack against the ROK 1st Division and 6th Division. According to 3RAR's war diary, the 1st Division 'disintegrated'. The diggers emerged from their New Year's Eve celebrations to see South Korean soldiers, in Jack Gallaway's words, 'moving at a solid jog trot towards the south, unencumbered by weapons or equipment and glancing fearfully over their shoulders as they ran'.

With the right flank of I Corps and the left flank of IX Corps wide open, the 27th Brigade was sent north with instructions to hold open the road for the US 24th Division and the ROK 6th Division to withdraw through Uijongbu. 3RAR was ordered to the village of Tokchong, ten kilometres north of Uijongbu, to block the main road south to Seoul.

Assisted by two Pershing tanks, a section of American mortars and air strikes by Mustang fighters, the Australians were able to fight off outflanking movements by Chinese forces converging from the north-west and north-east, before driving off a Chinese force that had attempted to block the road further south. Meanwhile, orders came through from IX Corps HQ that a general retreat was underway. With the withdrawal route now reopened, the battalion moved on roads teeming with refugees and fleeing ROK soldiers to establish a new rearguard for the brigade's withdrawal the following night to Seoul. The cost to 3RAR was four men wounded.

By dawn on 2 December the diggers were gathered in the grounds of a former agricultural college in north-east Seoul. It was another galling experience for the battalion and for the brigade as a whole, which had yet to be defeated in battle or forced to relinquish a significant position but was swept up again in a general retreat that cost it every metre of ground it had fought for. 'The spectacle of troops in retreat and of refugees in flight . . . [was] both disheartening and pitiful,' the brigade diary reported.

The stage was now set for the long-planned withdrawal of the Eighth Army across the Han River, with the 27th Brigade covering the bridgehead. Chinese attacks along the 24th Division front on the night of 2–3 January dislodged units of the US 19th Regimental Combat Team. By morning, according to the brigade diary, the situation was 'not very clear'. With the 24th Division having lost contact with the Chinese, 3RAR was instructed to send out a strong fighting patrol, supported by twenty Patton tanks, with orders to move up the main road and engage any enemy force it encountered. To Ben O'Dowd, who would be leading the mission, it sounded like a 'very messy' operation:

> If the enemy fired on us while we were approaching their defences, well and good; we could about turn and make for home, having achieved our aim. If, however, the Chinese let us get among them or, worse, through them before declaring their presence, the Diggers would be shot up from both sides. If this happened, we were supposed to dismount and engage the enemy while the tanks turned round, then remount and go for home . . . no account was taken of the fact that we might have to recover casualties and load them onto tanks under fire.

The time set for A Company to move off was 10 a.m. but almost immediately the mission ran into problems. O'Dowd, in the command tank, found that he was unable to communicate by radio with his platoon commanders. The only solution was for officers and men to cling to the sides of tanks as they trundled up the Uijongbu road.

At the 24th Division forward defences, O'Dowd stopped to gather the latest information. He found the situation even more 'confused' than he had been led to believe. Chinese troops were reported to have got behind the 21st Regimental Combat Team, making the operation even more hazardous. The diggers had learnt to be sceptical of US patrol reports, which sometimes identified enemy who were not there, but on this occasion they were only too happy for the sightings to be believed. News also came through that US Air Force planes had mistakenly attacked the 21st Regimental Combat Team's forward battalion. There were no complaints in A Company when the mission was aborted.

With the Chinese threatening to break through, Ridgway scrapped plans for a line along the Han River and decided to pull back to a new defensive line south of Seoul. Again, the 27th Brigade would form the rearguard, with orders to hold the Seoul–Uijongbu road while the 19th and 21st Regimental Combat Teams withdrew through their positions.

As usual, the hurried UN evacuation was marked by chaos and confusion, exacerbated by reports—or rumours—of enemy soldiers attempting to infiltrate UN lines disguised as refugees. The where-abouts and intentions of the main enemy force was unclear, but it appeared that the Chinese were not actively following up the offensive they had begun on New Year's Eve. '[I]t was difficult to know what was going on,' the brigade diary noted. '[T]he only information forthcoming was that we were evacuating.'

It was nearly dark when the Australians reached their blocking position on a snow-covered mountain ridge in the northern suburbs of Seoul. Expecting to be there for no more than a couple of hours, the diggers had brought only their weapons and ammunition. In the event, they were kept waiting all night by the US 1st Cavalry Division, which never arrived, withdrawing instead via a bridge across the Han River several kilometres to the east.

Chinese troops sent to probe the battalion's positions were driven off with the help of tank and mortar platoons, and by 6 a.m. on 4 January everything was quiet. Two hours later the battalion crossed the railway bridge over the Han, waved off by army engineers preparing demolition charges. The last brigade vehicle, belonging to the Argylls, was across by 10 a.m. With that, the Eighth Army

abandoned Seoul.* Blowing up the bridge seemed unlikely to stop
the Chinese, Jack Gallaway thought, since the river was frozen solid
'and looked as if it would carry a Centurion tank'.

The retreat to Yoda-ri, more than 150 kilometres away, was excru-
ciatingly slow along icy roads crowded with refugees. Drivers found
it hard to stay awake and six diggers were injured when their truck
slid down an embankment. It was ten at night when the battalion
reached Yoda-ri, only to have to double back 30 kilometres to a new
defensive line, codenamed Line D. This was intended as an intermediate position before a final fallback to a more robust Line E,
100 kilometres further south (and within range of the evacuation
port of Pusan), but the decision by the Chinese not to press home
their advance convinced Ridgway that Line D could be held.

With any further move on hold, the diggers got down to the
business of patrolling in weather that was worsening by the day.
Heavy snow fell on the night of 9–10 January; by morning it
was up to 45 centimetres deep. That morning, A Company and
C Company patrolled to a depth of 6000 metres but found no trace
of the Chinese divisions that had kicked the UN army out of Seoul.

The combination of harsh weather and the relentless retreat was
affecting the diggers' health and threatening their morale. Captain
Don Beard, who had accepted a demotion from the rank of major
to take on the job of regimental medical officer, soon had his hands
full dealing with cases of frostbite. Tender, swollen and trench feet
required the evacuation of as many as a dozen diggers a day to
hospital in Japan. Many returned from patrols suffering from acute

_____

* In the early part of the war, the Americans usually blew up bridges after retreating over them. Len Opie recalled seeing 'hundreds of people' watching as a young
Korean boy walked across a bridge 'and we kept our fingers crossed because we
knew it was going [to explode] at a certain time. And he just got over it and the
bridge went up and they raced down and rescued him.' As the front line became
more fluid, the Americans were more likely to leave bridges intact so that they
could be reused when lost ground was retaken.

snow glare, although this could be alleviated by rubbing charcoal beneath the eyes.

Demoralisation was harder to deal with. The entry for 6 January in the brigade war diary warned of a 'general disinterestedness in the war . . . beginning to creep in'.

> It was unfortunate but true that Officers were talking seriously and openly about the superiority of the Chinese troops over those of the Allies and of the possibility of a general evacuation of South Korea . . . members of the Brigade were not guilty of this defeatist attitude although the average soldier was puzzled by the poor military situation and had lost confidence in the steadiness and discipline of some United Nations units.

Neither the Americans nor the ROK troops had done much to inspire faith in their fighting ability. The eagerness of both to 'bug out' rather than hold their ground had made the Chinese appear a more formidable enemy than they were, and dragged the disciplined and well-led 27th Brigade into an unseemly stampede. The arrival of the ROK 6th Division on the brigade's left flank had done little to restore confidence. Understrength and ill-equipped, the South Koreans had been forced by lack of transport to undertake several long marches in the course of the general retreat and were perceived by Brigade HQ as a 'tired division'. A worrying 2000-metre gap existed between the brigade's left and the right of the ROK division; the diggers patrolled this gap day and night to stop the Chinese from infiltrating.

But the Chinese were nowhere to be seen. Despite some 'highly exaggerated and loose reporting' by neighbouring units, the brigade's own patrols reported no contact across the length of its front. The only sightings were by American and South Korean patrols on their flanks. A patrol by the ROK 6th Division reported engaging a company of Chinese troops on 10 January; on the same night, a patrol by the US 5th Regimental Combat Team reported seeing

'200–300' enemy with camels and dogs. The Americans, the war diary noted dryly, were 'preparing to shell this reported enemy circus'.

But if the Chinese cameleers were illusionary, the freezing winter temperatures were achingly real. On 12 January the mercury fell to minus 19 degrees Celsius, and the next day it hit minus 26 degrees—enough to freeze oil, starter motors and even brakes.

With the Australians still finding no sign of the Chinese in front of their own lines, a C Company platoon was sent by truck to the town of Ichon, around 25 kilometres to the north, to follow up reports of enemy soldiers in the area. The patrol failed to lure out any Chinese but came under fire from four Royal Navy aircraft. Fortunately, no diggers were hit.

Two days later an A Company platoon, led by Lieutenant John Church, returned with orders to clear the high ground in the vicinity of Ichon and spend the night there. This time the Chinese did make an appearance. At around 10.30 p.m. a heavy mist lifted to reveal a party of 40 to 50 Chinese troops in dark clothing, moving in single file towards Corporal Jim Everleigh's forward outpost. The diggers waited until several of the Chinese had passed before opening fire, killing twenty enemy soldiers without loss.

Church suspected that the patrol they had ambushed might be part of a larger force and decided to withdraw. As Church's platoon pulled back, the Chinese launched a mortar attack and infantry assault on the position the diggers had just left. A jeep sent back to fetch return transport flipped over on the icy roads and Church's men were obliged to cover most of the distance on foot. By 4.30 a.m. they were safely back with the battalion.

It was now clear that the nearest Chinese units were at Ichon, more than 30 kilometres north of Line D, and that the Eighth Army had continued retreating from an enemy that, in O'Dowd's words, had 'long . . . given up the chase'.

As a result of the action on 16 January, Coad decided that future patrols should be at company strength. These patrols were under strict instructions not to engage with any enemy force they were not able to annihilate.

Over the next few days the diggers took turns with the US 5th Infantry Regiment to carry out overnight patrols to Ichon. On 20 January, A Company was sent out with instructions to confirm reports that an enemy force was occupying high ground about 3000 metres north of the town. Information from local villagers also suggested that the Chinese had laid telephone lines in the area.

Soon after dark, a reconnaissance patrol consisting of Lieutenant Angus McDonald and four ex-commandos set off with orders to search for signs of enemy occupation on the slopes below the company's position, in the adjacent valley and on the hills on the other side. They were to return by first light on 21 January. If the company came under attack while the patrol was out, McDonald was under orders not to come in behind the enemy but to circle around and lead his men back across 30 kilometres of no-man's land to battalion lines.

It was not long before a company-strength group of Chinese was spotted moving south in what O'Dowd guessed was an attempt to get behind his position and set an ambush on A Company's withdrawal route.

At around 1 a.m. the Chinese attacked O'Dowd's forward outpost, killing Lance Corporal John Andrew. Bugles and whistles heralded a second attack, this time against 2 Platoon with mortars and medium machine guns. Recognising this as part of a classic Chinese encircling manoeuvre, O'Dowd ordered the company to withdraw to a village ten kilometres further south, where 3RAR signallers had set up a relay wireless station to improve communications. 'The trap was being set for us that night,' O'Dowd wrote later, 'and it might have worked had we not observed the force going around us, silhouetted against a background of snow. We beat the trap by no more than five minutes.'

No sooner had the company taken up its new position in the village than it came under attack from Chinese machine guns

and mortars. A Company was now in exactly the same predicament it had just escaped from: pinned down by a frontal attack
while enemy troops worked their way around to the rear in order to
ambush the diggers as they returned to the battalion. Once again,
O'Dowd was forced to withdraw – this time to an abandoned
village, from which he was able to contact battalion HQ and call
for transport.

Not everyone made it back to battalion lines: McDonald's reconnaissance patrol had pushed on beyond its original objective and
spent the next few days attempting to circle back to Ichon, often
through waist-deep snowdrifts, only to discover that A Company
had already left. By now McDonald's men were exhausted. After
running into a large Chinese patrol they tried to hide in a village.
Private Tom Hollis described his capture:

> We went in this house and it had two rooms. We got one
> [Korean] . . . but the other bloke got away. Angus [McDonald]
> said, 'Look out the back, Tom, and see if we can get out.'
> I looked out the back and there was . . . a ten foot wall . . .
> So I said, 'Yes, pretty right.' Anyhow, next thing we heard
> this grunting . . . [Corporal Don] Buck was at the front door,
> and he looked out the front door and there was a heap of
> [Chinese] there.

Around 60 Chinese soldiers had set up a machine gun to shoot
anyone coming out of the hut. Realising that they were surrounded,
the diggers put down their weapons and surrendered.

> They took us down to a hut, one by one, and interrogated
> us. Now, I don't know what McDonald, [Private Ted] Light
> and [Corporal Laurie] Buckland said, but when I went down
> there they said . . . because these are high-ranking officers and
> they could speak English . . . 'If you were put back in the

line, what would you do?' I said, 'I'll go back in the line and keep fighting, we came over here to fight you' . . . apparently when Buck went down he said similar words. That's when they segregated us and they took the other three away. They put them into an indoctrination camp somewhere and . . . then they let them go . . . they said Buck and I needed further education.

McDonald, Buckland and Light spent about three weeks in captivity, but the Chinese held on to Hollis and Buck for more than two and a half years, during which time they were regularly subjected to communist indoctrination lectures. Hollis was obdurate to the end, parroting Chinese propaganda only when his captors threatened him with starvation, but he recognised that things would have been much worse if he had been caught by the North Koreans. 'They wanted . . . the Chinese to give us over to them [and] they would have shot us . . . the Chows stuck with us and saved our lives.'

By the end of January, General Ridgway had got the Eighth Army moving north again. Three American divisions, one each from I, IX and X Corps, advanced on 25 January, capturing significant ground. But it was a tentative advance, with a codeword ('RAIN') in place for a hasty retreat to the safety of Line D should the situation 'suddenly deteriorate'. The diggers knew exactly what that would look like.

Depleted by cold-weather casualties, combat losses and R&R trips to Tokyo, the battalion badly needed reinforcements. While morale remained strong, there was concern at Brigade HQ in Japan that the bitter cold and harsh living conditions in Korea were taking their toll. In late January the battalion was told to ship out 60 'jaded and war weary' soldiers for replacement by 'eager' 27th Brigade volunteers. On the last day of the month, 3RAR was put back on two hours' notice to move.

18

MAXIMUM DAMAGE

The momentum of the war was shifting again. The communists had retaken Seoul but in the process they had outrun their own supply lines. A month since MacArthur's assertion that Chinese troops were 'fresh, completely organised . . . and apparently in peak condition for actual operations', General Peng's army was paralysed, short of weapons and equipment and with up to half of frontline soldiers suffering from frostbite.

Despite being under orders from President Truman to exercise 'extreme caution' in his public remarks and to clear any statements with the State or Defense departments, General MacArthur continued to rail against the restrictions imposed on him by the Joint Chiefs of Staff. Spurning their advice to fight on with what he had, he again criticised the failure to make use of the 'great potential' of Chiang Kai-shek's Nationalist army to reinforce UN troops in Korea and attack 'vulnerable areas' of the Chinese mainland. In addition, he proposed blockading the Chinese coast and bombing Chinese munitions factories. Such measures, MacArthur argued, would not only 'release the pressure upon our forces in Korea' but 'severely cripple and largely neutralise China's capability to wage aggressive war', and thus 'save Asia' from being overrun by communists.

The joint chiefs turned down all MacArthur's demands, reiterating the need to inflict 'maximum damage to hostile forces in Korea' without sacrificing the safety of his troops or compromising his 'basic mission' to protect Japan.

MacArthur was predictably enraged, reminding them that his orders had been to fight the 'North Korean invasion army', not the Chinese, and pointing out the 'self-evident fact' that his force was not strong enough to hold a position in Korea and simultaneously protect Japan. 'The troops are tired from a long and difficult campaign [and] embittered by the shameful propaganda which has falsely* condemned their courage and fighting qualities,' he cabled the joint chiefs on 10 January, adding that the soldiers' deteriorating morale posed 'a serious threat to their battle efficiency'. The military position was 'untenable', he declared, but his army could 'hold on for any length of time up to its complete destruction', if that was what Washington desired.

Alarmed by MacArthur's depiction of an exhausted and demoralised army, the joint chiefs decided they needed to see the situation for themselves. General Collins, the army chief of staff, and his air force counterpart, General Vandenberg, left for Tokyo on the evening of 12 January.

In Korea, Collins visited all Corps Headquarters and saw and talked to the commanders of most divisions. To MacArthur's chagrin, he reported the morale of all the UN troops except the South Koreans to be much better than MacArthur had painted it, singling out the 'British and others' (by which he presumably meant the Australians) and the French for special praise. He found even the South Koreans in better shape than he had expected, but

---

*   Had MacArthur forgotten about the big bug-out, not to mention all the smaller bug-outs? The wording of his 10 January cable suggested a commander dangerously detached from the battlefield realities of the war he was fighting.

acknowledged that they were in absolute terror of the Chinese, and were prone to break and run whenever the Chinese attacked.

Overall, Collins concluded that morale among American troops was improving rather than deteriorating, a fact he attributed largely to the confidence and energy of Ridgway's leadership—and, in particular, to the fact that Ridgway, unlike MacArthur, took pains to visit the front in what he euphemistically termed 'difficult times'.

Collins also found the military situation more encouraging than MacArthur's cables had led him to believe. In the west ('the best tank country in Korea', as he described it to Acheson), he considered Ridgway's position 'very strong'. American air superiority in the east meant serious trouble there was unlikely. The Eighth Army's major vulnerability was in the centre. Even so, Ridgway felt, there would be no need to evacuate for at least three months.

Nor did Collins and Vandenberg find any evidence to support MacArthur's demands to take the war across the border. Collins concluded that attacking China would do little to improve the Eighth Army's position, while Vandenberg was content to keep attacking Chinese supply lines inside Korea. As for knocking out hydroelectric plants in the north that were vital to Chinese industry, Vandenberg had flown over one of the dams, describing it as an enormous concrete structure around 60 metres thick at the top and much thicker at the base. The air force had dropped one bomb on the dam to practically no effect. Any operation to destroy the dams, Vandenberg told Acheson, would be 'very difficult'.

Both American generals did their best to crack the mystery of where the Chinese had been hiding since the end of the New Year's offensive. Vandenberg flew over the area north of Wonju, a town in central Korea that had been the scene of heavy fighting in early January, but could see no sign of enemy soldiers. Although it had snowed three days before he made his trip, Vandenberg reported that he had seen no footprints or vehicle tracks—or indeed any trace at all of the Chinese divisions he was convinced were down there.

While Collins and Vandenberg were in Korea, President Truman tried to pep up his cantankerous and dispirited commander with a long telegram explaining his thinking about Korea and about the West's global conflict with communism, reassuring MacArthur that even if it became 'impracticable' for UN forces to stay in Korea, they would be able to fight on from offshore islands. If they were forced to withdraw, it would be made clear to the world that 'that course is forced upon us by military necessity and that we shall not accept the result politically or militarily until the aggression has been rectified'. The presidential telegram finished with the obligatory sop to the great man's ego. 'The entire nation is grateful for your splendid leadership in the difficult struggle in Korea and for the superb performance of your forces under the most difficult circumstances.' MacArthur replied tersely: 'We shall do our best.'

However Truman tried to spin his administration's war aims, MacArthur understood that they had changed: the chimera of a reunified non-communist Korea was gone and American hopes now rested on being able to negotiate a return to the pre-war division along the 38th parallel. How to achieve this was the subject of a meeting between the joint chiefs, key officials of the State Department and the executive secretary of the National Security Council and his deputy in Washington on 13 February 1951. According to a memorandum of the meeting, it depended on 'whether we can step up the punishment being inflicted on the enemy'. As General Vandenberg put it, America's air superiority was such that 'there are not enough targets left in North Korea to keep the air force busy', and 'while we are punishing the Chinese on the ground, we are trading irreplaceable Americans for expendable Chinese. The question is not only how long will the Chinese be willing to take punishment but also how long will the US public be willing to take American losses, even at the ratio of 20 Chinese to one American.'

But a more urgent question dominated the meeting: where should Ridgway attempt to stabilise the line? In theory, the more territory held by the UN side at the time of a ceasefire the better, but the State Department judged it politically unnecessary—and even harmful—either to retake Seoul or to attempt to seize ground along the 38th parallel. From a military point of view, the most advantageous position for the Eighth Army was roughly where it stood now. General Collins even suggested that there was something to be said for 'fall[ing] back a bit from our present position', a move he said could be carried out without relinquishing hold of major rice-growing areas south of Seoul. While Ridgway's forces were 'close to the limit' of their capabilities, Collins felt that provided Chinese troop numbers remained approximately the same, the positions of the two sides were unlikely to move very much for the remainder of the war.

What 'very much' meant was anybody's guess.

19

NO MORE INTERMINGLING

The start of February brought the Australians much-needed respite from the freezing weather. While Lieutenant Colonel Ferguson reconnoitred routes for a possible move northwards, the diggers occupied themselves washing clothes, maintaining vehicles and weapons, and, in the diary's words, 'coping with the mud and resting'. Patrols were sent out to ascertain the state of the roads and to identify crossing places over the Han River that might be useful to the enemy. A photographer from *Life* magazine turned up to take some pictures of Australian soldiers.

In the hills to the north, two American divisions, the 1st Cavalry and the 24th Infantry, were struggling to maintain Ridgway's offensive in the face of dogged enemy resistance. To counter the steady build-up of communist forces in front of the 24th Division, the British Commonwealth Brigade—which now included New Zealand's 16th Field Regiment—was ordered to take up blocking positions at Yoju, on the west bank of the Han River.

Twenty kilometres north of Yoju, the US 23rd Regimental Combat Team and the newly arrived French battalion had established defensive positions around Chipyong-ni, a strategically important town that commanded roads to the west, north-east and south-east. A single-track railway ran through the town.

A week earlier, an American reconnaissance patrol—a total of around 60 officers and men travelling by jeep and armed to the teeth with automatic rifles, medium and heavy machine guns, mortars and rocket launchers—had been ambushed near a pair of railway tunnels five kilometres south-east of Chipyong-ni. A spotter plane accompanying the patrol had noticed the enemy force on a nearby hill, but due to poor radio communications was unable to warn the patrol leader.

Leaving ammunition and many of their heavy weapons behind, the Americans outran the enemy to reach a ridge above one of the tunnels, where they formed up in a tight defensive perimeter against at least two companies of enemy soldiers. Only air strikes coordinated by the pilot of the spotter plane prevented the Americans from being overrun in a battle that lasted all day and into the night. The Chinese were finally driven off after a reinforcement company broke through the encirclement just after midnight. By then three-quarters of the original patrol were casualties. What became known as the Battle of the Twin Tunnels was clear evidence of a Chinese intention to hold Chipyong-ni.

The area was also significant for another reason. General Ridgway had ordered Almond to close the gap between X Corps and the unprotected right flank of IX Corps, and Chipyong-ni lay roughly on the boundary between the two formations. The Chinese would have known this from interrogating American soldiers taken prisoner at the twin tunnels, who came from both X Corps and IX Corps. Chipyong-ni made an obvious target for a counterattack to blunt or even turn back Ridgway's offensive.

The town was encircled by low hills and ridges rising above the rice paddies. Most of the buildings were made of mud, sticks and straw; half had been flattened during earlier fighting.

A defensive perimeter based on occupying the surrounding hills would have been impractically long. Instead, the 23rd Regimental Combat Team's commander, Colonel Freeman, opted for a tight perimeter a couple of kilometres wide, taking in high ground on three sides and rice paddies on the fourth.

From their base at Yoju, the diggers went out on daily patrols aimed at clearing enemy troops west of the Han River. After a visit from Lieutenant General Bryant Moore, commander of IX Corps, on 9 February, the patrol area was widened to include Chipyong-ni. The next day, with two Chinese field armies gathering unseen in the nearby hills, Bruce Ferguson went to make contact with the Americans and French at Chipyong-ni.

When scouting ahead or visiting his forward troops, Ferguson was generally accompanied by his intelligence officer, Alf Argent, a radio operator carrying a portable wireless set, and a couple of snipers for personal protection. Sometimes he also took his artillery commander and an American officer from the heavy mortar company. But for the risky trip to Chipyong-ni, Ferguson travelled with a platoon-strength Australian patrol.

While the 23rd Regimental Combat Team dug in at Chipyong-ni, the Eighth Army continued to push northwards, but the advance was stopped in its tracks on the night of 11 February, when the Chinese launched a major counteroffensive, with two columns driving deep into X Corps' sector. The attack splintered two ROK divisions and turned Ridgway's offensive into a rolling withdrawal.

Mossman's official history reported a heavy loss of equipment by X Corps, including 155-millimetre howitzers. 'While there is nothing sacrosanct about a piece of artillery, compared to the loss of the lives of men,' Ridgway wrote to Almond in the immediate aftermath of the retreat, 'I don't expect to hear again of such loss as reported to me this morning of five 155 [howitzers] . . . It is prima facie indication of faulty leadership.'

A subsequent inquiry into the debacle absolved American commanders for the losses in men and equipment, attributing those instead to the 'sudden and complete defeat of the ROK 8th Division with little or no warning to the [US] 2nd Division forces', and recommended there be no similar 'intermingling' of US and ROK forces in future.*

Before the Chinese attacked, Chipyong-ni was well behind X Corps' front line, but as Almond's units headed south, the Americans and French at Chipyong-ni were left occupying a perilous bulge in the UN front. By 13 February, infantry patrols were reporting 'increased enemy activity' on the north, east and west sides of Chipyong-ni, while spotter planes noted new enemy forces approaching from the north and east. It seemed only a matter of time before the Chinese moved to cut off Freeman's main supply routes.

With his garrison at risk of being surrounded, Freeman wanted permission to give up his positions and fall back to Yoju. Almond and his division commanders approved the move, and at noon on 13 February Freeman formally recommended the 23rd Regimental Combat Team and the French battalion pull out of Chipyong-ni the following morning.

But events were moving fast. A reconnaissance report of a strong Chinese blocking force on the main supply route south convinced Freeman that there was no time to lose: his withdrawal from Chipyong-ni should begin as soon as possible. By now, Almond had submitted Freeman's original request for a withdrawal beginning the following morning to General Ridgway. Ridgway, however, was having none of it, and nor was MacArthur, who had flown in that day from Tokyo to confer with the Eighth Army commander.

MacArthur reiterated that the purpose of the war was not to capture territory but to kill the enemy's soldiers while conserving his own. At the same time he emphasised the importance of holding the

---

* According to Mossman, Ridgway accepted this explanation but did not withdraw a warning he had given to all corps commanders, in which he stated that the 'loss or abandonment to enemy of arms and equipment in usable condition is a grave offense against every member of this command. I shall hereafter deal severely with commanders found responsible.'

line at the Han River. The garrison at Chipyong-ni stood directly in the path of Chinese forces attempting to sweep through the Han River valley and envelop Ridgway's western forces. Holding the town was vital. There could be no retreat from Chipyong-ni, Ridgway told Almond. Should the garrison be encircled, Almond would have to send a force to relieve it.

Told he would have to stay and fight it out, Freeman set about toughening his defences, posting tanks near the outer perimeter, making arrangements for air strikes and the resupply of food, ammunition and medical equipment by air, and creating an inner ring to be manned at night by engineers fighting as infantry. With artillery, machine guns and anti-personnel mines covering all likely avenues of enemy attack, Freeman made sure that any attempt to penetrate the perimeter would be fiercely resisted.

Outside Chipyong-ni, the diggers continued their patrols. On 13 February it was the turn of Ben O'Dowd's A Company to make contact with the defenders at Chipyong-ni. This time they ran into an 'unidentified' party of eight enemy soldiers, who at the sound of Australian gunfire 'disappeared without returning fire'. At Chipyong-ni, a staff officer showed O'Dowd a map indicating in red the location of enemy attacks and patrol actions. It seemed to O'Dowd that the garrison was almost entirely encircled by red marks. As the Chinese closed in, Freeman pounded them with artillery and air strikes, but the situation looked ominous. The diggers were relieved to make it out before the circle closed.

At midnight on 13 February news reached 27th Brigade headquarters that the garrison at Chipyong-ni was under heavy attack. During the night an American reconnaissance patrol was caught by the Chinese at a crossroads south-east of Chipyong-ni. Two companies tried to run the gauntlet in their vehicles and were massacred by Chinese troops firing from the ridges.

After a chaotic morning conference, the Commonwealth brigade was given the task of clearing the main supply route to the besieged garrison, while a task force from the US 5th Cavalry Regiment would simultaneously attempt to reach Chipyong-ni via an alternative route.

By 1 p.m. the brigade was ready to go, led off by the Middlesex Regiment. They had advanced no more than a couple of kilometres when they were fired on by enemy soldiers occupying a ridge overlooking the road. By late afternoon the Middlesex men had taken the ridge. After repelling a counterattack, they dug in for the night, with the Australians just behind and guarding their left flank. The Chinese counterattacked repeatedly during the night but each attack was beaten off.

The next day the brigade's orders were changed. Its job was now to fight its way through to Chipyong-ni and relieve the 23rd Regimental Combat Team, advancing along the road on which the reconnaissance company had been massacred less than 24 hours earlier. To achieve this, the brigade would first need to capture a feature identified on the map as Hill 195 but remembered by all as 'The Doctor'—and it would have to accomplish the task with its left flank unprotected and its right guarded only by the brittle ROK 6th Division.

As O'Dowd described it later, Hill 195 was 'broad, bald and devoid of any form of cover. It rose gently from a gully to its crest, providing an excellent, unimpeded field of fire for the enemy throughout its entire length. There was no room for flanking, no option but to approach straight uphill into the enemy's fire.'

The plan called for B Company to push the enemy off the high ground on the right of the road, while A Company attacked Hill 195 on the left. A preliminary artillery bombardment by the New Zealanders had little effect: any shell that overshot the horseshoe-shaped summit, even by a few metres, tumbled down harmlessly into the hollow. In the end, Ferguson decided the attack could not wait.

B Company went first but soon ran into heavy machine-gun and mortar fire. The Chinese on the right side of the road were too strong to be dislodged, and B Company was forced to withdraw.

That left A Company to assault Hill 195 with its right flank completely exposed.

Between the road and the slope of Hill 195 lay a long stretch of open ground. Soon after crossing the start line, men started falling. The shooting from the right intensified as the diggers from A Company scrambled uphill, but worse was to come. As they closed to within a couple of hundred metres of the top, the diggers came under rifle and machine-gun fire from Chinese on the left, who were dug in along a ridge running parallel with Hill 195—a ridge that O'Dowd had been promised was clear of enemy soldiers.

A Company was now caught in a deadly crossfire, pinned down and in the open. 'There was too much small-arms fire coming from all sides and further progress was absolutely impossible without taking further casualties,' O'Dowd wrote later. 'It was now late afternoon and the battlefield was littered with the dead and wounded. Enemy fire was so effective that we could move neither forward nor back.'

Clearly, the Chinese were determined to prevent any relief force from reaching the UN garrison at Chipyong-ni. As darkness fell, O'Dowd was ordered to withdraw. The battle for The Doctor had cost three diggers their lives; another fourteen were wounded.

While 3RAR struggled to make headway along the main supply route, Colonel Marcel Crombez set off with his 5th Cavalry task force on a more westerly road. Around twelve kilometres from Chipyong-ni, Crombez was forced to wait while his engineers repaired a demolished bridge. The delay meant that relief would not reach the garrison at Chipyong-ni until at least the next day. The following morning, with his infantry tied down by Chinese troops shooting from a ridge above the road, Crombez decided that his only chance of reaching Chipyong-ni by nightfall was with tanks.

Twenty-three American tanks—a combination of Pattons and older Shermans—would drive the final ten kilometres and break the encirclement. To deal with anti-tank mines and to protect his tanks from enemy soldiers attacking from close up, Crombez had infantry and engineers ride on the tanks.

It was a terrible road, even by Korean standards, bordered by mountain slopes on one side and rice paddies on the other. A couple of kilometres short of Chipyong-ni, the road ran through a deep cutting, an obvious danger point. Every time the column stopped, the infantry would dismount to protect the tanks while the engineers removed landmines. When the column was ready to move again, the troops were supposed to climb back on. Any soldier left behind was either to find his way back to UN lines or wait to be picked up when the tanks returned from Chipyong-ni. At least, that was the plan.

Halted by an enemy force at the village of Koksu-ri, the tanks swung their turrets in search of targets, knocking off the soldiers riding on the back. After others dismounted to take cover from enemy machine guns and mortars, the column moved off without warning, leaving at least 30 American infantrymen behind. Beyond the village, another firefight ended with more troopers left behind. The final ambush was at the cutting, where Chinese troops perched on the embankments hurled satchel charges and blasted the tanks with mortars and captured American bazookas. Three tanks were damaged but all made it through. Of the 160 American infantrymen riding on the tanks when they crossed the Han River 24 hours earlier, only 23 were still clinging on when the column broke through the Chinese lines around Chipyong-ni.

While the two relief forces fought their way north, the Chinese were doing everything they could to wipe out Freeman's garrison. On the night of 14–15 February, they succeeded in penetrating the UN lines, seizing foxholes inside the perimeter and nearly overrunning Freeman's 155-millimetre howitzer battery before daylight enabled the Americans to bring their artillery and air power into play. Throughout the next day, the Chinese fought tenaciously against American counterattacks supported by air strikes, artillery and tanks. Only the arrival of Crombez's relief force prompted the Chinese to abandon the battlefield.

The official history reported nearly 5000 PRC casualties in the battle for Chipyong-ni at a cost of 52 UN soldiers killed, 259 wounded and 42 missing. The successful defence of Chipyong-ni by an isolated American force against a numerically far superior enemy represented a major defeat for Mao's 'volunteer' army and marked a turning point in the war. Encouraged by the success of Colonel Crombez's armoured attack, Ridgway now began planning a new offensive aimed at clearing the enemy from the area around Chipyong-ni and the mountains to the south-east.

It was unlike the Chinese to leave their dead behind, and the discovery of 600 enemy dead, as well as arms and equipment, confirmed that the Chinese had left the hills around Chipyong-ni in a hurry. A force comprising the 27th Brigade and elements of the US 5th Cavalry and the ROK 6th Division was quickly deployed to block their entry into the Han River valley. In keeping with earlier communist offensives, intelligence now suggested that the Chinese and North Koreans were withdrawing en masse from the scene of the battle, and indeed from the entire central region. Determined to deny his enemy any respite while inflicting as many casualties as possible, Ridgway expanded his initial plans for a single-corps offensive to an operation involving both IX Corps (including the 27th Brigade) and X Corps advancing in tandem. The aim of the operation was to trap and destroy the Chinese below a new defensive line running roughly east from Chipyong-ni. The attack, due to start on 21 February, was code-named Operation Killer—a name that did not go down well in Washington but which Ridgway kept despite protests from the army chief of staff.[*]

---

[*] 'The term "Operation Killer" has had a most unfortunate effect,' an official at the Bureau of Far Eastern Affairs informed Dean Rusk on 14 March. 'This slogan has stuck in the public mind as representing the objectives, nature and meaning of the whole action in Korea. I fear that to many people Korea now means only killing, a process of killing Americans, Chinese and Koreans.'

The day before the attack was launched, General MacArthur arrived in Korea for one of his flying visits. MacArthur had been told in broad terms about the coming offensive and was eager to claim credit for it. Since taking over as Eighth Army commander, Ridgway had gone to great lengths to stop the sort of media leaks that had compromised previous UN initiatives in Korea. While keeping reporters informed about his plans, he insisted on an embargo until the operation was underway. By and large the reporters accepted his terms. Ridgway was therefore horrified to hear MacArthur announce, at a press conference before his return to Tokyo, that he had 'just ordered a resumption of the offensive'. As well as potentially tipping off the Chinese, it was a naked attempt by MacArthur to steal the limelight for an operation he had neither planned nor ordered.

Speed was now imperative if Ridgway was going to cut off the retreating Chinese, but a spell of unseasonably warm weather turned roads into quagmires and rivers into rapids filled with floating ice. Bridges were washed away and roads and railway lines buried under landslides. The UN offensive crawled slowly towards a new line, designated the Arizona Line. Getting his troops out of their vehicles had been a priority for Ridgway since he took command, and 3RAR's war diary recorded the diggers slogging on foot across 'tortuous and rugged' country, supported by 'approximately 150 Korean native porters' carrying ammunition, food and water.

The arrival on 19 February of the first Canadian troops—the 2nd Battalion, Princess Patricia's Canadian Light Infantry (the Princess Pats, for short)—had increased the 27th Brigade's strength from three battalions to four and transformed a previously understrength brigade into what the diary described as a 'powerful fighting force'.

Two days later the brigade went into action, with the Princess Pats and the Argylls advancing side by side. The combination of thick mud and difficult terrain meant progress was slow; by the end of the first day they had hardly gone ten kilometres. The following morning the Canadians were stopped by Chinese troops dug in above a pass. After three attempts to dislodge the Chinese failed, 3RAR was ordered to seize a ridge overlooking the pass from the east. The ridge connected two hills, Hill 523 and the more imposing Hill 614. The first was taken without opposition, but when a platoon from B Company advanced on Hill 614, the Chinese opened up with rifles and machine guns, wounding one Australian. With darkness falling, B Company abandoned its attempts to take Hill 614 and dug in for the night on Hill 523.

Kenneth Travers and his mate 'Poddy' Barber had a lucky escape after being jumped by two Chinese soldiers. 'They sneaked up and they stuck a rifle straight into Poddy's head . . . but Poddy grabbed it and . . . he said, "Shoot him and get him off me!" . . . they were leaning over so he couldn't get up . . . he let the rifle go and dropped backwards and . . . they both jumped out.'

Travers had taken off his boots to exercise his feet and had to scamper back to the company position without them (the quarter-master gave him a new pair in the morning). When he was sent out the next day to check for enemy dead, Travers found his boots riddled with bullet holes. 'They had just fired into the pits,' he said.

During the night, the New Zealand gunners and an American heavy mortar crew kept up a steady barrage on suspected Chinese positions, while Korean porters hauled ammunition and supplies up the snow-covered hillside.

As well as blocking the battalion's advance, the Chinese on Hill 614 posed a direct threat to B Company on Hill 523. At first light on 24 February, 6 Platoon was ordered to take Hill 614 by a frontal assault. The ridge connecting the two hills was so narrow that no more than one section—around a dozen men—could scramble along it at once; flanking manoeuvres were impossible. As they began climbing the final steep rise to Hill 614, the diggers came under intense mortar and machine-gun fire from Chinese who had withstood the artillery and mortar barrage. 'Anyone came up that spur, they had four machine guns straight on them,' Travers recalled. 'You couldn't see them and you couldn't hit them . . . they were knocking us over like pins . . . It scared the hell out of me.'

The sides of Hill 614 had been stripped of heavy timber and all that was left was low scrub: if a man near the top was hit, there was nothing to stop him falling all the way to the bottom. One digger was killed and six wounded before the platoon withdrew.

The Canadians on their left had also taken casualties, but when a helicopter arrived to collect two badly wounded soldiers, it evacuated only the Canadian, leaving a seriously injured digger behind. The day ended with 3RAR back where it had started.

The next day Ferguson called in air strikes on Hill 614 while restricting the Canadians and 3RAR to aggressive patrolling. One Australian patrol reached within grenade range of the summit of 614 before being beaten back at a cost of one dead and two wounded. On their left flank, a Canadian patrol probing an approach to the ridge discovered foxholes but no enemy soldiers. The following morning, 27 February, began with napalm strikes on the enemy positions, together with artillery and heavy mortar fire. Still the Chinese refused to be dislodged.

D Company was now given the chance to do what B Company had been unable to do. Len Opie was enjoying a cup of cocoa a couple of hundred metres back when his platoon commander said, 'Get your gear, Len, we are going up the hill.' It was to be a platoon-strength attack, with Opie's section in the lead. 'I had about seven in the section, I suppose—and we weren't given any instructions at all, except that there was a hill and we had to take it.'

Artillery fire and air strikes had shorn away the vegetation, robbing the diggers of cover. Charging ahead with his Owen submachine gun, Opie tossed grenades—some captured from the Chinese—into enemy foxholes, aiming them at the hillside so that they rolled down and exploded. As well as the Owen, he carried the .303 rifle he had been issued on enlistment and had kept ever since.

After his ammunition ran out, he grabbed weapons from enemy soldiers he had killed.

The Chinese decided they'd had enough. Battered and demoralised, they fled the battlefield, leaving behind fifteen dead. After its successful attack, 12 Platoon returned to D Company and Opie was infuriated to see B Company taking credit for having nearly captured the hill. For his actions that day Opie was awarded the Distinguished Conduct Medal. He was one of only five Australian soldiers to receive the award during the Korean War. Many felt it should have been a Victoria Cross.

A half-hearted counterattack by a small Chinese force in the early hours of 28 February was easily driven off, enabling the diggers to consolidate their hold on Hill 614 and clearing the way for the brigade to resume its advance.

In Korea, there was always another hill to take, another ridge to attack, and 3RAR's next objective was Hill 587. Initial resistance forced C Company to dig in several hundred metres short of the objective, but during the night most of the Chinese defenders withdrew and the following morning Hill 587 was easily captured. Grenades, guns, ammunition and food scattered around the foxholes were evidence of another hasty exit. The battalion's next move would be far more challenging.

On 3 March the 27th Brigade came back under the command of the US 1st Cavalry Division for a new operation, codenamed Woodbine, aimed at pushing the front line twenty kilometres further north and bringing UN forces within striking distance of Seoul.

More porters were brought up; each of the brigade's four battalions now had at least 100. Although 'not nearly so useful as mules', as the diary put it, Korean porters were 'indispensable and the next best thing in this hilly country'.

Intelligence suggested that the Chinese had built strong defensive positions on the steep-sided hills and would fight hard to hold them. 3RAR's objective was Hill 410, with the Princess Pats attacking the adjacent Hill 532. A ridgeline connected the two peaks. Despite the milder weather, thick snow still covered the summits and slopes.

Ferguson's plan was for O'Dowd's A Company to attack up the east spur, while Bill Keys' D Company took the west spur leading to the summit of Hill 410. Realising that A Company would have to cross the valley floor and begin its ascent in full view of the enemy, O'Dowd sent Lieutenant John Church's 2 Platoon into the valley under cover of darkness to look for signs of enemy occupation. The platoon was to stay in the valley all night and to spend the next day observing enemy movement on the slopes. At one point during the night, Chinese soldiers holding magnesium flares came close to one of Church's patrols; since it was essential not to give their presence away, the diggers resisted the urge to fire.

As a result of delays in bringing up ammunition and supplies, the start of Operation Woodbine was put back by 24 hours, meaning another jittery night in the valley for 2 Platoon. As darkness fell on 5 March, O'Dowd sent his trusted number two, Reg Saunders, to tell Church to hold tight until the rest of the company came down the following night in preparation for a dawn attack. O'Dowd later wrote:

> [T]he enemy did not appear to be dug in below the 410 ridge but did have an unobstructed view down the steep east spur and into the wide valley floor. This made it certain we would be shot up and mortared if we emerged from the timber line in daylight, taking casualties all the way across the valley floor to the cover of the timber line on the opposite side . . . It was my intention to make a silent approach up the east ridge, with the hope of jumping the enemy before dawn.

Trouble started as soon as A Company began moving down the steep track that led to 2 Platoon's position on the valley floor. The snow, trampled down by the diggers two nights earlier, had frozen, turning the track into something resembling a ski ramp on which men found it impossible to stay upright. Soldiers skidded on their backsides in the dark, along with dropped weapons, ammunition boxes and equipment, all careening down the icy slope that would give the coming battle its nickname: the Battle of the Slippery Slide.

As dawn broke, 1 Platoon began its attack on the eastern spur, drawing a hail of mortar and small-arms fire that immediately caused casualties. The narrow ridge forced the platoon to move in single file and the diggers were soon pinned down.

B Company now moved from its assembly area and began to follow A Company up the ridge. Stan Connelly recalled the gruesome sight that confronted him at the bottom of the slope:

When I moved up to take part in that action A Company had already been in and there were half a dozen of their members dead at the bottom of the ice slide. They'd got to the top of the hill, been shot down and . . . careered down the hill along this great long strip of ice . . . It looked as though it had been man-made but in fact it was just a freak of nature . . . we were moving in single file to get along the track and I saw these A Company guys lying with their eyes open and dead at the bottom of the slope.

Above them, the diggers from A Company could not lift their heads without risking a sniper's bullet. They were too close to the enemy for artillery support. The American mortar crew dropped a few bombs on the ridge but they were unable to staunch the accurate fire from Chinese rifles, machine guns and mortars. Tom Muggleton recalled the Chinese being 'absolutely brilliant with a 60-millimetre mortar. They could lob it on a pin . . . [we] took a lot of casualties through the 60-millimetre mortars.'

Connelly was sure he would die that day:

It was enough of a task to scramble up the side of this very steep ridge, but when we got to the top and had a peep over, [we saw] the ridge was so narrow that there was just a walking track . . . [It was] no more than three foot wide . . . and there was an enemy machine gun nest right on the track. They couldn't get it with artillery because the peak was too narrow, the only way they could attack it was to come along the track and to do that you're in single file, easily picked off, impossible to press the attack home.

It was late afternoon when B Company reached the top of the ridge. Word went around that they were going to be ordered over the top. 'We were still on the side of the ridge peeping over the top,' Connelly recalled, 'with the machine gun opening up every time they saw a head pop up . . . that looked like the end of it to me.'

With A Company unable to move, Ferguson ordered D Company to have a go at the western spur. They would have support from artillery and heavy mortars. Shooting intensified as the diggers got closer to the summit. Two Americans passing back instructions to the mortar crew were hit, along with their radio. Given the ferocity of enemy machine-gun fire, casualties so far were light—one dead and several wounded—but blizzards during the afternoon reduced visibility to zero, meaning the wounded had to be carried for kilometres down precipitous tracks to the aid post, an agonising journey that could take several hours.

Near the top the ridge flattened out, enabling 11 Platoon to launch a frontal attack with support from platoons on each side. As 11 Platoon neared the crest, a phosphorous bomb fell short, burning several diggers. But the battle for Hill 410 was nearly over. A desperate fight with small arms and grenades ended with the Chinese positions on the hillside being overrun, although the summit remained in enemy hands. A number of Chinese soldiers were shot as they tried to escape.

As D Company consolidated its position, a shell landed on 10 Platoon. Who fired it was never established, but the explosion killed three diggers and wounded three more—a tragic ending to an all-day battle that had cost the lives of twelve Australian soldiers and left 31 wounded, with the battalion still frustratingly short of its objective. The Canadians, too, had been stopped just short of the summit.

In the end, B Company did not go over the top and Stan Connelly survived. 'We stayed on the peak of the ridge but just below,' he recalled. 'I actually slept for half the night [and] spent the other half on watch . . . the next morning the sun came up bright and early and we stepped up onto the track and the enemy had gone. Withdrawn without any further bother. A lucky day.'

The diggers found the ridge expertly fortified, with deep trenches and bunkers. Weapon pits were camouflaged with pine branches to protect them from air strikes. As on previous occasions, the Chinese had left in a hurry, abandoning large numbers of hand grenades, mortar tubes and bombs, Soviet ammunition, food and 'a few dead'.

'The enemy's sudden withdrawal from excellent defence positions caused considerable surprise,' the brigade diary reported. 'He had withdrawn not only on the brigade front but on most other fronts.' Eighty-two enemy dead were counted in the vicinity of Hill 410.

Three days later, Major O'Dowd was wounded in a battle for another hill. Two diggers were killed. O'Dowd was evacuated to a British military hospital in Japan, while the brigade was given a few days off. Rest and recreation were top of the agenda for the diggers, along with night training and the replacement of American winter gear with Australian uniforms. Reinforcements were marched in and hot showers laid on, courtesy of the US Army. Someone dreamt up the idea of a rugby league competition, but only one game was played before the battalion received a warning order to join the US 24th Division. The Eighth Army was advancing again.

20

SACKED

While the Commonwealth troops relaxed, Seoul changed hands for a fourth time. Abandoned by the Chinese without a fight, the now devastated South Korean capital was reoccupied by ROK troops on 16 March 1951. There was none of the triumphalism that accompanied the city's capture after the successful Inchon landing in September 1950. MacArthur could not resist another flying visit to Korea, but this time he did not enter Seoul.

The fighting during the first half of March had yielded mixed results for Ridgway. While the Eighth Army had retaken plenty of territory, it had been far less successful at destroying enemy soldiers and equipment. The Chinese and North Korean armies had proved infuriatingly good at staying out of reach of the advancing UN forces. Ridgway's answer was Operation Courageous, an advance designed to carry the Eighth Army north to a new line, the Benton Line, about eight kilometres south of the 38th parallel, and in the process trap and destroy the North Korean I Corps and the PRC's 26th Group Army.

A rift was now opening in Washington between those seeking a 'peaceful and honourable' settlement based on a return to the pre-war status quo and those prepared to risk a wider war— potentially an atomic war—to achieve the larger purpose of humbling Mao's China, in the first place by driving the communists back across the 38th parallel.

The same Bureau of Far Eastern Affairs official who had written to Dean Rusk deploring the name Operation Killer also warned of the American public's 'misgivings and profound uneasiness' about the continuation of the war:

> Those who approved our resistance in Korea now find the present situation completely confusing and baffling. Even when the idea of obtaining the most favorable conditions for a peaceful settlement is presented they still appear to feel that we are remiss in not taking some decisive action which would end the slaughter.

Ridgway told news reporters on 12 March that it would be a 'tremendous victory' if the war ended on the 38th parallel. Australian newspapers quoted Ridgway saying it would be an 'incalculable defeat for Communist China if she fails to drive the Allies into the sea'.

> Communist losses are now piling up in the ratio of 60 for every Allied casualty ... We have the initiative, and we have broken up all Communist attempts to seize it from us ... Communist China, having set out to destroy the United Nations' forces in Korea, must concede it a defeat if she fails.

Press speculation that Ridgway was planning to halt his forces at the 38th parallel sent the South Koreans into a panic, prompting Pyo Wook Han, the embassy's worried first secretary, to advise Rusk that if this were to happen, 'no future security would be possible for Korea' and 'the Korean people would suffer a great loss in morale and might become disillusioned with the United Nations'. At a meeting three days after Ridgway made his statement to the press, Rusk assured Han that no decision had been made about whether UN forces would cross the 38th parallel and insisted that 'neither the United States nor the United Nations had, in any sense, abandoned their basic objectives for a unified and independent Korea'.

At a meeting between senior State Department officials and the joint chiefs on the morning of 15 March, General Collins commented that the Chinese 'have been dumb enough to fight us with their best troops' and had 'take[n] a terrible beating' that had 'filled up their hospitals' and would make it 'very hard for them to replace their losses'. There would be 'no place for the Chinese to hold' if the Eighth Army was successful in taking the strategic town of Chunchon, Collins said. 'We have our momentum up and we may be able to go a considerable distance without much fighting.' Admiral Sherman said he 'personally favored the taking of Pyongyang'.

General MacArthur chose the same day, 15 March, to declare, in an interview with the president of United Press, that he did not have the forces to defend either the 38th parallel or any other line across the peninsula. If he had such a force, he said, and the logistical resources to maintain it, he would be able to 'drive the Chinese communists back across the Yalu' and hold the river as the main line of defence for a unified Korea.

At a meeting with General Ridgway and Ambassador Muccio in Pusan, also on 15 March, President Syngman Rhee raised the issue of crossing the 38th parallel, speaking in what Muccio described as a 'rambling fashion' of 'vague plans to telegraph President Truman and General MacArthur concerning the necessity of bombing Manchuria'.*

The United Nations was now overwhelmingly in favour of ending the war as soon as possible. America's allies, aghast at President Truman's earlier mention of the bomb, were screaming for a settlement.

Back in January, in response to MacArthur's request for permission to blockade the Chinese coast and bomb Manchuria, the joint chiefs—with Truman's blessing—had clarified MacArthur's instructions: he was to continue to fight and to inflict casualties on the enemy, and should evacuate his forces only if it was necessary to save his command. In reply, MacArthur had warned that he could not defend a position in Korea and protect Japan at the same time, and that fighting on under the current restrictions risked the 'complete destruction' of his army. MacArthur could hardly have conveyed more clearly his repudiation of the president's war policy. The transformation of the Eighth Army under Ridgway had given the lie to MacArthur's prophecy of doom, while at the same time goading him into an act of open rebellion.

On 19 March, Secretary of State Acheson, Defense Secretary Marshall and the joint chiefs met to explore the possibilities of peace in Korea. They also discussed the draft of a proposed statement by President Truman on the Korean situation. The next day they cabled MacArthur with the gist of the presidential announcement:

---

*   At the meeting, Ridgway took Rhee to task for the ROK army's habit of 'bugging out'. According to Ridgway's memorandum of the meeting, he told Rhee that 'this was war we were in, and not peace time manoeuvres or training. Therefore, I expected that senior commanders whose troops disintegrated under attack, and above all those whose troops abandoned equipment, would be sternly and summarily dealt with. I said it was one thing for a senior officer who felt he could not hold his ground to withdraw his units intact, either on his own initiative or with proper superior authority, but it was quite another, and [a] very serious matter, for him to give up the equipment which we had such difficulty in supplying, and which was so vital to the enemy in waging war against us.'

that with communist armies largely expelled from South Korea, it was time to discuss the conditions for peace, and that diplomatic efforts should be made *before* any significant advance north of the 38th parallel. Judging the parallel to have no military significance, the joint chiefs wanted MacArthur's thoughts on what freedom of action he would need 'for the next few weeks' to provide security for his forces and maintain contact with the enemy.

MacArthur's response was brief and predictable: 'Recommend that no further military restrictions be imposed upon the United Nations Command in Korea.' The inhibitions that already existed, he said, made it 'completely impracticable' to attempt to clear North Korea.

With MacArthur sulking in Tokyo, Truman and his advisers drew up a statement indicating that, in light of Ridgway's recent successes on the battlefield, Washington was ready to talk peace. Implied in the president's speech was that a negotiated settlement would see both sides back where they were at the outbreak of war, at the 38th parallel.

Drafted in close consultation with America's Korean War allies, including Australia and New Zealand, Truman's statement made the case for a pragmatic peace over punishment and recrimination. But before it could be issued, General MacArthur made a pronouncement of his own, in flagrant violation of the president's December directive that all public statements on foreign policy must be cleared through Washington.

On 24 March, without alerting Washington, MacArthur issued his *pronunciamento*. Operations, he declared, were continuing 'according to schedule and plan', and South Korea was 'substantially cleared . . . of organized Communist forces'.

Of even greater significance than our tactical successes has been the clear revelation that this new enemy, Red China, of such exaggerated and vaunted military power, lacks the industrial capacity to provide adequately many critical items essential to the conduct of modern war.

He lacks manufacturing bases and those raw materials needed to produce, maintain and operate even moderate air and naval power, and he cannot provide the essentials for successful ground operations, such as tanks, heavy artillery and other refinements science has introduced into the conduct of military campaigns.

As well as taunting an enemy that had repeatedly got the better of him on the battlefield, MacArthur threatened to do exactly what the joint chiefs had forbidden him to do: expand the war beyond Korea and into China.

The enemy . . . must by now be painfully aware that a decision of the United Nations to depart from its tolerant effort to contain the war to the area of Korea, through an expansion of our military operations to its coastal areas and interior bases, would doom Red China to the risk of imminent military collapse.

Washington first got wind of MacArthur's statement from the radio; the full text was obtained from the press ticker and handed to Dean Acheson at 11 p.m. on 23 March. It was recognised at once as an act of naked insubordination, an attempt to sabotage a peace initiative before it began. According to Halberstam, Acheson said, 'I couldn't send a message to the Chinese after that. [MacArthur] prevented a cease-fire proposition right there. I wanted to kick him into the North China Sea.'

At midnight Acheson cabled the US embassies in all thirteen nations contributing fighting units to the UN force in Korea with a copy of MacArthur's text and a covering note saying that the statement was 'not authorized, expected or representative of the views of this Govt'.

Truman's immediate concern was to muzzle MacArthur before he could say anything else; the question of how to discipline him could wait. Meanwhile, Rusk got to work formulating a response to placate America's allies.

The Norwegian ambassador called on Warren Austin, US ambassador to the United Nations, wanting to know the meaning of MacArthur's *pronunciamento*. Austin disingenuously suggested that 'General MacArthur merely intended to indicate that as commander of UN forces he was prepared to discuss a cease-fire'. Asked whether MacArthur's comments implied that America was now intending to attack the Chinese mainland, Austin assured the Norwegian that US policy had not changed.

For nearly a fortnight Truman appeared to wrestle with the problem of what to do with MacArthur. By the time he sought the opinion of his top advisers, he had made up his mind that MacArthur had to go. The last straw came on 5 April, when a Republican congressman read out a letter he had received from General MacArthur openly endorsing the use of Chinese Nationalist forces to fight the communists—a proposition repeatedly ruled out by Washington. On 11 April Truman went on US television to announce that he had sacked his supreme commander and replaced him with General Ridgway.

That day, 3RAR's war diary recorded MacArthur's dismissal as the third item of radio news. During the night, there had been a fall of snow. March had been a generally quiet month for the Australians; April would be anything but.

21

DON'T YOU COME BACK WITHOUT IT

On 25 March the Commonwealth troops, now under command of the US 24th Infantry Division, were shunted 80 kilometres north as part of the general advance towards the Benton Line. It was a miserable day for moving—the worst weather they had seen for a fortnight. Several vehicles broke down or got stuck in the mud and it was 2 a.m. before the last stragglers arrived at their destination. On 28 March all four battalions of the 27th Brigade began advancing. With Basil Coad on leave in Hong Kong, a new commander, Colonel Brian Burke, took charge. Meeting only token resistance, the brigade cleared all the features in its path, picking up a few frostbitten Chinese prisoners along the way.

'[The] 27 Brigade were clearing the lines, hills on either side, and that was one of the things that 27 Brigade did that the Americans didn't do,' Sergeant Ron Perkins recalled. 'The Americans would just clear up the roads . . . we would clear the hills before we would move on the road . . . that's why we never got trapped like the Americans did.'

As the brigade advanced, American engineers went to work removing mines, fixing bridges and improving the road. By 31 March, all battalions had reached their objectives.

From the Benton Line the Eighth Army was to advance to a new line, the Kansas Line, just north of the 38th parallel. From there Ridgway planned a limited attack, codenamed Operation Dauntless, against a communications centre around 40 kilometres north of the parallel that was likely to play a key role in any new Chinese offensive. Excitable reporters dubbed this area the Iron Triangle. The purpose of Dauntless was to disrupt enemy activities rather than seize territory; if the enemy counterattacked in strength, the UN forces were to pull back to the Kansas Line.

On April Fool's Day 1951 the Australians were delivered by truck to a position eight kilometres north of the town of Kapyong, around 60 kilometres north-east of Seoul. The 27th Brigade, now under command of IX Corps, had orders to advance up the Kapyong Valley. At 7.30 a.m. on 3 April the diggers moved off. During the day, they encountered small-arms fire from disorganised groups of enemy soldiers who were not dug in and appeared to be withdrawing. By nightfall the battalion had reached its intermediate objectives and was camped a couple of kilometres south of the 38th parallel. Small parties of enemy soldiers tried to infiltrate the Australian positions but were beaten off. The following morning the body of a Chinese soldier was found in the D Company area.

Later that day, after evicting an enemy force from Hill 523, 3RAR sent a patrol across the 38th parallel. An intelligence summary in the battalion diary reported that small enemy parties were fighting 'delaying actions' against infantry units, only to withdraw in the face of artillery and mortar fire. The Argylls had a much tougher time, losing two officers in a fierce battle for another hill, before air strikes, including napalm, forced the Chinese to retreat.

As well as barbed wire and entrenchments, the vacated PRC positions were infested with mines and booby traps. The Argylls suffered several casualties after running into a minefield that consisted entirely of American mines laid several months earlier by the ROK army. Brigade HQ was well aware that ROK troops had laid mines along the 38th parallel and had tried unsuccessfully for several days to get details of their exact location; the information was still being translated when the Argylls wandered into the minefield. Casualty figures for 6 April showed six Commonwealth soldiers wounded by mines, one American killed and another wounded.

Booby traps caused further casualties. One technique favoured by the Chinese was to plant American 60-millimetre mortar bombs in trees; a soldier brushing past the tree would dislodge the bomb, which would explode when it hit the ground.

More hills lay ahead but the dire state of the roads brought the Commonwealth troops to a temporary standstill. By the morning of 8 April the brigade was on the move again, reaching the Kansas Line that day.

During the previous ten days, the 27th Brigade had taken a succession of objectives codenamed after trees (Willow, Cherry, Poplar) and flowers (Crocus, Gladiola, Narcissus). Now it was confronted by a series of hills and ridges codenamed after fishes. Pike, Sole and Kipper were all taken quickly against minimal opposition, but the Chinese were determined to defend a hill codenamed Sardine.

The job of taking Sardine was initially handed to the Middlesex Regiment. After Sardine was captured, a company of diggers was to pass through the Middlesex positions and take the next hill, codenamed Salmon.

An initial attempt to capture Sardine on 13 April was beaten off by the Chinese and the day ended with the hill still in enemy hands. Dramatic news then reached the Commonwealth troops: Brigade HQ and two battalions, the 1st Argylls and 1st Middlesex, were to be relieved and shipped out, the latter to be replaced by the 1st Battalion King's Own Scottish Borderers and 1st Battalion King's Shropshire Light Infantry. Such an announcement could hardly fail to make an impression on the minds of the soldiers preparing to make another assault on Sardine.

Overnight, however, the task became even more difficult. In the early hours an enemy force attempted to infiltrate a nearby hill, codenamed Cod. First light revealed a platoon of Chinese soldiers occupying a position on the ridge between Cod and Sardine, threatening the Middlesex company that had been tasked with taking Sardine. Rocky outcrops made it hard to close with the enemy and it was midafternoon before the Chinese platoon was driven off. At the same time the Princess Pats were struggling to make headway against a strong Chinese force defending an adjacent hill, codenamed Turbot. By the end of the day, both the Middlesex company and the Canadians had been forced to withdraw.

The diggers were not impressed. 'The Middlesex had an obvious morale problem,' O'Dowd wrote later. 'With their battalion close to relief and a return to the good life in Hong Kong, they regarded this as a rather inappropriate time for heroics.'

It wasn't just the Australians who thought the Middlesex could have tried harder. An entry in the brigade diary noted that the 'premature announcement' of relief during 'active operations' had tended to 'restrain any aggressive action by the units concerned'.

Whether news of its relief took the fight out of the Middlesex Regiment or not, it was clear that the Chinese were well dug in on Turbot, Sardine and probably Salmon as well, and that dislodging them would not be easy.

Colonel Ferguson went up for a recce, travelling on a Harley-Davidson motorbike ridden by Private Bob Parker, a member of the Signals Platoon who had been pressed into the role of despatch rider. With him, as usual, were his intelligence officer and a couple of snipers. Taking Ferguson to visit a company of diggers on the ridge above the road, Parker rounded a bend and, he recalled, ran smack into an American machine-gun post.

They pulled us up and said, 'You can't go up there, it's dangerous.' And old Ferguson said, 'I am going up.' The Americans

[were] sitting behind their machine gun and I was sitting on my bike [with] my Owen gun slung across my shoulder . . . [I] pointed [it] at them and I said, 'I beg your pardon?' [and they said,] 'Okay, you Aussies, but you're mad.'

Ferguson's motorbike jaunt produced no useful intelligence, although Parker remembered it entertaining the Americans. Meanwhile, new plans were made to attack all three hills the following day, but only after the enemy positions had been softened up by air strikes, heavy artillery and mortar fire. Once the Middlesex company had captured Sardine, A Company of 3RAR was to move through them and attack Salmon, leaving the Canadians to have another go at Turbot.

By 10 a.m. on 15 April, the Canadians had captured Turbot. Simultaneously, the Middlesex company was close to taking Sardine when it came under fire from its own supporting artillery. With the assault breaking down in confusion, the diggers were handed the task. As Jack Gallaway put it, 'Brigadier Burke, who was forward with Bruce Ferguson to observe the attack, told [the Middlesex] to get out of the way and let the Australians do the job.' In O'Dowd's version, Burke said, 'Drop-kick will do it'—a phrase that immediately grabbed his attention, as 'drop-kick' was how the brigadier often referred to 3RAR, and the nearest company was A Company.

Captain Reg Saunders' stint as acting commander of A Company was over due to O'Dowd's unexpected return from hospital in Japan.*

---

*   Saunders was later given command of C Company. An AIF veteran who had seen plenty of action during the last war, Saunders was the first Indigenous man to be commissioned in the Australian Army. As a company commander in Korea, he raised eyebrows among American soldiers. Ron Perkins recalled being with a group of diggers when an American officer asked, 'You have got a black officer?' The Australians said, 'Yes.' 'Who is he in command of? The whole company? You mean he's got white men under him?' 'Of course he has,' the diggers told him. 'He's a bloody good officer, you'd never fault him anywhere. He almost walks on water.'

O'Dowd arrived just in time to lead the attack on Sardine. Ferguson told him, 'The Brits have been unsuccessful twice and now all eyes are on the Australians. Don't you come back without it.'

The diggers had their work cut out. Sardine and Salmon were the last two hills on a razorback ridge. A Company was on a parallel ridge, separated from Sardine by a thickly wooded gully. From his vantage point on this ridge, O'Dowd had watched the Middlesex fail twice by descending into the valley and attacking uphill against intense machine-gun and rifle fire from the Chinese on the summit. Rather than replicate this head-on approach, O'Dowd decided on a two-pronged assault, with Lieutenant Harold Mulry's 3 Platoon making the initial attack, supported if necessary by Sergeant George Harris's 2 Platoon looping around to attack the Chinese left flank.

The distance between the start line in the gully and the defenders on Sardine was too short to allow a barrage from artillery and heavy mortars, so O'Dowd requested artillery fire just beyond the ridgeline to distract the Chinese while 3 Platoon moved into position. Once the artillery stopped firing, the battalion's medium machine guns would take over.

The Chinese waited for Mulry's forward sections to get halfway up the hill before letting go with machine guns, rifles and a hail of grenades. Luckily for the diggers, the enemy's grenades were far less lethal than their own, but several men were wounded. O'Dowd decided that pressing on with a frontal attack would be too costly and ordered Mulry to hold his position while Harris's 2 Platoon felt its way around the Chinese left flank.

As soon as the Chinese became aware of the flanking manoeuvre, the firing against 3 Platoon began to fall away. That was all the incentive Mulry—a 'fearless war horse', in the words of his company commander—needed. Urged by O'Dowd to have another go, Mulry galloped uphill with his men, prompting the enemy to break and run. O'Dowd let 3 Platoon pursue them for a while before calling them back to consolidate their position on Sardine in preparation for an attack on Salmon the next day by C Company.

Bob Parker and another despatch rider had to abandon their motorbikes in the wooded gully in order to join a party of foot-sloggers delivering hand grenades to the diggers on top of Sardine. It was now that Parker's map-reading skills deserted him. 'All of a sudden there is shrapnel and explosions and things going off around us,' Parker recalled. 'We had taken a wrong turn and got in between the enemy and our mob.'

It was dark and Parker and his mate took shelter in a mud hut. Before long a Chinese patrol went past.

> We heard all of this noise . . . and we looked outside and there were about 20 Chinese coming along. And we didn't have the hand grenades ready, [they] didn't have any detonators in them . . . We had our Owen guns, of course, but there were twenty of them and we just sat there very quietly and away they went and away we went . . . and found where we went wrong.

Eventually the pair found the right track and made contact with the diggers on top of Sardine. They kept their mistake to themselves. '[They asked us,] "What took you so long?" [and we said,] "Oh, we had to slow down for a bit."'

Capturing Sardine cost A Company eight men wounded, mostly by Chinese grenades. According to O'Dowd, most of the injured diggers returned to duty after being patched up by the medics. Except for sporadic enemy mortaring, the company had a quiet night. By the following morning the Chinese troops on the ridge leading to Salmon had vanished, although an enemy patrol was spotted at its base and dispersed with rifle and machine-gun fire. At 8.30 a.m. Reg Saunders' C Company moved off with orders to take Salmon. Brigadier Burke and his staff joined Ferguson on Sardine to watch the attack. As Saunders' men began to advance, the Chinese lost their nerve and fled, enabling C Company to capture Salmon without firing a shot.

To the Americans, the fighting in the fish hills was little more than a clearing-up operation leading to the establishment of a new front line, designated the Utah Line. 'On the east flank of the advance,' Mossman wrote in his official history, 'the British [*sic*] 27th Brigade of the IX Corps had cleared minor 40th Army forces from Paegun Mountain above the headwaters of the Kapyong River to reach line Utah.'

But the Commonwealth troops, and especially the Australians, were justifiably proud of their success. Relieved by the 19th Regiment of the ROK 6th Division, they were trucked all the way back to a reserve area near Kapyong. According to Bartlett:

> There were still some patches of snow on the hills but the wild azaleas were already in bloom and the trees were coming out in fresh leaf . . . A flagpole had been erected in the [3RAR] battalion headquarters area and fatigue parties were laying out stone-edged paths ready for a long stay.

Advance parties from Brigade HQ and the Argyll and Sutherland Highlanders were soon on their way to Hong Kong. The remaining Argylls and the Middlesex battalion were expected to be gone by the end of the month. For the first time since January, the diggers had their own cooks with them. An entry in the war diary for 17 April 1951 showed the battalion looking forward to some decent rest, with beer and movies laid on and three hot meals a day instead of American C rations. The fighting seemed far away at last.

22

WHY YOU FIGHT SO BRAVELY?

From around 9 April, as Eighth Army forces closed in on the Kansas and Utah lines, rolling clouds of smoke began appearing ahead of the UN troops. An entry in the diggers' war diary for 15 April noted that visibility that day was poor due to smoke from surrounding 'bush fires'. By the middle of April, clouds of smoke nearly twenty kilometres deep were drifting over the I, IX and X Corps fronts. Air reconnaissance confirmed that groups of as many as 500 enemy troops were setting fire to grassland and scrub, while some observers reported the use of smoke generators. Fires that had been put out by the rain were rekindled. Visibility was further reduced when moist sea air settled over the battlefront, turning the smoke into smog.

The obvious purpose of the smoke was to hide enemy troop movements, but the only evidence of PRC troops near the front line was a handful of captured prisoners. American commanders, however, suspected that the Chinese were regrouping in preparation for a new offensive. A 'survey of all sources' by Eighth Army intelligence, cited by Mossman, concluded that the Chinese were planning to attack sometime between 20 April and 1 May, although daily intelligence summaries continued to describe the enemy as maintaining a 'defensive' attitude.

In the absence of clear evidence of an enemy offensive, Lieutenant General James Van Fleet—who had succeeded Ridgway as commander of the Eighth Army*—decided to push ahead with the second phase of Operation Dauntless, a 'bite and hold' operation that would see I and IX Corps advance towards the Wyoming Line.

Van Fleet launched his offensive on 21 April. By the end of the day, two IX Corps divisions, the ROK 6th Division and the US 1st Marine Division, had advanced between five and ten kilometres beyond the Kansas Line against virtually no opposition. In the I Corps zone further west, the US 24th Division held its position to allow the ROK 6th Division to move alongside. Neither corps uncovered any evidence that the enemy was preparing to attack. On the evening of 21 April, the I Corps commander, General Milburn, advised Van Fleet that the 'enemy attitude remains defensive'.

That night, the head of Eighth Army intelligence, Colonel James Tarkenton, was still unable to give Van Fleet a concrete prediction of when the impending enemy offensive would begin. But, as Tarkenton had warned earlier, lack of clear evidence of an enemy attack was no guarantee that an attack was not coming. The Chinese had already proved themselves masters of concealment, hiding whole armies almost to the moment they moved into position before an attack.

Signs of an imminent Chinese attack were growing. Overnight patrols by I Corps reported signs of a stronger than expected Chinese presence near the Imjin River. On 22 April, both IX Corps divisions continued to advance against minimal opposition but enemy resistance in the I Corps zone was building. A Chinese prisoner captured by the marines during the afternoon told interrogators that the communists were planning to attack that day. The official

---

*   Van Fleet arrived in Korea at 12.30 p.m. on 14 April. Ridgway left for Tokyo at 7 p.m. the same day to replace MacArthur as supreme commander.

history noted that a Chinese artillery officer taken prisoner by the Turkish Brigade told his captors that his division's guns were positioned to support an attack due to start after dark.*

At first light on 22 April, air reconnaissance revealed heavy concentrations of communist troops in forward areas north of I and IX Corps. Intelligence would identify these as belonging to the 60th Infantry Division of the newly arrived 20th Group Army. While the Chinese were gathering evenly across the I Corps front, in the IX Corps zone it was clear that enemy formations were making for the notoriously flaky ROK 6th Division.

Artillery and air strikes inflicted casualties on the Chinese without disrupting their military preparations. At 7 p.m. the commander of 24th Division, General Blackshear Bryan, advised I Corps headquarters that he expected the enemy to attack his division in about two hours—a prediction that, in Mossman's words, 'proved correct almost to the exact minute'. By then the ROK 6th Division was in headlong retreat.

Attacking without artillery support, Chinese forces struck the South Koreans at 8 p.m., immediately cracking open the division's flanks and pouring through huge gaps in its defences. Against American advice, the Korean commander had placed his reserves directly behind his forward units, with the result that both came under almost simultaneous attack. In the initial assault, Chinese forces drove through a central gap, some looping behind the ROK 2nd and 19th Regiments, while others went after the 7th Regiment, which was supposedly in reserve. The two forward regiments quickly disintegrated, abandoning weapons and vehicles as they fled. Before long the 7th Regiment joined the exodus.

---

* It was a feature of the Korean War that while the average American or Australian infantryman knew little or nothing about his side's strategic plans, Chinese soldiers were often remarkably well informed about forthcoming operations and willing to share this information with their captors. Despite the shortage of competent linguists in US intelligence, POWs often proved the best source of information.

With terrified ROK infantry swarming in all directions, the fire support units were in danger of being overrun. All communications with the ROK regiments had been lost and the Chinese were close enough for the gunners of the NZ 16th Field Regiment to hear small-arms fire in front of one of their batteries. At 4 a.m. the decision was taken to save the valuable guns. With South Korean soldiers streaming past them, the New Zealanders began to pull out. American artillery units caught up in the Korean retreat were forced to abandon most of their weapons; only the New Zealanders managed to withdraw with their guns and equipment intact.

By dawn on 23 April, the remnants of the three shattered ROK regiments were five kilometres south of the Kansas Line, having retreated fifteen kilometres during the night. In the process they had left the flanks of the US 24th Division and 1st Marine Division invitingly open to the Chinese. At 6.10 a.m. the New Zealanders informed 27th Brigade headquarters, with heroic understatement, that the situation was 'obscure and did not look too good'. According to Jack Gallaway, news of the communist offensive 'did not cause any great concern' to the diggers, who were safely in reserve and looking forward to celebrating Anzac Day with the New Zealanders and the Turkish Brigade.[*]

With the forward positions of both the I and IX Corps now at risk of encirclement, Van Fleet gave orders for defensive positions to be established in depth along the Kansas Line. This meant pushing the South Koreans—around 2500 men—north to the Kansas Line to join up with the withdrawn 1st Marine Division. The 27th Brigade was warned by IX Corps headquarters that it might be required to take up a blocking position in the Kapyong Valley if the Chinese broke through the South Koreans. According to historian

---

[*]   Gallaway had been injured in a vehicle accident during the withdrawal from Seoul. Although a lively witness to the battalion's first months in Korea, he had no personal experience of the Battle of Kapyong.

Michael Kelly, Brigadier Burke had only learnt of the offensive 90 minutes earlier when he turned on his wireless while shaving. Burke sent his battalion and company commanders out at once to recce the surrounding area.

The capture of Seoul was the primary goal of the Chinese spring offensive, General Peng having allegedly promised the city to Mao Zedong as a May Day gift. The way to the South Korean capital was through the Kapyong Valley, a historic invasion route to the city and one that had been used by the Chinese themselves in December.

On the morning of 23 April, the 27th Brigade was virtually all that stood between more than 300,000 communist soldiers and their objective. According to Gallaway, '[N]o one considered this situation unusual. The reconnaissance of possible defensive positions and the preparation of them for future occupation was routine when in reserve.'* The coming hours, however, would be far from routine.

The area to be defended was six kilometres north of the town of Kapyong, at the junction of the Kapyong River and a stream fed by valleys to the north and north-east. The junction was guarded on the east by Hill 504 and on the west by the taller Hill 677. To the north-west stood the impressive 800-metre-high Sudok San. O'Neill's official history described these three hills as a 'naturally strong position well suited to blocking a major advance'.

Burke's problem was that he did not have enough troops to form a mutually supporting defensive line. The front line between Hill 504 and Sudok San, which faced the oncoming Chinese, was

---

* O'Neill cited American intelligence reports of 337,000 communist troops involved in the main thrust for Seoul and 149,000 in the central sector, with another 214,000 in reserve—a total of more than 700,000 men. Facing them were 418,500 UN troops, including 152,000 South Koreans, 245,000 Americans, 11,500 Commonwealth soldiers and 10,000 from other contributing nations.

nearly seven kilometres wide. Instead of a continuous line, Burke would have to make do with putting a battalion on each of the key features. With the Argylls having already left for Hong Kong, Burke assigned 3RAR to defend Hill 504, the Princess Pats to Hill 677, and the Middlesex Regiment, who were still expecting to be relieved, to Sudok San.

Adding to Burke's problems was an order from IX Corps HQ to put a blocking force in the valley to prevent the South Korean withdrawal from becoming a rout. Burke told Ferguson to position his headquarters on the road nearly two kilometres behind the rifle companies, opposite a few deserted houses that had once been a small village. For protection, Ferguson held on to a section of medium machine guns, two anti-tank guns, the mortar platoon and the Assault Pioneers. Ferguson explained later that the siting of his HQ was intended as 'a morale booster for the South Koreans who would be encouraged to stop, stand and fight'.* But the decision made life harder for Ferguson, who would soon find himself fighting two battles, one for Hill 504 and the other for his own battalion headquarters.

At 10 a.m. Burke lost another of his battalions. The previous night's chaotic retreat had cost the ROK 6th Division all its artillery, so the New Zealanders were ordered further up the Kapyong Valley to provide fire support. Fearing another debacle, Burke sent the Middlesex battalion forward to protect the Kiwi gunners. This meant Sudok San would be undefended. Worse, it left 3RAR's left flank exposed and created a three-kilometre gap between the Australians and the Canadians.

---

* As acting platoon commander, Sergeant Fred From rounded up a large number of fleeing Korean troops and persuaded them to dig in and help defend the battalion HQ. He described his recruitment method to Jack Gallaway: 'His Korean interpreter challenged every soldier who approached the perimeter. Those who answered in Korean were invited to join the Australians, those who did not were shot.'

By early afternoon the situation had deteriorated further. Ordering the ROK 6th Division forward was one thing; getting the troops to move was another. As the prospect of the Koreans advancing to the Kansas Line became ever more remote, IX Corps headquarters ordered the 27th Brigade to occupy the blocking positions proposed by Burke that morning.

A handful of American tank and artillery units—two companies of the US 2nd Chemical Mortar Battalion, a field battery of 105-millimetre howitzers and a company of Sherman tanks from the US 72nd Tank Battalion—gave the brigade extra firepower.

The New Zealand gunners and the Middlesex battalion were now twelve kilometres further up the valley, close enough to fire on the Chinese infantry. But by 6 p.m. the ROK 6th Division's right flank had folded. With Korean troops flooding back, along with their US Army advisers, the Kiwis' commanding officer decided it was time to go. At 8 p.m. the artillery stopped firing and the regiment, with infantry clinging onto its guns and vehicles, set off down a road crowded with fleeing ROK soldiers and civilian refugees. An hour later Burke had his artillery and his third battalion back.

Ferguson now got to work organising 3RAR. He put Captain Norm Gravener's D Company on the summit of Hill 504, which offered excellent fields of fire and an unobstructed view across the Kapyong Valley, and stationed A and B Companies astride the north–south road, O'Dowd's A Company on a spur dominating the road from the east and Darcy Laughlin's B Company on a separate ridge dominating it from the west. B Company's task was to secure the valley and hold the left flank until the Middlesex battalion moved into position on its left. Reg Saunders' C Company, in reserve, would occupy another spur 300 metres behind A Company, with instructions to reinforce Laughlin, if necessary, and to counterattack if the enemy overran either A Company's or B Company's position.

Deployed at various locations on the valley floor were the fifteen Sherman tanks of the US 72nd Tank Battalion, commanded by First Lieutenant Kenneth Koch. Each tank was armed with a 76-millimetre cannon, one .50-calibre and two .30-calibre machine guns. A written record of Ferguson's orders suggested that the American tanks were 'under command' of Captain Laughlin and Major O'Dowd, but according to Bob Breen the pair never had operational control of the tanks, which were commanded through-out by Koch. It would be more accurate to say that Koch's tanks and Ferguson's rifle companies were fighting simultaneous battles, the former on the valley floor and the latter on the hills and ridges overlooking the road, each aimed at stopping the Chinese from driving through the Kapyong Valley towards Seoul.

At around 3 p.m. on 23 April the rifle companies began moving into position. The official history described Hill 504 as being 'crowned by a steep-sided, narrow, U-shaped ridge, the two arms of which lead down via spurs running to the north-west'. The men of D Company faced a 'long and difficult climb to the summit, carrying their weapons, ammunition, food and communications equipment'.

Holding the summit of Hill 504 was crucial; losing it would enable the Chinese to fire down on the two companies dug in on its western slope and jeopardise the Australians' ability to hold the road. But putting D Company on the summit meant accepting a 400-metre gap between it and A Company on the more westerly of the two spurs. As O'Dowd saw it, he could either spread his men thinly across his allocated area or occupy a critical point in strength. Since the priority was to deny the enemy the use of the road, he chose a spot at the lower end of Hill 504. From their positions on the slope facing the road, O'Dowd's platoons could support each other against attacks from the north and fire across the valley floor against enemy troops threatening B Company, but they were of little use to Gravener's men on the summit.

While the ground occupied by B Company was suitable for digging, other areas were too rocky. Joe Vezgoff was with C Company, lower down the ridge that led to the summit of Hill 504. 'It was hard, rocky ground . . . with scrubby trees . . . no soil,' Vezgoff recalled. Some men were able to squeeze into crevices or between rock formations and form defensive positions. O'Dowd's men had to make do with piling loose rocks around them for protection from enemy fire. The low heather scrub covering the slope was tinder-dry from the harsh Korean winter.

According to Bob Breen's detailed analysis of the battle, there was 'no mood of urgency among the Diggers or feeling of impending danger' as they took up their positions. The information they had received from their commanders was that they should 'settle in for a quiet night' before either developing defensive positions where they were or moving forward. They had done this many times before without firing a shot.

Private John Beresford recalled being told, 'There's nothing to worry about. We'll be moving first thing in the morning so just dig your pit and have tea and that'll be it.'

O'Dowd remembered the situation being 'a bit unreal':

There was a division of infantry [the ROK 6th Division] in front of us and the Divisional Headquarters was between us and Battalion Headquarters. In infantry, if you can see Divisional Headquarters you have got to be on leave. It was rather hard to take seriously that we would have to fight that night.

The haphazard organisation of battalion HQ, and in particular the failure to dig defensive positions, suggested that Ferguson himself was not expecting an enemy attack.

Around midafternoon, the first groups of retreating South Korean troops began passing the Commonwealth positions. As the afternoon wore on the trickle became a deluge. By the time darkness fell, the road was crowded with ROK soldiers, refugees and a growing number of Chinese infiltrators, whose aim was to isolate Laughlin's B Company from the three companies across the road on Hill 504 before attacking the battalion HQ area.

The sight of an ROK division in full retreat, casting off brand-new American weapons, clothing and equipment as it went, was nothing new to the Australians: they had seen the ROK 1st Division do the same thing on New Year's Day. Following a well-practised routine, honed during their months in Korea, the diggers checked their weapons, laid out spare ammunition and grenades, and waited.

Aware that Chinese soldiers would be hiding among the refugees, O'Dowd asked for permission to fire his machine guns over the heads of the human tide but Ferguson refused, on the grounds that he did not want to injure civilians. As predicted, Chinese infiltrators used the cover of darkness to get behind the forward companies. 'We were now isolated,' O'Dowd recalled, 'and an attack was only a matter of how long it would take for the Chinese to find us in the dark and get organised.'

Across the road, the men of B Company finished their digging and had a hot meal just before last light. In his report of the battle, Captain Laughlin noted that 'normal traffic was proceeding up and down the road' and there was 'no indication . . . that the situation would seriously deteriorate within a few hours'.

Due to the distance their units had to cover to get into position, the observers from the Kiwi artillery regiment and the heavy mortar battalion did not reach B Company's position until after dark—too late to accurately register their weapons. If B Company got into trouble during the night, it would have to manage without direct fire support.

The darkness did not last. Before long, a full moon rose in the sky, suffusing the landscape with white light. 'The evening was cool and fine,' Laughlin wrote in his report of the battle, 'with visibility good for hundreds of yards.'

Small parties of South Koreans had been retreating along the road since 7 p.m., but by 9 p.m. Laughlin knew that things were rapidly deteriorating. 'Trucks packed with ROK soldiery were coming down the road at reckless speeds running down foot soldiers in their efforts to get rearwards,' he wrote in his report. 'Soldiers were no longer walking to the rear but jogging along and displaying all signs of complete panic.'

At around 9.30 p.m. the Chinese launched their first attack against the American tanks on the valley floor: small groups of soldiers, initially mistaken as friendly, tried to close with the tanks. It was only when they began firing that they were recognised as enemy. The attack, probably at platoon or company strength, targeted five tanks in front of Laughlin's B Company.

The five Shermans were sited several hundred metres forward of the nearest infantry support, at a ford over the Kapyong River. It was lucky for the Americans that the full moon made it difficult for PRC fighters to approach undetected, although tank commanders risked being shot in the head as they directed fire from open hatches. Despite the lack of infantry protection, the Shermans in front of B Company beat off their attackers before withdrawing to pre-arranged positions forward of B Company.

As soon as the tanks began to withdraw, the Kiwi gunners were ordered to put fire on the road ahead of the tanks. At the same time, Laughlin called for the heavy mortars to lay down a barrage on the valley floor roughly 500 metres ahead of the line between A Company and B Company. The difficulty of ranging the guns and mortars in the dark meant it was some time before the barrage was effective.

Except for those serving B Company, on the west side of the road, and the anti-tank platoon, all the telephone lines from Ferguson's HQ crossed the road and were soon cut by vehicles fleeing the

Chinese. Lines were no sooner repaired than they were torn up by American tanks moving along the valley, making it impossible for Ferguson to speak directly with his units on the east side of the road. He was now cut off from all his rifle company commanders except Laughlin.*

By now heavy fighting had broken out in the battalion head-quarters area. It began just before 10 p.m., with Chinese soldiers attacking the assault pioneers and the mortar and anti-tank platoon positions. According to an account written by Major Jack Gerke, who commanded Headquarters Company during the battle:

> a wave of Chinese troops surged across the ford, attacking the platoon of tanks, the regimental police and signallers defending the low ground near the road and ford . . . Chinese attacking the LMG section and pioneers near the cemetery were forcing them back under weight of numbers . . . In the dark the CCF had infiltrated through and around BHQ and established a road block, stopping all movement to the rear.**

---

* A VHF wireless set was available but these worked best when both parties were within line of sight. Ferguson's decision to site his personal caravan in a gully, with a steep ridge between him and the forward companies, made using the wireless, in Gallaway's words, a 'chancy proposition'. According to Gerke, damage to wireless sets meant that the battalion wireless network did not work and communication was only possible through the artillery net. This, however, was 'very poor', and the limited distribution of sets made it impossible for orders to be passed to individual company commanders. It was not until seven o'clock the following morning that effective communication was established.

** According to a covering note dated 3 July 1952 and signed by Captain L. G. Clark of Australian Army Headquarters in Melbourne, this was an 'authentic account' of the Battle of Kapyong 'prepared under the supervision of Maj. J Gerke, DSO, who interviewed as many of the officers and NCOs from the various companies as was possible'. Gerke's account, the note said, was 'as accurate as it is possible to obtain'. Bob Breen cautioned, however, that Gerke was 'a fighter, not a writer', and 'did not have the time or the scholastic training to produce a definitive account' of the battle. Significantly, Gerke was unable to speak to key veterans of Kapyong, including O'Dowd, Gravener, Laughlin and Saunders, when researching his account.

Lieutenant Cecil 'Ces' Evans, in command of the machine-gun platoon, called for tanks to fire on the roadblock and nearby houses; after the tanks had finished firing, 40 Chinese dead were counted in a single house.

As each Chinese machine gun was knocked out of action, another opened up. With all batteries on the move, Ferguson was unable to call up artillery support. Soon after midnight, he lost the US 2nd Chemical Mortar Battalion, which had been deployed around 500 metres south of battalion headquarters. Shaken by the attack on Ferguson's HQ and afraid of being trapped by Chinese troops moving south, the Americans had taken to their heels.

Puzzled by the sound of silence where there had once been heavy mortar fire, Gerke sent the company sergeant major and a driver to investigate. According to the official history, 'they reported that the area was deserted, although some of the mortars were still in position on the ground and the company's vehicles were packed ready for movement'. The Americans had apparently fled, abandoning most of their equipment, and did not stop running until they found refuge around sixteen kilometres to the east. All 50 of the battalion's vehicles would be recovered undamaged from the paddy fields the day after the battle.

At about 10.30 p.m. the Chinese launched a second and much more determined attack against the tanks in front of B Company. Once again, tank commanders had to direct fire from open hatches, with their heads and upper bodies exposed to sniper fire. Without proper infantry protection, the Shermans were vulnerable to Chinese soldiers clambering over them and dropping grenades or satchel charges through the open hatch. Within minutes the commander of each tank was hit by rifle fire; the platoon leader was shot between the eyes and killed. The only way to get the Chinese infantry off the tanks was for the tanks to close their hatches and hose each other with machine-gun fire.

The Shermans revved up their engines and began pulling out, either to join the battle at battalion HQ or to take their wounded to the rear. Breen reported that B Company's second-in-command, Lieutenant Jim Young, sprinted down the slope without a weapon and persuaded one tank crew to stay a bit longer, only to find himself stumbling into a group of enemy soldiers, who, luckily for Young, were more interested in attacking the tank than they were in killing him.

In the end, the tanks in front of B Company withdrew. 'The Yanks called out to us and told us they were leaving,' Corporal Clem Kealy told Gallaway. 'They offered to take us out with them but there were Chinese between us and them so we stayed where we were.'

Another platoon of American tanks now arrived, taking over from the platoon that had just left. Protected by A Company and B Company riflemen on the ridges, Lieutenant Wilfred Miller's Shermans fired steadily on the columns of Chinese troops advancing down the road.

Probing attacks by enemy infiltrators—including an attack on Laughlin's headquarters—were repelled.

Kealy commanded the outpost section on the highest point of the feature, a small knoll at the northern end. At 11 p.m. he reported seeing four or five groups of enemy soldiers up to 50 strong to his left and right moving down the road to the company's main position. Artillery fire succeeded in scattering some groups. After Kealy reported that his section was under attack by 30 enemy, Laughlin ordered him to break contact and withdraw immediately to the main position.

A concerted assault on B Company's position now appeared inevitable. Just before 1 a.m. Lieutenant Len Montgomerie's 4 Platoon reported a group of about 40 enemy soldiers advancing up the hill towards their position. Montgomerie's men succeeded in driving off the Chinese with mortar, rifle and machine-gun fire. The encounter lasted less than an hour and resulted in heavy losses for the enemy. The moonlight was again a priceless asset to the Australians, who used it to pick out targets as far away as 100 metres.

While Laughlin's men were fighting off their attackers, the Chinese made their first move against A Company on the east side of the road. Out on a limb in a forward listening post, Lance Corporal Pat Knowles and Private Tim Coffey of 1 Platoon were feeling jumpy. 'About 2030 hrs we heard a collection of voices below our positions,' Knowles wrote later.

> This I promptly reported to 1 Platoon headquarters and returned to the listening post. At 2100 hrs the voices started up again accompanied by the cocking of weapons, this I promptly reported to 1 Platoon headquarters. I then made sure everyone in 1 Platoon was aware what was going on, then returned to my post. At 2130 hrs a company runner, Pte Roy Holloway, came down to our position and said to me, 'Pat, I have a message for you from O'Dowd. Now there is nothing personal in this as O'Dowd gave it me.' I said, 'OK, let's have it' to which Roy replied, 'Shut up and stop panicking, there is no-one down there.'

But O'Dowd was wrong. Under cover of darkness, the Chinese were preparing to attack. As O'Dowd described it later, the initial contacts came as a 'series of enemy probing patrols bumping into our forward weapon pits at various points, searching for soft spots' and the diggers 'shooting them back into the dark'.

These encounters were clearly the prelude for a full-scale attack aimed at evicting A Company and B Company from the high ground on both sides of the road. Failure to achieve this before daylight would leave the Chinese troops on the valley floor exposed not only to a deadly barrage by US tanks and artillery, Australian mortars and Kiwi gunners, but also to bomb, rocket and napalm attack from the air.

The assault on A Company followed the usual pattern: a flurry of bugles and whistles as commanders assembled and organised their men, followed by silence as the Chinese soldiers crept up the hill in their noiseless rubber shoes; the clatter of enemy grenades hitting the rocky ground before exploding, and finally the infantry assault as Chinese soldiers rose up in the moonlight, burp guns blazing. O'Dowd wrote later:

> Our effective killing range was to about ten metres, and our killing time two to three seconds—the time it took for their heads and shoulders to appear above the edge of the ridge and for them to run to the forward pits. As soon as shapes appeared out of the gloom our soldiers would produce as much rapid fire as each individual weapon was capable [of].

A single-shot rifle was not much use in close-range fighting like this, and the diggers' preferred weapon was the Australian-made Owen submachine gun. Though sturdy and reliable, the Owen fired low-velocity 9-millimetre bullets that did not always penetrate the thickly padded uniforms worn by the Chinese.

'Each time they knocked them back, the Chinese just disappeared for a while,' Sergeant George Harris recalled. 'The bugles would start again and 1 Platoon would cop it again. In between assaults the wounded and dead were brought back and fit men were repositioned by section commanders into forward positions . . . the whole position was in danger of being overrun.'

After each attack the Australian casualties were removed to the reverse slope, where the medic, Corporal Nobby Clark, and his stretcher-bearers did what they could for the wounded, while fit men were drafted in to occupy the vacant weapon pits.

According to O'Dowd's account, the Chinese attacked across the whole front of the company's position, with Lieutenant Fred Gardner's 1 Platoon, nearest the road, taking the worst of it early on. Casualties did not concern the Chinese, who surged forward over the bodies of their own dead and wounded. But Gardner was losing men with each attack. By midnight, all three of 1 Platoon's Bren gunners had been hit and only thirteen out of the original 30 men were capable of fighting on. With the platoon at risk of being overrun, O'Dowd gave permission for Gardner and the other survivors to withdraw. The Chinese immediately occupied 1 Platoon's former position and held it for the rest of the night.

'About 0230 hrs a Chinese started blowing his whistle, giving three bursts each time, he was obviously calling for reinforcements,' Pat Knowles recalled.

> After about half an hour of this Major O'Dowd sang out, 'For Christ's sake, get that bastard.' Well, we couldn't see a bloody thing, we couldn't hear a movement and the tension was getting a bit ripe, we could hear the moaning from the wounded and were expecting another attack at any moment. So remembering what I had been taught in my previous army service as an armourer i.e. the average person fires high at night, I took aim at the sound, dropped my front sight about one inch and fired. No more whistle blasts for the rest of the night.

A steady mortar barrage of both high explosive and incendiary bombs continued until daylight, the latter setting fire to the dry heather. The combination of thick smoke, burning heather and exploding ammunition caused further misery for the wounded lying out in the open.

The sound of heavy fighting to the rear told Laughlin that groups of enemy soldiers were still going around his flanks. The next attack against his own position came at 3.30 a.m., with a feint against 5 Platoon coinciding with an assault on 6 Platoon by a force of about 60 Chinese striking from three sides. Despite the presence of two Sherman tanks between 5 Platoon and 6 Platoon, the Chinese succeeded in penetrating the company's perimeter and attacking the company headquarters with rifle and machine-gun fire. With the help of the tanks, 6 Platoon counterattacked and drove off the PRC soldiers, who lost as many as half their strength killed before withdrawing.

At 4.45 p.m. the Chinese launched their final assault against B Company. A force of between 50 and 70 enemy soldiers hit the company's right flank, but this time the Chinese were unable to breach the perimeter. B Company suffered no casualties in repelling the attacks.

As the sun came up, Laughlin was able to see Chinese troops in the valley between B Company and the eastern ridge occupied by A Company and C Company. The Chinese had little cover and were forced to withdraw northwards, harassed all the way by tank, artillery and machine-gun fire. The valley floor made an 'excellent killing ground', Laughlin wrote in his battle report. Hundreds of PRC soldiers were killed or wounded.

On the eastern side of the road, A Company was having a much tougher time of it. The fighting at battalion headquarters had made it impossible for Ferguson to direct the battle, so it fell to O'Dowd, as senior company commander on the spot, to coordinate the efforts of the other three rifle companies.

The position of A Company on the slope was still precarious. Shortage of manpower meant that O'Dowd had to leave an undefended stretch of rising ground between 2 Platoon and 3 Platoon. If the Chinese discovered the gap, they could potentially tear the company in two. Just before dawn, they found the gap and put a machine gun in there. Pat Knowles was crouching in a weapon pit with three others, just in front of 2 Platoon, when the Chinese machine-gunner opened up.

[He] gave us hell for about 20 minutes. He obviously had a good idea where we were but probably couldn't see us, but he raked our little area with all the spite he could muster . . . we were going to get nowhere lying where we were, so I agreed to go back to company headquarters for instructions. I waited till 'Charlie' changed magazines and took off . . . I explained what was happening [and] Lt Gardner directed us to pull back . . . I then made my way back to my old position, waited for 'Charlie' to change magazines and dived back to rejoin my three companions . . . we waited for 'Charlie' to change magazines and dived back down the hill again. 3 Platoon then sent a patrol . . . to flush out the machine gunner, who was pretty well concealed in a hole in a gully. I looked up my mate Tim Coffey to find he had been badly wounded.

Another digger, Private Bill Jillett, was killed in the attack on the Chinese machine-gun nest, one of 50 casualties suffered by A Company that night.

As dawn broke, the enemy was still in possession of 1 Platoon's old position, but that was about to change. The job of taking it back was given to 3 Platoon and they went about it with gusto. To compensate for their lack of artillery support, and to mitigate the use of artillery by the enemy, the Chinese preferred to fight at night. Daylight drastically altered the terms of the battle: the Chinese, so dangerous in the dark, now found themselves caught in the open, scrambling for cover among loose rocks and clumps of heather. The Australians showed no mercy. According to Sergeant George Harris, the Chinese 'turned and ran away. They didn't feel like fighting us any more. We were just getting them in the back as they ran away . . . they were hiding in thickets or creek beds or down towards the river . . . [We were] picking them off everywhere.'*

Anxious to preserve ammunition when resupply was far from guaranteed, O'Dowd eventually called his men off.

Captured enemy positions were often booby-trapped but on this occasion something else awaited the attackers: a wounded digger who had been inadvertently left behind when 1 Platoon pulled out during the night. Realising that the Australians were preparing to retake the position, the Chinese moved the injured man into a weapon pit, where he would be safe from the flying bullets. 'He was recovered by 3 Platoon,' O'Dowd wrote later, 'and we were indebted to the enemy for his life.'

As well as recovering a wounded mate, A Company had regained all the ground it had lost during the night, but there were not enough fit men to occupy it. 'It was my 24th birthday on the 24th of April, which was the second day of Kapyong, and I didn't think I would see another one,' Perkins recalled.

Gardner told Pat Knowles to go through the dead and wounded diggers and strip them of their ammo, a job Knowles said he 'did not relish'. As he did the rounds of the hill, Knowles was 'amazed at the drag marks, blood, cotton wool and bandages where the Chinese had dragged their dead and wounded away during the night'.** When

---

* Such easy killing did not sit well with some diggers. Stan Connelly said he felt no compunction about shooting an attacking enemy, but 'I never have and I never would shoot them in the back as they ran away . . . It seemed to me to be not fair. Not fair play . . . I know sometimes some of the old diggers will say they enjoyed a turkey shoot or some such thing but I think that's just bombast. Hyperbole . . . I don't think it happened very often and certainly I didn't personally experience it.'

** If the Chinese were unable to carry away their dead, they usually tried to hide them to conceal the scale of their losses. According to John Beresford, the diggers 'rarely found a dead body'. At Kapyong, Beresford recalled coming under enemy mortar attack while he was helping some wounded diggers. An Australian officer suggested getting the wounded men to safety inside a Chinese dugout. When Beresford went to investigate, he found a large bunker opening off the dugout. The floor was covered with rice straw, but when Beresford moved one of the bales he discovered as many as 50 dead Chinese soldiers hidden under the straw.

Gardner did a body count he found he had just nine men left from the previous night's strength of nearly 30. Including the ammunition taken from casualties, each man had about fifteen rounds.

With PRC troops infiltrating behind his position, O'Dowd was unable to evacuate his casualties. The medics could only treat wounded men with what they carried in their bags. '[T]hey had nothing to relieve pain, no morphia, no effective means for averting shock except for a few blankets and sleeping bags,' O'Dowd recalled. Most of the wounded had to lie all night on the frozen hillside without shelter. Dressings for wounds ran out and there was no water. While lying there, some of the injured men were burnt by fires started by Chinese incendiary rounds. O'Dowd was not alone in believing that if it had been possible to keep the wounded warm and treat them for the shock and pain, some who died might have survived.

It was now several hours since O'Dowd had been able to speak to his commanding officer, Ferguson, who had radioed a pessimistic situation report to Brigadier Burke at 1.40 a.m. from the headquarters of the Middlesex battalion, several kilometres south of his own HQ. The fight at battalion HQ had been intense, with every man in the machine-gun section either killed or wounded and the pioneers suffering numerous casualties. Sergeant Edwin Milwood of the anti-tank platoon was fatally wounded, and two signallers trying to reconnect the telephone line to A Company were killed.

Exactly what Ferguson was doing during the attack on his headquarters is unclear; he might have been using his vehicle to shuttle between his HQ and the more secure Middlesex HQ. At around 4 a.m. Ferguson asked Burke to send a company of Middlesex soldiers to clear the route to his HQ, presumably for the purposes of resupply and the evacuation of casualties, and to help defend the HQ area.

The Middlesex soldiers accomplished the first task, dislodging the Chinese from positions overlooking the road, before being forced to withdraw by enemy fire coming from high ground further west. By 5 a.m., according to Gerke's account, the Chinese had driven the pioneers and machine-gunners from their position near the cemetery. With the HQ area vulnerable to enemy firing down, Ferguson made the decision to withdraw his command post as soon as it was light. As the Chinese occupied high ground on both sides of the road, dominating movement on the road and in the valley, the Australians had to seek whatever cover they could find in the riverbed and in broken ground nearby. During the withdrawal, Ferguson's own vehicle had a front wheel blown off, but by 9 a.m. he had established his new headquarters forward of the Middlesex position, overlooking the western end of the valley, four kilometres to the rear.

Not everyone made it. Ferguson's despatch rider, Private Bob Parker, ended up being taken prisoner. Parker was hit in the hip and thrown into a roadside ditch after coming under fire from three enemy machine guns. Unable to run, he crawled through the mud, firing his Owen submachine gun until he ran out of bullets. He recalled the incident half a century later:

I said, 'Oh, shit!' I pushed the Owen gun into the dirt and covered it up, then . . . I stood up and I put my hands out and looked at them, and they just come charging at me. The chap in front was the squad leader and he had an American BAR [Browning automatic rifle], and he was firing that from the hip and all the others were firing burp guns, and . . . I said, 'Oh, hell!' You know, there could not have been a more scared person around the place. Anyway, they all raced over to me and patted me on the back . . . They said, 'Why you fight so bravely?' [I thought] they can't be meaning me, they must mean the battalion . . . They were all looking at me . . . I still had a slouch hat on because I used to wear a slouch hat when I was riding the motorbike. The chin strap was round my neck and the hat was on my back, hanging down the back here, and they were all looking at it, and I think that's probably what saved my life because they wanted to get an Aussie.

Sources differ on whether Ferguson's headquarters was ever actually 'overrun' by the Chinese, but Laughlin evidently believed it since he used the word in his battle report, stating that B Company was then ordered to withdraw across the road, through Reg Saunders' C Company, and to take up a position between C Company and D Company, completing a battalion perimeter on the high ground east of the road. According to Laughlin's battle report, tanks would cover the withdrawal until the diggers made contact with friendly troops.

Before pulling out, Laughlin ordered a count of enemy dead: 173 bodies were found around the company perimeter and in the valley. Lieutenant Koch boasted that his tanks had killed 500. Many more enemy dead lay in front of A Company. A clearing patrol led by the company sergeant major rounded up 39 Chinese prisoners, who would now have to be brought along.

During the night, the Chinese commanders had failed in their efforts to push A Company off the ridge, but they realised that if D Company could be dislodged from the summit of Hill 504, O'Dowd's depleted troops would be unable to hold. This time they would not wait for darkness.

23

WAVES OF CHINESE

The first attempt to infiltrate D Company's position happened around 4 a.m. on 24 April, when six Chinese soldiers reached the company perimeter. One was shot and one captured. At 6 a.m. a large enemy force was seen approaching A Company's right flank. According to Gerke's account, the enemy was 'dressed very similarly to our own troops, and equipped in a similar manner, and so was mistaken for some of our own troops and allowed to close in on the platoon's perimeter'. The Chinese troops gathered in front of Lieutenant John Ward's 12 Platoon.

At around 7 a.m. the Chinese launched their first assault. 'Waves of Chinese throwing grenades followed waves of other Chinese firing automatic weapons,' Gerke wrote. 'Each wave was about five seconds apart, only support for this attack coming in the form of mortar fire onto D Company's front.'

D Company's commanding officer, Norm Gravener, told Bob Breen that 12 Platoon was 'hit hard' and had 'seven to eight casualties, which was not too bad considering the strength of the attack'.

The Chinese, Gravener recalled, had a difficult time locating 12 Platoon's position in the trees after they came over the ridge. 'To get to Ward's perimeter, the Chinese had a long, hard climb followed by a 50-metre dash. I was also able to direct artillery fire [from the NZ 16th Field Regiment] onto them as they made their way up the ridges.'

The same pattern of attack was repeated by the Chinese every 30 minutes until 10.30 a.m., each assault beaten off with machine-gun fire and grenades at heavy cost to the enemy. 'After each attack failed the Chinese forces appeared to move back to low ground out of range,' Gerke wrote, 'where they would re-form and after shouted encouragement from those in command, another attack would be launched . . . with the help of cross fire from C Company, terrific casualties were inflicted on the enemy.'

While D Company clung to the summit of Hill 504, B Company abandoned its own position across the valley. The sight of Laughlin's men moving out came as a nasty surprise to O'Dowd. Ferguson was at the Middlesex HQ, several kilometres to the rear and therefore (as O'Dowd put it) 'not in a position to understand' how withdrawing B Company would compromise the battalion's overall position. To O'Dowd it seemed inevitable that as soon as B Company vacated the low ridge overlooking the valley, the Chinese would move in and seize a position that would enable them to fire down on A Company's exposed left flank:

> I got hold of the Commanding Officer [Ferguson] as soon as I could and made the point that B Company must go back. There was no immediate response to this request and predictably it was not long before we were treated to glimpses of the Chinese throwing up dirt as they consolidated their easy gain.

At 9.30 a.m. Ferguson—perhaps at Burke's insistence—ordered Laughlin to reoccupy the position he had just left. Whether it was made by Burke or Ferguson, the decision to move B Company back to its former position was prompted by the news that the US 5th Cavalry Regiment—a force equivalent to a British brigade—would soon be arriving to relieve pressure on 3RAR.

Two of Laughlin's platoons, 6 Platoon and 4 Platoon, had crossed the valley floor and withdrawn safely inside the C Company perimeter on Hill 504. When Laughlin's order came through to turn around and go back, 5 Platoon, commanded by Lieutenant Ken McGregor, was still at the bottom of the feature. Irked at being told to go back over ground his men had already covered, McGregor asked Laughlin, 'How expensive do you want it to be?' Laughlin did not reply.*

Laughlin's battle report noted only that 'small enemy parties' were observed in the company's old position after the withdrawal. Apparently, he believed that if 5 Platoon acted quickly, it could retake the position before the Chinese had time to occupy it in strength.

Between McGregor and the company's former position was a small knoll on the valley floor, nicknamed 'the Honeycomb' by the diggers on account of the network of bunkers and trenches dug by the Chinese earlier in the war. Some enemy soldiers—Laughlin estimated 'perhaps 10 to 15'—had been seen going into one of the old trenches, which would now have to be cleared before B Company

---

*   Ferguson's order for B Company to pull out has been the subject of controversy ever since. By Laughlin's account, the operation, supported by American tanks, was conducted 'in good order', the only casualty being one soldier shot in the arm as the company prepared to move out. Breen considered that Ferguson's decision to withdraw B Company from its commanding position across the road 'made no sense at all', although it must have been made with the concurrence of his brigade commander. Breen conceded that Brigadier Burke 'must have assessed that the Australians were surrounded and cut off' and 'would probably have agreed with Ferguson if he had suggested withdrawing B Company in preparation for a withdrawal of the remainder of the forward companies'. Neither Burke nor Ferguson left a record of why or when the decision to withdraw B Company was made.

could launch its attack on the ridge above. Stan Connelly was part of the section ordered to attack the Honeycomb.

> We charged and we began to get shot down. I remember my good friend Gene Tunney on my right falling . . . and then my big mate Rod Gray on my left went down, shot through the chest . . . there were so many bullets coming that it was like walking, running into a very stiff breeze . . . most of the section had been knocked out and I'm within ten foot of the Chinese trench when bang, something hit me . . . It just blew the legs out from underneath me and I crashed to the ground carrying this bloody great Bren gun and all the ammunition . . . I'm carrying about 80 pound of gear and equipment and I'm sprawled out on the ground and I know I've been hit and I don't know where.
>
> I can hear the Chinese talking to each other in the trench . . . I'm thinking what they're saying to each other is, 'Will we shoot these guys in the head and make sure they're dead?' because we'd be thinking the same thing . . . I wasn't sure whether I could get up and I certainly wasn't sure whether I could walk or run. Anyhow, when you've got battle gear on . . . you can unstrap [your] belt and just shuck all the gear. Everything will come off and fall away from you except the Bren gun, which is on a sling across my neck, so . . . I slipped the Bren gun sling off my neck and unclipped the belt and jumped to my feet and then I realised that I'd been shot through the right thigh so I sort of hopped and skipped and jumped and . . . after about 20 or 30 yards I was able to dive down below a low mound . . .
>
> So there we are, most of the section blown away and . . . we can see there's about 70 or 80 Chinese in [the trench], not the eight or ten that we expected, and we're pinned down because they've got covering fire from the hill we'd vacated the night

before, so nobody's moving, everybody's pinned down and we're back . . . where we started.

Eight members of Connelly's section were hit in the attack. A bullet smashed Lieutenant McGregor's jaw, leaving him dazed and bleeding. Sergeant Don Frazer took over command. Those who were unhurt kept firing at the Chinese to give injured mates a chance to crawl away. Some of the wounded played dead.

With McGregor's section pinned down and unable to move, Laughlin ordered Lieutenant Len Montgomerie's 4 Platoon to have a go. This time it was no spur-of-the-moment improvised attack but a platoon-strength assault, with supporting fire from a machine-gun section and the remaining members of 5 Platoon.

In desperate hand-to-hand fighting, Montgomerie's men cleared the Honeycomb trench by trench against 'fanatical' Chinese resistance. After coming under fire from enemy troops on a second knoll closer to the ridge, the leading elements of Montgomerie's platoon charged into them with bayonets fixed, prompting some Chinese soldiers to drop their weapons and flee. The bodies of 81 dead Chinese were found at the Honeycomb and around the second knoll. Three diggers were killed in the assaults and two more wounded.

With dozens of wounded diggers awaiting evacuation, Ferguson called the medic, Captain Don Beard, who recalled their conversation:

> He said, 'I've arranged with an American tank regiment for a squadron of tanks, we'll go up there with ammunition and see if we can get the casualties out. Will you come with me?' I didn't want to go because I had only just got out of the battle. However, of course I said, 'Yes, sir.'

As soon as they spotted Koch's tanks moving up the valley, the Chinese started firing. Inside the tanks, Ferguson, Beard and Ferguson's intelligence officer, Alf Argent, listened to the clatter of bullets striking the turret as they moved towards the battalion's position.

Having recaptured both knolls, Ferguson and Laughlin discussed retaking B Company's former position on the ridge. Reoccupying the position would enable B Company to cover the arrival of the 5th Cavalry, but at what cost? The position was now strongly held by the Chinese. Dislodging a large enemy force would require a major attack and would likely cost Australian lives.

Despite 4 Platoon's success in clearing the two knolls, Ferguson decided against trying to recapture the company's old position. He did, however, ask O'Dowd whether he thought the battalion could hold its position for another night. O'Dowd gave a guarded reply: holding on was possible, he said, but only if the Americans controlled the high ground to the rear and on the battalion's left flank, and only if the forward companies were resupplied with ammunition, food and water, radios and batteries.

While Ferguson assessed the situation, a party from A Company got to work unloading ammunition and preparing the wounded for evacuation. Beard described the scene to historian Michael Kelly:

> [T]he Americans gave covering fire from the tanks while we offloaded the ammunition and got on the casualties. I was only able to get one or two casualties inside and time was running short . . . I said to the CO, 'Well, the only thing is we'll have to lash the casualties onto the sides of the tanks and go helter-skelter as fast as we can down the track and hope not too many are hit.'

American crewmen gave up their places inside the tanks to ride outside, comforting and holding on to the wounded diggers. On the outward trip, when they were delivering ammunition to the rifle companies, the Shermans drew heavy fire from the Chinese, but when they returned with the wounded, the Chinese stopped firing.

The tanks made several trips with wounded diggers strapped to their sides, and each time the Chinese held their fire. According to Beard, Ferguson himself made at least three return trips to bring back wounded Australian soldiers.

O'Dowd's men had been hoping for grenades and ammunition for their Owen submachine guns; what they received instead was ammunition for Vickers machine guns, which had to be removed from the belts by hand before it could be loaded into their rifle and Bren gun magazines. Designed for a range of 3000 metres or more, the high-velocity Vickers ammunition soon stripped the barrels of their rifles and Bren guns. '[Y]ou put that in a rifle and it belts the hell out of your shoulder,' Ron Perkins recalled, 'and in fact eight or ten rounds out of that in a rifle, you can throw the rifle away because [the ammunition] is far too powerful for it.'

As for food, water and medical supplies, there was none.

Around 11.30 a.m. the Chinese resumed their assault on the summit of Hill 504, battering themselves against 12 Platoon's defences for another two hours until at least 30 bodies lay in front of the Australian position. The speed with which each wave of attacks was prepared and launched, despite casualties, and the effectiveness of mortar and grenade support left the diggers in no doubt that the Chinese were following a well-rehearsed drill.

Between assaults, 12 Platoon was able to bring up reinforcements and evacuate the wounded from the forward section commanded by Corporal Bill Rowlinson. In order to hold the position, every weapon pit had to be manned. Although wounded in the leg, Rowlinson refused to be relieved and was later awarded the Distinguished Conduct Medal for his courageous leadership under fire. No less courageous was the company's medical orderly, Private Ron Dunque, who was constantly exposed to the enemy's machine guns as he scuttled from weapon pit to weapon pit, treating the wounded and supervising their evacuation. Dunque was later awarded a Military Medal.

By early afternoon news reached Brigade HQ that the 5th Cavalry would not be coming after all. Convinced that 3RAR would not be able to survive another night of Chinese attacks, Brigadier Burke decided to withdraw the Australian battalion. Ferguson, who had returned to the Middlesex position, contacted O'Dowd by radio. 'Sometime after midday,' O'Dowd recalled, 'the commanding officer came on the air to advise me that there was no relief coming our way and I had approval to take a shot at getting the rifle companies out.'

The battalion was to withdraw along the four-kilometre ridgeline that ran south-west from Hill 504 to the ford below the Middlesex Regiment's forward companies. Despite having spent most of the night fighting off enemy attacks on his position, O'Dowd now had to start drawing up detailed plans for the timing, route and method of the withdrawal.

Meanwhile, the Chinese had resumed their attack on D Company. The second wave of assaults began around 11.30 a.m. and ceased around 1.30 p.m., with the diggers retaining control of the summit. Still under orders to hold his position, Gravener prepared his men for what seemed likely to be a difficult night, tightening his perimeter by withdrawing 12 Platoon into the centre of the company. The withdrawal was carried out under fire but the Chinese initially failed to notice what was happening and continued mortaring the vacated area. It was around 3 p.m. before they attacked and occupied the position.

The official history stated that after artillery failed to drive the Chinese from the old 12 Platoon area, Gravener called for air attacks. Breen disputed this, insisting that the request for air support—meaning strafing, rockets and napalm—must have come from Ferguson or the brigade staff. Whoever made the call, the strike went disastrously wrong. After arriving overhead, the pilot of a spotter aircraft dropped a flare on what he assumed to be the target. Sergeant Ray McKenzie told Breen what happened next:

I saw a US Marine Corsair line up and start a run on our position. I was angry about this because our marker panels were clearly visible. I saw the big silver bomb [a napalm tank] leave the plane and watched it fall in the D Company area, on 10 Platoon, where I had been two minutes before. The napalm exploded and took all the oxygen out of the air. I felt like I was breathing heat.

Private Keith Gwyther, one of the seven diggers from D Company who, on arriving in Korea, had absconded to join the Americans for fear of missing out on the fighting, was in a nearby weapon pit. In an account he later gave to the Melbourne *Argus*, Gwyther described how he had camouflaged his foxhole with fallen leaves that were 'shrivelled . . . into ashes' by the heat of the burning napalm.

Fortunately, the pilot of another Corsair realised his compatriot's mistake and pulled out of the attack, but the napalm killed two diggers and wounded several others, as well as destroying valuable weapons and ammunition. Only quick thinking by the radio operator saved Gravener's wireless set, the loss of which would have made it impossible to communicate with the Kiwi gunners, whose support would be essential when the order came to withdraw.

Napalm ignited the dry heather. As ammunition exploded all around him, Ron Dunque rushed to help the injured. The diggers liked to have their grenades lined up along the edge of their weapon pits, and when Dunque reached for the hand of one soldier, a grenade went off, throwing him down the hill. George Harris likened the men burnt by napalm to 'roasted meat. Their face and hands had been barbecued. [Lance Corporal Harold] Giddens was particularly bad. His hands had been reduced to stumps and he had some shocking facial scars.'

The Chinese tried to exploit the accident by attacking Lieutenant Russ McWilliams' 11 Platoon, but the napalm had missed McWilliams' men and they succeeded in beating off the attack.

Dunque was kept busy evacuating wounded men from his section while under fire from the enemy. Although wounded himself in the head and leg, Dunque made six trips carrying injured men over his shoulder back to the company position.

While D Company clung to its position on the summit, O'Dowd got to work planning a fighting withdrawal along a route that—for all he knew—might already have been blocked by the Chinese (perhaps the enemy force Gravener had reported moving along his right flank). Timing was critical. The enemy had had all day to observe the battalion's actions and O'Dowd considered it an 'absolute certainty' that they would renew their assault after dark. 'He had had plenty of time to set himself for this so it would be bigger and more educated than the night before and if we were still around when it happened, withdrawals were out.' O'Dowd wanted daylight fields of fire to enable his men to hold back the Chinese and protect the battalion's rearguard long enough for it to 'get a clean break come dusk, permitting us to disappear into the night'.

Besides the likely enemy blocking force sitting across his escape route, O'Dowd identified two other problems: the Chinese soldiers occupying B Company's old position would have a clear view of the withdrawal taking place across the road and, unless kept busy, they would almost certainly attack the companies moving back along the ridge. The enemy force attacking Gravener's men on Hill 504 was also bound to follow up any withdrawal, making D Company's exit extremely hazardous.

To deal with the enemy across the road, O'Dowd asked the Kiwi gunners to lay down a combination of smoke and high explosive on B Company's old position. The artillery was to start firing at 4 p.m.

To clear the withdrawal route I ordered B Company to push down the escape route to the ford closest to the 1st Middlesex and secure both sides. If they found enemy astride the escape route they were to attack and drive them off. If they were unable to shift the enemy they were to keep him busy until I could get there with another company.

The likelihood of being pursued along the ridge by the Chinese led O'Dowd to adopt a leapfrog-style withdrawal, in which one company stood its ground while another prepared to fall back and the third moved. In effect, the battalion would be withdrawing through a series of blocking positions, with companies leapfrogging backwards all the way to the ford. With his radio operator, Ron Perkins, in tow, O'Dowd spent the coming hours evaluating potential fallback positions.

When B Company's commander, Darcy Laughlin, received his orders, he startled O'Dowd by asking, 'What do you want me to do with my prisoners?' By his own admission, O'Dowd had 'completely forgotten' that Laughlin's men had captured around 30 Chinese. Since releasing them was out of the question ('they knew too much') and he was loath to shoot them ('War Crimes Tribunals were hanging WW2 officers by the score for just that sort of thing'), O'Dowd told Laughlin to take the prisoners—whom Gallaway described as 'thoroughly domesticated'*—with him.

Just before 4 p.m., O'Dowd told B Company to begin its withdrawal. The other companies were waiting for the Kiwi gunners to open up. Four o'clock came and went with no guns firing: the wind had changed direction, meaning the smoke shells had to land on a different spot to be effective. Unwilling to wait while the New Zealanders re-targeted their guns, O'Dowd instructed Reg Saunders' C Company to get moving.

---

* According to Private Don Parsons, the Chinese prisoners had attached themselves to B Company's sergeant-major, Eric Bradley. 'With his great height, red hair and pipe permanently in his mouth, he was probably the only Australian they could recognise and there was no way they were going to leave him.'

Next to go was A Company, led by O'Dowd's second-in-command, Captain Bob Murdoch. As Murdoch prepared to move out, a platoon of American tanks lurched into position in the valley and started firing at the Chinese across the road—a welcome intervention. Shortly afterwards, the New Zealanders began their barrage, some shells landing dangerously close to the tanks and forcing at least one to back off.

With C Company and A Company positioned behind D Company to discourage follow-up by the enemy, Gravener was ordered to pull out. The Chinese, however, had chosen this moment to launch another attack on the summit, making it too risky for D Company to break contact. After beating off the attack, Gravener began thinning out his troops, helped by accurate fire from the New Zealanders, whose shells at times exploded no more than 150 metres forward of the diggers. According to Gravener's battle report, this ferocious barrage 'completely frustrated [enemy] attempts to follow-up further', enabling D Company to get away. 'As they [the Chinese] . . . started to stream down the hill, the New Zealand artillery got the lot of them,' Ron Dunque recalled. 'Bang, bang, bang. I saw the whole front row . . . disappear.'

Some of the diggers were reluctant to abandon their position. According to Len Opie, a few members of D Company felt they were holding on alright and demanded to know why they were being ordered to pull out. '[We said] "We might as well stay." And they said, "Well, you are not going to have too much ammunition left, you've got to withdraw, [that's] the order."'

Not all the diggers managed to escape. Private Gwyther was alone in a weapon pit when a shell exploded nearby, collapsing the mud walls and knocking him out cold. When he came to, there were Chinese soldiers swarming around him.

'My head was addled, my mouth was dusty, and I was half covered by dirt,' Gwyther told the Melbourne *Argus*. 'I looked up and saw Chinese dragging machine-guns, mortars, bazookas and rifles . . . Some were digging in two or three yards on either side. Others were burying dead guys up on the knoll. Those Chinese with the spades would probably bury me if they knew.'

Private Ron Dunque remembered seeing 'thousands of Chinese . . . lining up [on] the top of the hills, ten deep . . . as we left our position and withdrew, they came up.'

Still half-dazed, Gwyther got rid of his field glasses, compass and two grenades and was gathering up his remaining gear when a Chinese soldier came towards him, dragging a shovel. The soldier spotted him. 'He let out a holler, and they all came streaming down.'*

While Private Gwyther was being marched into captivity, the diggers put their Chinese prisoners to work. As he shuttled back and forth between fallback positions, O'Dowd was startled to find himself surrounded by enemy soldiers. They turned out to be prisoners helping to transport Australian wounded, but O'Dowd was furious to see several carrying weapons. When he demanded to know why, an escort answered, 'You don't expect the bloody wounded to carry [the weapons], do you?'

The Chinese continued to menace the diggers as they withdrew along the ridge. By the time O'Dowd reached the ford across the Kapyong River, B Company, C Company and D Company were already across, leaving Murdoch's A Company stuck on the last fallback position.

During the withdrawal, most of the diggers had drunk what little water they carried. John Beresford tried to eat a cracker but his mouth was so parched that he was unable to swallow it. As they came down off the ridge, he and his mates spotted what they thought was a creek. There was a 'human stampede', Beresford recalled,

---

* Gwyther told Dunque later that he had seen him heading away from the position in a 'half run' but had decided not to call out, because if Dunque had come back they would both have been captured.

as the thirsty diggers rushed towards the water. After guzzling all they could, they walked through paddy fields to reach the ford across the river. Looking back the next morning, they could see their own tracks and realised that what they had thought was a creek was really a filthy drainage ditch. 'You wouldn't let a dog drink out of it,' Beresford said, 'but we did.'

With Murdoch struggling to make a clean break from the enemy, O'Dowd worried that A Company men would be badly shot up while trying to cross the ford in the moonlight.

In the dark a party led by Murdoch became separated from the rest of the company after coming off the ridge too soon. At a fork in the track, Murdoch had taken the wrong turn, reaching the river some distance short of the ford. Realising his mistake, he led his men along the river bank to the ford, while the Chinese, assuming the diggers had already crossed the river, waded in after them, enabling A Company to break contact and complete its withdrawal. When Murdoch's party finally arrived, it was from the wrong direction.

As fire controller for a mortar section, Ron Perkins had been issued with a set of binoculars. 'They didn't issue us with cases,' he recalled. 'They were frightened we might put them away and not use them.' Perkins kept his binoculars in a Chinese case he had souvenired early in the fighting. At Kapyong he had been forced to fight as a rifleman, and his binoculars stayed in their case. 'Two days later, I think it was the 26th [of] April, I took them out to clean them . . . and there was just little bits and pieces hanging on the strap.' Gazing at his shattered binoculars, Perkins realised the case had saved him from a Chinese bullet. 'Luck of the draw,' he told himself.

By 11.30 p.m., the withdrawal—described in the official history as 'difficult and brilliantly executed'—was complete. As they crossed the river, each element was personally checked through by Colonel Ferguson before moving to the battalion's new position.

Few actions are more difficult and dangerous than a fighting withdrawal in the dark over rugged terrain while carrying wounded comrades. 'The urge to run, to put distance between oneself and danger, is instinctive,' O'Dowd wrote later.

Add to this the mental state of men who have been under severe stress for a prolonged period and you can begin to make excuses. At Kapyong no excuses were necessary. The men took up fall-back positions quietly and efficiently and when ordered to move did so in an orderly manner. In consequence the operation went off like a training exercise back in Australia.

The Australian withdrawal took seven hours and was carried out at a cost of just one man captured: Private Keith Gwyther. Initially listed as missing, and later as missing believed killed, Gwyther was only reported to be alive in January 1952, after being allowed to write home from a North Korean prison camp. He endured more than two years of captivity, including bouts of brutal punishment and torture inflicted by the North Koreans after each of his three escapes, and was eventually released on 9 August 1953. Gwyther was mentioned in despatches for his outstanding conduct while in captivity.

24

AT LAST I FELT LIKE AN ANZAC

The dogged defence conducted by 3RAR at Kapyong, supported at crucial moments by American tanks and by the artillery of the NZ 16th Field Regiment, blunted the Chinese spring offensive. On 25 April, Anzac Day, Australian troops returned to their former battalion headquarters area and recovered equipment that had been left behind during the withdrawal.

With the Australians gone, it was the turn of the 2nd Battalion of Princess Patricia's Canadian Light Infantry on Hill 677 to face the advancing Chinese. Shortly after midnight on 25 April, the Chinese attacked the battalion's left flank. Like the diggers the previous day, the Canadians were isolated and exposed to enemy attack from all sides. In danger of being overrun, the Canadians had no choice but to call down artillery fire on their own position. This action, together with a counterattack by American tanks, eventually caused the Chinese attack to falter and enabled the Canadians to hold on.

The next day, the US 5th Cavalry Regiment made its belated counterattack, but the Americans were driven back. It would be several weeks before the Kapyong Valley was back in the United Nations' hands.

Between them, 3RAR and the Princess Pats had fought an entire enemy division to a standstill, buying time for General Van Fleet to reorganise his army and halt the Chinese advance north of Seoul, at what became known as the 'No-name Line'. Within a few weeks of the Battle of Kapyong, the Korean War had settled into a virtual stalemate that would continue for the remainder of the war.

A nearly simultaneous battle between the advancing Chinese and the British 29th Brigade demonstrated what might have happened to the diggers if the battle had played out differently. Like Brigadier Burke at Kapyong, the commander of the 29th Brigade had been assigned a sector too broad to cover with the manpower he had available. The Chinese attacked across the Imjin River around midnight on 22 April, exploiting a gap between the 1st Battalion of the Gloucestershire Regiment and the 1st Battalion of the Royal Northumberland Fusiliers. Over two days and three nights, the encircled and outnumbered Gloucesters fought off waves of Chinese attackers. Efforts to relieve them failed. When it proved impossible to resupply the Gloucesters and evacuate their wounded by air, they were given permission to break out if they could. Just 39 soldiers rejoined the brigade; the rest were either killed or captured. The battalion's total casualties were more than 600. The Gloucesters' doomed but courageous stand was credited with enabling the rest of the 29th Brigade to make an orderly withdrawal to a new line above Seoul. By then, the Chinese spring offensive had stalled and the capital was safe.

To O'Neill, the outstanding feature of the Battle of Kapyong was the unflagging morale of the diggers as they fought off relentless Chinese attacks during the night of 23 April and then held their positions for most of the next day, cut off from any hope of relief and under constant fire from the enemy. The biggest test of their morale was the withdrawal itself, carried out by 'exhausted men in considerable danger without giving way to depression, fear or panic of any kind'.

In recognition of their 'extraordinary heroism and outstanding performance' during the Battle of Kapyong, 3RAR, the Princess Pats and A Company of the US 72nd Tank Battalion were awarded a Presidential Unit Citation by President Truman. The NZ 16th Field Regiment, without whose support the diggers might have suffered the same fate as the Gloucesters, was awarded a Presidential Unit Citation by the South Korean president, Syngman Rhee. President Truman's citation concluded:

> The 3rd Battalion, Royal Australian Regiment; 2nd Battalion, Princess Patricia's Canadian Light Infantry; and Company A, 72nd Heavy Tank Battalion, displayed such gallantry, determination, and esprit de corps in accomplishing their missions under extremely difficult and hazardous conditions as to set them apart and above other units participating in the campaign, and by their achievements they brought distinguished credit on themselves, their homelands, and all freedom-loving nations.

Several members of 3RAR received individual awards, including its commander, Bruce Ferguson, who was described in the official history as 'an outstanding fighting soldier and battalion commander in the finest traditions of the First AIF and the Second AIF'. The citation for his Distinguished Service Order (DSO) noted his 'outstanding leadership', which was reflected in the 'magnificent performance' of his battalion.

The commander of an American tank platoon, Lieutenant Wilfred Miller, who accompanied Ferguson on repeated trips to evacuate Australian wounded, left a more nuanced account of his leadership:

I observed him personally on our forays into and out of the area of the encircled Australian soldiers, during which time Colonel Ferguson was calm, acted like he was in total command of the situation, and that his organisation would triumph. He demonstrated great concern for his wounded and his encircled men and had no apparent regard for his personal safety. He exposed himself to enemy fire by getting out of the tank, speaking to the wounded, and walking among his troops as if it was just a practice drill back in Australia.

According to the official history, the recommendation for Ferguson's award was approved 'with unusual speed' and he received his DSO from Lieutenant General Robertson on 1 May 1951.

The Battle of Kapyong took a heavy toll on the Australians. Thirty-two diggers were killed and 59 wounded. Unlike other battles fought by the UN army, it was not decided by artillery or tanks or air strikes, but by Australian soldiers on the ground, often fighting hand-to-hand, often in the dark, with the weapons they carried and the ammunition they could scrounge.

'Officers study, train and plan,' Ben O'Dowd wrote later, 'but it is all a negative exercise unless they have soldiers with the courage and determination to give expression to such plans.'

At Kapyong A Company fought off wave after wave of fanatical attacks all through one night. They fought from half-made weapon pits. They removed their dead and wounded and occupied their weapon pits to await the next onslaught with a good chance of a similar fate . . . fully aware of the chance of survival if seriously wounded. They knew they were cut off with what looked a poor chance of escape. In these circumstances any panic or break in morale would have been disastrous. I don't believe this possibility existed. They gave as good as they got, fought it out and won.

That a battalion could withdraw and still win was confirmed by the text of the Presidential Unit Citation:

Towards the close of the second day, the 25th of April, the enemy breakthrough had been stopped. The seriousness of the breakthrough on the central front had been changed from defeat to victory by the gallant stand of these heroic and courageous soldiers.

Norm Gravener, who led D Company off the summit of Hill 504, told Breen that after crossing the ford they were 'welcomed . . . like lost brothers. We were rather dishevelled—rather black from all the fire—very tired and, I might add, very relieved.' To Reg Saunders, 3RAR's achievements at Kapyong represented the supreme validation: '[W]e came to the Middlesex lines, passed through them and on Anzac Eve we dug in among friends. At last I felt like an Anzac and I imagine there were 600 others like me.'

Ben O'Dowd died in 2012 at the age of 93. Over the years he was asked many times about the Battle of Kapyong, but he never gave a pithier summation than this: 'The diggers won the Battle of Kapyong. There was nothing the officers could do. It was a matter of whether the diggers had the guts to go on with it or not. And they did.'

EPILOGUE

After the failure of Mao's 1951 spring offensive, the Korean War lapsed into stalemate. In October 1951, 3RAR lost twenty men killed and 89 wounded at the Battle of Maryang San, part of a UN offensive against a Chinese salient. Over five days of heavy fighting, the diggers pushed a larger enemy force from a strongly held position on Hill 317. After the Australians were withdrawn, the Chinese retook the hill and kept it for the remainder of the war. Thereafter the Korean War became a static affair reminiscent of the trench warfare of World War I.

The killing stopped when the armistice came into effect at 10 p.m. on 27 July 1953, but the war did not end. It left behind a legacy of mutual antipathy, distrust and fear between North Korea and South Korea, marked by periodic border skirmishes, kidnappings, espionage and other provocations.

The number of military incidents across the peninsula jumped from 42 in 1965 to nearly 300 in the first half of 1967. In January 1968, with war raging in Vietnam, 31 North Korean special forces soldiers infiltrated the South with orders to kill the South Korean president. The plot was uncovered and all but two members of the assassination squad either committed suicide or were killed.

After one of the North Koreans surrendered, he was deemed a defector by Pyongyang and his parents and siblings were executed.

In the same month as the botched assassination raid, an American spy ship, the *Pueblo*, was attacked and boarded off the North Korean coast. The crew were captured and held in North Korean prison camps for nearly a year, where they were subjected to various kinds of torture and abuse before being released.

Two decades later, North Korean agents detonated a bomb aboard a civilian airliner bound for Seoul, killing more than 100 passengers and crew, most of them South Korean. The motive for the bombing was allegedly to discourage visitors from attending the 1988 Seoul Olympic Games.

In 2010 a South Korean naval ship was sunk by a torpedo fired by a North Korean submarine. More recently, after years of diplomacy aimed at reducing tensions on the peninsula, the outlaw regime in Pyongyang revived its nuclear and ballistic missile program, ramping up its anti-Western rhetoric and demolishing the inter-Korean liaison office in the border town of Kaesong.

As the 70th anniversary of the armistice approached in July 2023, a senior UN official lamented the fact that the tensions left by the Korean War 'persist and remain unresolved, even after seven decades'. During the previous eighteen months, North Korea had test-fired 90 ballistic missiles, making a mockery of a UN resolution prohibiting it from conducting any launches using ballistic-missile technology. Russia and China, the regime's long-term friends on the Security Council, ensured there were no repercussions.

ACKNOWLEDGEMENTS

Many diggers left lively accounts of their Korean War experiences, some in the form of handwritten diaries and journals, others in digitised interviews recorded for the Australian War Memorial's oral history collection or filmed for the Australians at War Film Archive. Some, including Ben O'Dowd and Jack Gallaway, published books. Together, they gave me a soldier's perspective on events described briefly in brigade and battalion diaries and analysed at length in Professor Robert O'Neill's official history of the war. I am grateful to Robyn van Dyk and the staff at the AWM for help in finding them.

For the larger strategic story, especially concerning the military and intelligence failures that surrounded China's entry into the war, I have relied on declassified CIA intelligence reports and diplomatic material contained in the Korean War volumes of *Foreign Relations of the United States*, a long-running series first published in 1861. For the Battle of Kapyong, my primary source of information was the detailed battle reports written by O'Dowd and his fellow company commanders.

BIBLIOGRAPHY

Australian War Memorial (physical and digitised items)

27 Infantry Brigade HQ war diary, September to December 1950, AWM373, WO281/709

27 Infantry Brigade HQ war diary, January to April 1951, AWM373, WO281/710

3 Battalion, The Royal Australian Regiment war diaries, July 1950 to April 1951, AWM85, 4/18 to AWM85, 4/28

'A Rifleman's View of the Battle of Kapyong' by Lance Corporal Pat Knowles PM, AWM2020.22.249

'Bengazi to Sinanjui: A true account of a soldier's experiences' by Keith Lindsay Lewtas, AWM2019.22.109

Diary of Keith Lindsay Lewtas, 1946, AWM2019.22.67

Diary of Keith Lindsay Lewtas, 1946–1950, AWM2019.22.65

Diary of Keith Lindsay Lewtas, 1951–1952, AWM2019.22.66

Diary of Keith Lindsay Lewtas, 'Korean Campaign', 1950–1951, AWM2019.22.107

Interview with Major Len Opie, S02654

Interview with Major Tom Muggleton, S02652

Interview with Private Bob Parker, S02658

Interview with Private Thomas Hollis, S02298

Interview with Sergeant Fred Rennie, S02649

Memoir by Private Harry Kammermann, AWM2020.22.244

'The Battle of Kapyong: From the inside' by Lieutenant Colonel Ben O'Dowd, AWM2020.22.250

Australians at War Film Archive

Interviews with Donald Beard, John Beresford, Keith Brunes, Raymond Burnard, David Butler, Stan Connelly, Ronald Dunque, Roy Freeman, Jack Gallaway, Keith Langdon, Thomas Muggleton, Ben O'Dowd, Len Opie, Bob Parker, Ronald Perkins, Len Reader, Kenneth Travers, Joseph Vezgoff and Raymon Wilson

Books, articles etc

Appleman, R. E., *Disaster in Korea: The Chinese confront MacArthur*, Texas A&M University Press, College Station, 1989

Appleman, R. E., *South to the Naktong, North to the Yalu (June–November 1950)*, Center of Military History, US Army, Washington D.C., 1992

Azotea, C., *Intelligence Failures of the Korean War*, School of Advanced Military Studies, Fort Leavenworth, 2014

Bartlett, N., *With the Australians in Korea* (third edition), Australian War Memorial, Canberra, 1960

Bates, P., *Japan and the British Commonwealth Occupation Force 1946–52*, Brassey's Ltd, London, 1993

Belmonte, L., 'Anglo-American Relations and the Dismissal of MacArthur', *Diplomatic History*, vol. 19, no. 4, Autumn 1995

Bernstein M. D., 'Delaying Action at Kapyong', *Military Heritage*, vol. 10, no. 5, April 2009

Blaxland, J., Kelly, M. & Higgins, L., *In from the Cold: Reflections on Australia's Korean War*, ANU Press, Acton, 2020

Brands, H. W., 'The Redacted Testimony that Fully Explains Why General MacArthur Was Fired', *Smithsonian Magazine*, 28 September 2016

Breen, B., *The Battle of Kapyong*, Headquarters Training Command, Georges Heights, 1992

Chilcote, T. C., *The Battle of the Twin Tunnels: Korea*, US Army War College, Pennsylvania, 1988

Christensen, T. J., 'Threats, Assurances, and the Last Chance for Peace: The lessons of Mao's Korean War telegrams', *International Security*, vol. 17, no. 1, Summer 1992

CIA, 'Analysis of Intelligence at the Outbreak of the Korean War and Chinese Intervention', www.cia.gov/readingroom/docs/CIA-RDP79R01095A000800010001-2.pdf

CIA, 'Study of CIA Reporting on Chinese Communist Intervention in the Korean War', October 1955, www.cia.gov/readingroom/docs/CIA-RDP86B00269R00030 0040002-2.pdf

Cohen, E. A., 'The Chinese Intervention in Korea, 1950', in *Baptism by Fire: CIA Analysis of the Korean War*, CIA Center for the Study of Intelligence, 2013

Combat Studies Institute, *The Battle of Chipyong-ni*, Army University Press, Fort Leavenworth, 2019

Culp, R., 'North Korean Invasion and Chinese Intervention in Korea: Failures of intelligence', master's thesis, Louisiana State University, 2004

Department of State, *Foreign Relations of the United States, 1950, Vol. VII—Korea*, US Government Printing Office, Washington, ebook generated 2018

Department of State, *Foreign Relations of the United States, 1951, Vol. VII, Part 1—Korea and China*, US Government Printing Office, Washington, ebook generated 2018

Faulkner, A., *Stone Cold: The extraordinary true story of Len Opie, Australia's deadliest soldier*, Allen & Unwin, Crows Nest, 2016

Fehrenbach, T. R., *This Kind of War: A study in unpreparedness*, Pocket Books, New York, 1964

Gallaway, J., *The Last Call of the Bugle: The long road to Kapyong*, University of Queensland Press, St Lucia, 1994

Garratt, J., *Task Force Smith: The lesson never learned*, School of Advanced Military Studies, Fort Leavenworth, 2000

Gugeler, R. A., *Combat Actions in Korea*, Center of Military History, US Army, Washington, 1987

Halberstam, D., *The Coldest Winter: America and the Korean War*, Hyperion, New York, 2007

Hao Yufan & Zhai Zhihai, 'China's Decision to Enter the Korean War: History revisited', *China Quarterly*, no. 121, March 1990

Hastings, M., *The Korean War*, Michael Joseph, London, 1987

Haynes, J. M., 'Intelligence Failure in Korea: Major General Charles A. Willoughby's role in the United Nations Command's defeat in November 1950', master's thesis, US Army Command and General Staff College, Fort Leavenworth, 2009

Horner, D. & Bou, J., *Duty First: A history of the Royal Australian Regiment*, Allen & Unwin, Crows Nest, 2008

Kelly, M., 'Victory Against All Odds', *Britain at War*, 16 March 2021

Knight, P. G., 'MacArthur's Eyes: Reassessing military intelligence operations in the forgotten war, June 1950–April 1951', PhD thesis, Ohio State University, 2006

Matray, J., 'Dean Acheson's Press Club Speech Re-examined', *Journal of Conflict Studies*, vol. 22, no. 1, 2002

Mobley, R., 'North Korea: How did it prepare for the 1950 attack?', *Army History*, no. 49, 2000

Mossman, B., *Ebb and Flow: November 1950–July 1951*, Center of Military History, US Army, Washington DC, 1990

Nagai, Y., 'The Korean War: An interpretive essay', *Japanese Journal of American Studies*, no. 1, 1981

National Security Council Report, NSC 68, 'United States Objectives and Programs for National Security', US National Archives, http://digitalarchive.wilsoncenter.org/document/116191

O'Neill, R. J., *Australia in the Korean War 1950–53*, volumes 1 & 2, Australian War Memorial and the Australian Government Publishing Service, Canberra, 1981 & 1985

Poats, R., *Decision in Korea*, The McBride Company, New York, 1954

Ridgway, M. B., *The Korean War*, Doubleday, Garden City, 1967

Rose, P. K., 'Two Strategic Intelligence Mistakes in Korea, 1950', *Studies in Intelligence*, Fall–Winter 2001

Salmon, A., *Scorched Earth, Black Snow: Britain and Australia in the Korean War*, Aurum, London, 2011

Sawyer, R. K., *Military Advisors in Korea: KMAG in peace and war*, Center of Military History, US Army, Washington DC, 1988

Schnabel, J. F. & Watson, R. J., *The Joint Chiefs of Staff and National Policy, Volume III 1950–1951, The Korean War, Part One*, Office of Joint History, Washington, 1998

Stewart, R. W., *The Korean War: The Chinese intervention*, US Army Center of Military History, https://history.army.mil/html/books/019/19-8/CMH_Pub_19-8.pdf

Traynor, C., 'Fraternising with the Enemy: The British Commonwealth Occupation Force and its interactions with Japanese citizens, 1946–52', master's thesis, University of Western Sydney, 2018

Vanderpool, G., 'COMINT and the PRC Intervention in the Korean War', originally published in *Cryptologic Quarterly*, www.nsa.gov/portals/75/documents/news-features/declassified-documents/cryptologic-quarterly/comint_prc_intervention.pdf

Warner, K., 'Combating Cold Korea', US Army Heritage and Education Center, November 2010

Weathersby, K., 'Dependence and Mistrust: North Korea's relations with Moscow and the evolution of Juche', US–Korea Institute at SAIS, 2008

Weathersby, K., '"Should We Fear This?" Stalin and the danger of war with America', Cold War International History Project, Working Paper No. 39, Washington DC, 2002

Weathersby, K., 'The Korean War Revisited', *Wilson Quarterly*, Summer 1999

Weathersby, K., 'The Soviet Role in the Early Phase of the Korean War: New documentary evidence', *Journal of American-East Asian Relations*, Winter 1993

Wood, J., *The Forgotten Force: The Australian military contribution to the occupation of Japan 1945–1952*, Allen & Unwin, Crows Nest, 1998

Woodrow Wilson International Center for Scholars, 'New Romanian Evidence on the Blue House Raid and the USS Pueblo Incident', E-dossier #5, March 2012 www.wilsoncenter.org/sites/default/files/media/documents/publication/NKIDP_eDossier_5_The_Blue_House_Raid_and_the_Pueblo_Incident.pdf

INDEX